Culinary Infrastructure

Over the past two centuries, global commodity chains and industrial food processing systems have been built on an infrastructure of critical but often-overlooked facilities and technologies used to transport food and to convey knowledge about food. This culinary infrastructure comprises both material components (such as grain elevators, transportation networks, and marketplaces) and immaterial or embodied expressions of knowledge (cooking schools, restaurant guides, quality certifications, and health regulations). Although infrastructural failures can result in supply shortages and food contamination, the indirect consequences of infrastructure can be just as important in shaping the kinds of foods that are available to consumers and who will profit from the sale of those foods.

This volume examines the historical development of a variety of infrastructural nodes and linkages, including refrigerated packing plants in Nazi-occupied Europe, trans-Atlantic restaurant labour markets, food safety technologies and discourses in Singapore, culinary programming in Canadian museums, and dietary studies in colonial Africa. By paying attention to control over facilities and technologies as well as the public–private balance over investment and regulation, the authors reveal global inequalities that arise from differential access to culinary infrastructure.

This book was originally published as a special issue of *Global Food History*.

Jeffrey M. Pilcher is Professor of Food History at the University of Toronto, Canada, and the author of several books, including *¡Que vivan los tamales! Food and the Making of Mexican Identity* (1998), *Planet Taco: A Global History of Mexican Food* (2012), and *Food in World History* (2d ed., 2017).

Culinary Infrastructure

Edited by
Jeffrey M. Pilcher

LONDON AND NEW YORK

First published 2018
by Routledge
2 Park Square, Milton Park, Abingdon, Oxon, OX14 4RN, UK

and by Routledge
711 Third Avenue, New York, NY 10017, USA

Routledge is an imprint of the Taylor & Francis Group, an informa business

© 2018 Taylor & Francis

All rights reserved. No part of this book may be reprinted or reproduced or utilised in any form or by any electronic, mechanical, or other means, now known or hereafter invented, including photocopying and recording, or in any information storage or retrieval system, without permission in writing from the publishers.

Trademark notice: Product or corporate names may be trademarks or registered trademarks, and are used only for identification and explanation without intent to infringe.

British Library Cataloguing in Publication Data
A catalogue record for this book is available from the British Library

ISBN 13: 978-1-138-56426-8

Typeset in Minion Pro
by RefineCatch Limited, Bungay, Suffolk

Publisher's Note
The publisher accepts responsibility for any inconsistencies that may have arisen during the conversion of this book from journal articles to book chapters, namely the possible inclusion of journal terminology.

Disclaimer
Every effort has been made to contact copyright holders for their permission to reprint material in this book. The publishers would be grateful to hear from any copyright holder who is not here acknowledged and will undertake to rectify any errors or omissions in future editions of this book.

Contents

Citation Information	vii
Notes on Contributors	ix
Introduction: Culinary Infrastructure	1
Jeffrey M. Pilcher	
1. Culinary Infrastructure: How Facilities and Technologies Create Value and Meaning around Food	5
Jeffrey M. Pilcher	
2. Frozen Food and National Socialist Expansionism	32
Julia S. Torrie	
3. Food Safety as Culinary Infrastructure in Singapore, 1920–1990	55
Nicole Tarulevicz	
4. A Museum's Culinary Life: Women's Committees and Food at the Art Gallery of Toronto	80
Irina D. Mihalache	
5. Developing Constipation: Dietary Fiber, Western Disease, and Industrial Carbohydrates	102
Sebastián Gil-Riaño and Sarah E. Tracy	
Index	133

Citation Information

The chapters in this book were originally published in *Global Food History*, volume 2, issue 2 (September 2016). When citing this material, please use the original page numbering for each article, as follows:

Chapter 1
Culinary Infrastructure: How Facilities and Technologies Create Value and Meaning around Food
Jeffrey M. Pilcher
Global Food History, volume 2, issue 2 (September 2016), pp. 105–131

Chapter 3
Food Safety as Culinary Infrastructure in Singapore, 1920–1990
Nicole Tarulevicz
Global Food History, volume 2, issue 2 (September 2016), pp. 132–156

Chapter 4
A Museum's Culinary Life: Women's Committees and Food at the Art Gallery of Toronto
Irina D. Mihalache
Global Food History, volume 2, issue 2 (September 2016), pp. 157–178

Chapter 5
Developing Constipation: Dietary Fiber, Western Disease, and Industrial Carbohydrates
Sebastián Gil-Riaño and Sarah E. Tracy
Global Food History, volume 2, issue 2 (September 2016), pp. 179–209

CITATION INFORMATION

The following chapter was originally published in *Global Food History*, volume 2, issue 1 (2016). When citing this material, please use the original page numbering for the article, as follows:

Chapter 2
Frozen Food and National Socialist Expansionism
Julia S. Torrie
Global Food History, volume 2, issue 1 (2016), pp. 51–73

For any permission-related enquiries please visit:
http://www.tandfonline.com/page/help/permissions

Notes on Contributors

Sebastián Gil-Riaño is Assistant Professor in Department of History and Sociology of Science at the University of Pennsylvania, USA. His research focuses on the twentieth-century history of scientific racial conceptions in the Global South.

Irina D. Mihalache is Assistant Professor of Museum Studies at the Faculty of Information, University of Toronto, Canada. Her academic background in communication and cultural studies, paired with her interest in food studies, has developed into a research agenda which inquires about the intersections between food and museums.

Jeffrey M. Pilcher is Professor of Food History at the University of Toronto, Canada, and the author of several books, including *¡Que vivan los tamales! Food and the Making of Mexican Identity* (1998), *Planet Taco: A Global History of Mexican Food* (2012), and *Food in World History* (2d ed., 2017).

Nicole Tarulevicz is a tenured Senior Lecturer in the School of Humanities at the University of Tasmania, Australia. She is the author of *Eating Her Curries and Kway: A Cultural History of Food in Singapore* (2013) and a recipient of the Association for the Study of Food and Society (ASFS) Award for Pedagogy (2013). She was elected to the Board of ASFS in 2014.

Julia S. Torrie, PhD, is a Professor of History at St. Thomas University in Fredericton, Canada. Her research explores the social and cultural history of Germany and its neighbours, especially France, in the mid-twentieth century. In addition to journal articles and book chapters on tourism, photography, civilian aid, and popular protest, she has written a comparative, transnational study of civilian evacuations, *For Their Own Good: German and French Civilian Evacuations, 1939–44* (2010).

Sarah E. Tracy is Assistant Adjunct Professor at UCLA's Centre for the Study of Women and Institute for Society and Genetics, USA. Her work draws on feminist science and technology studies (STS), food studies, sensory studies, and postcolonial studies.

Introduction: Culinary Infrastructure

Jeffrey M. Pilcher

This volume develops the framework of culinary infrastructure in order to focus attention on essential but often-overlooked facilities and technologies used to transport food and to convey knowledge about food. Although scholars have noted the importance of infrastructural components such as grain elevators, refrigerated cars, and marketplaces within food systems and commodity chains, the contributors to this volume expand the range of this critical infrastructure by focusing on less obvious physical facilities as well as the knowledge infrastructure that has become increasingly important in modern culinary cultures. These essays seek to highlight linkages between the material nature of food systems and production, on the one hand, and the symbolic and social realm of culinary cultures, on the other, thereby helping to bridge material–cultural divisions within the interdisciplinary field of food studies.

In the first essay, I define the concept of culinary infrastructure and survey the historical development of important components of the physical and knowledge infrastructure around food. I first became interested in this intersection when writing a book called *The Sausage Rebellion* on early-twentieth-century efforts to introduce Chicago's refrigerated, industrial meatpacking model to Mexico, whose failure I attributed in part to local preferences for the taste of freshly slaughtered meat. A comparative article on meat in Paris, New York City, and Mexico City that I co-authored with Roger Horowitz and Sydney Watts developed this argument further within the framework of market cultures.[1] I addressed the subject of infrastructure explicitly in my next book, *Planet Taco*, which sought to explain U.S. influence on the transnational emergence of a Mexican restaurant industry as a result not only of fast food chains such as Taco Bell, but also of Mexican culinary professionals' reliance on a North American infrastructure of media and critics, culinary education, food suppliers, and tourist markets. This institutional dependency shaped for a time the possibilities of what counted as a fine-dining Mexican restaurant, with broad implications for high-value agricultural exports more generally, at least until Mexico developed a rival infrastructure of its own.[2] In the current essay, I bring together these two threads—industrial systems for transporting food and the knowledge systems of culinary practice and social distinction—in order to show that a common and broad-based infrastructure runs through the entire food system, determining value and meaning around food. Paying particular attention to control over infrastructure and the public–private balance over investment and regulation, I point to inequalities that arise from differential access among producers and consumers as well as rival nations. I conclude that infrastructural systems serve as crucial sites of power in determining what kinds of foods are available in markets and who will profit from their sale.

The first case study, by Julia Torrie, illustrates the complex relations of power deriving from control over infrastructure, in particular, the construction of frozen food processing plants in Nazi-occupied France during World War II. The technology of frozen food appealed to the National Socialist regime not only as an exemplar of modernity and centralization, but also as a means to extract agricultural production from conquered territories, thereby thwarting potential Allied naval blockades, which had starved Germany into submission during World War I. Within a year after the fall of France, German engineers had expanded existing refrigerated warehouses at the Atlantic port of La Rochelle, while also installing industrial machinery for quick freezing, which had been licensed in 1939 from the American firm of Charles Birdseye. Torrie observes that German infrastructural investments were not entirely opposed by French experts, who had carefully followed German experiments with frozen food preservation in the pre-war years. She interprets this tacit acceptance not as collaboration but rather as an understanding that these improvements would benefit French agriculture long after the war's end. Experts recognized German intentions of using the food for their own war effort, but existing French refrigerating had been underutilized because of the widespread resistance to the taste of frozen foods. Therefore, these officials reasoned that the export of surpluses would not adversely affect the local population, at least at first, before food shortages became intense. Torrie concludes that the wartime use of refrigerated technology indeed contributed to the acceptance and spread of a European cold chain in the postwar era.

The intersections of physical and knowledge-based culinary infrastructure can be seen from the case of Singapore, an island nation completely dependent on imported foods and on migrants working in their renowned, multicultural hawker courts.[3] Nicole Tarulevicz focuses on concerns over food safety and the way new technologies (pest control and refrigeration), provisioning networks (hawker courts and markets), and official discourse (regulations and public information campaigns) were employed to manage the challenges of food provisioning in the tropics. Her essay highlights the importance of popular knowledge as a crucial element of culinary infrastructure and illustrates the ways that this popular knowledge has interacted with official, elite conceptions over the course of the twentieth century. Using examples drawn from the media, particularly advertisements and letters to the editor of the island's leading English-language paper, Tarulevicz examines the conflicting interests and beliefs of merchants, consumers, and the state. The experience of Singapore is particularly relevant for increasingly globalized food systems because of the effectiveness of the island's local networks in managing the demands of transnational supply chains and culinary cultures. Whether Singapore can continue as a model of effective culinary infrastructure remains to be seen, as an older generation of vendors retires without obvious

CULINARY INFRASTRUCTURE

replacements; their own children increasingly enter higher-status professions and immigration restrictions block newcomers from taking over the labor of cooking.

The next essay, by Irina Mihalache, identifies the museum as a novel facility of culinary infrastructure, examining efforts by the women's committees of the Art Gallery of Toronto to use food to attract new visitors during the 1960s. Intersections between culinary knowledge production and the physical infrastructure of provisioning were forged as the women's committees' pursued sponsorship from such prominent firms as Consumers' Gas Company and Canada Packers to support their cooking classes and men's lunches. In seeking to build a knowledge infrastructure to shape the city's food cultures, volunteers also found themselves forced to create a physical infrastructure of food production within the museum, often over the objections of male museum directors. Mihalache uses documentary evidence from the museum's archives to identify the social networks of committee members, both locally and through connections with culinary celebrities in the United States and the United Kingdom, for although high-status food was still French, Toronto's Anglo elite made little attempt to associate with culinary authorities in Paris, much less Montreal! This essay also contributes to the literature on museum studies by showing how the presence of food in restaurants and exhibits (such as the National Museum of the American Indian's Mitsitam Cafe and the National Museum of American History's Food: Transforming the American Table, 1950–2000, both branches of the Smithsonian Institution in Washington, D.C.) can make museums more inclusive institutions.[4]

The final chapter, by Sebastián Gil-Riaño and Sarah E. Tracy, adds still another dimension to culinary infrastructure by probing linkages between the economic infrastructure of the international grain trade and the embodied infrastructure of the digestive system, which moved food through the guts. Using a science and technology studies perspective, they analyze a *dietary fiber paradigm* advanced in the 1960s and 1970s by the British physician Denis Burkitt and his collaborators. Working in the former colonial societies of Uganda and South Africa, these medical researchers attributed a host of chronic diseases, including constipation, diverticulitis, appendicitis, and colon cancer, to the predominance of refined carbohydrates, which had become cheap and abundant as a result of modern culinary infrastructure. The growing incidence of these diseases in industrial societies, and their almost total absence in rural Africa, led researchers to track the transit time of food from consumption to defecation using hospital questionnaires and observation among prisoners. By measuring the stool size, composition, and frequency of bowel movements among racialized populations, Burkitt concluded that the consumption of fiber or roughage could help to avoid disorders associated with the modern, industrial diet. Gil-Riaño and Tracy observe that although Burkitt and his colleagues failed to transcend the racial categories of their era, they nevertheless showed the inadequacy of scientific research that normalized western populations and assumed the aberration of the "Other." By identifying the digestive disorders inherent within industrial food production, their influential studies pointed the way toward improved dietary health.

As these essays recognize, we live in a world of mobile food, and understanding the infrastructure that facilitates that movement, both physically and conceptually, is essential for the intellectual enterprise of food studies. Even those who reject the global and wish to create local food systems must recognize the necessity for local infrastructure in the form of seed exchanges, irrigation systems, farmers' markets, small-scale slaughter facilities, and agroecological knowledge, not to mention the fossil fuels that underlie so much of modern life. Industrial foods have become so pervasive in part because of massive infrastructural investments that have made food seemingly cheap and convenient, at least for consumers. A rival infrastructure built on local networks will be needed to create viable alternatives to the conventional food system

Notes

1. Pilcher, *The Sausage Rebellion*; Horowitz, Pilcher, and Watts, "Meat for the Multitudes."
2. Pilcher, *Planet Taco*, 199–201.
3. For more on Singapore's hawker courts, see Tarulevicz, *Eating Her Curries and Kway*.
4. Levent and Mihalache, *Food and Museums*. See also Green, "Public Histories of Food."

Bibliography

Green, Rayna. "Public Histories of Food." In *The Oxford Handbook of Food History*, edited by Jeffrey M. Pilcher, 81–95. New York: Oxford University Press, 2012.

Horowitz, Roger, Jeffrey M. Pilcher, and Sydney Watts. "Meat for the Multitudes: Market Culture in Paris, New York City, and Mexico City over the Long Nineteenth Century." *American Historical Review* 109, no. 4 (October 2004): 1055–1083.

Levent, Nina, and Irina Mihalache, eds. *Food and Museums*. London: Bloomsbury Academic, 2016.

Pilcher, Jeffrey M. *Planet Taco: A Global History of Mexican Food*. New York: Oxford University Press, 2012.

Pilcher, Jeffrey M. *The Sausage Rebellion: Public Health, Private Enterprise, and Meat in Mexico City, 1890–1917*. Albuquerque: University of New Mexico Press, 2006.

Tarulevicz, Nicole. *Eating Her Curries and Kway: A Cultural History of Food in Singapore*. Champaign: University of Illinois Press, 2013.

Culinary Infrastructure: How Facilities and Technologies Create Value and Meaning around Food

Jeffrey M. Pilcher

ABSTRACT

Culinary infrastructure comprises the diverse artifacts, organizations, and media that mobilize food or that organize and convey knowledge about food, thereby facilitating production and consumption, but without having those transformations as a direct goal. This infrastructure includes both material components (such as transportation and sewage networks, marketplaces and ports, refrigeration, and communication technologies) and immaterial or embodied expressions of knowledge (recipes and cooking practices, futures markets and intellectual property, quality certifications and health regulations). Although failures of infrastructure become apparent in the form of supply shortages or food contamination, the indirect consequences of infrastructure can be just as important in shaping the kinds of foods that are available to consumers and who will profit from the sale of those foods. By surveying a diverse variety of infrastructural nodes and linkages, this essay seeks to overcome fundamental divisions within the interdisciplinary field of food studies between economic and ecological dimensions of food supply and the social and cultural meanings within which they are embedded. Historical analysis of the technological and knowledge-based systems of infrastructure can also highlight both the imperial origins of industrial food production and the contingent and contested nature of food systems. The essay gives particular attention to struggles over the boundaries between public and private control of infrastructure.

Culinary infrastructure refers to the basic facilities and technologies used to convey food, and knowledge about food, not only from the proverbial field to the fork, but also across continents and cultures. Although often overlooked in favor of the more direct transformations effected by industrial food processing, the infrastructure that connects production and consumption has had its own far-reaching and often unanticipated consequences in creating the modern industrial diet. Consider the grain elevator, a structure consisting of multiple, round towers, like a giant pack of beer, commonly found along industrial water-fronts and railroad crossings. Devised in 1842 by Joseph Dart, a warehouse-man from Buffalo, New York, it facilitated the transfer of grain between carts, trains, barges, and ships. Whereas stevedores had worked long hours to haul unwieldy sacks of grain up and down ladders and across gangplanks, it took just minutes to lift grain into vertical storage bins using the elevator's steam-driven conveyor belts or to pour it directly into railroad cars and ship holds. The invention achieved savings in time and labor, but as the historian William Cronon observed, it caused even more significant changes in the nature of grain as a commodity. No longer could the final buyer evaluate an individual farmer's harvest according to weight, cleanliness, and taste because it had to be removed from the sack to move efficiently through the system. Once mixed with grain from other farms and rendered interchangeable according to grade, such as first- or second-class spring wheat, it could be traded on international commodity markets and futures exchanges, where it was bought and sold before it had even been harvested. Thus, an infrastructural facility designed to speed intermodal transfers had the unintended result of erasing grain's origins and material qualities, helping create a world of "food from nowhere."[1]

Although facilities for transporting, storing, and exchanging food date back to the ancient world, the concept of infrastructure emerged in the nineteenth century in response to the growing complexity of industrial systems. French engineers coined the term in 1875 while seeking to improve the national railroad network, whose inadequacies had contributed to defeat in the Franco–Prussian War.[2] Infrastructure is inherently plural, "a collective term for the subordinate parts of an undertaking," according to the *Oxford English Dictionary Online*, and it refers broadly to organizational and knowledge-based as well as physical structures and facilities.[3] Despite its omnipresence in the modern world in the form of roads, bridges, power lines, sewage pipes, marketplaces, and grain elevators, infrastructure tends to be ignored – until it breaks down. The French unhappily discovered this point in 1870, when they were unable to match the trainloads of Prussian soldiers rumbling with clocklike precision across their borders. Failures in the infrastructure of conveying food can have similarly disastrous consequences in supply shortages or food contamination. Even when functioning properly, infrastructure shapes the kinds of foods that are available to consumers and who will profit from the sale of those foods. This essay and its companion pieces in this special issue of *Global Food History* survey the broad reach of culinary infrastructure and identify crucial nodes and linkages that convey power by determining the nature and meanings of food.

Various components of culinary infrastructure have appeared in diverse studies on the industrial transformation and commodification of food, but never in a unified fashion. The commodity chain literature of rural sociol-ogy and geography, inspired by Immanuel Wallerstein's world systems theory, has described technological systems involved in global linkages of supply.[4]

CULINARY INFRASTRUCTURE

Interpretative social scientists such as the anthropologists Sidney Mintz and Arjun Appadurai meanwhile developed the food biography and the "social life of things" as perspectives for examining the ways that the movement of foods across societies has changed its values in fundamental ways.[5] The food regime approach of Harriet Friedmann and Philip McMichael adopted the perspective of international political economy to locate changing points of control over production and distribution.[6] Food systems analysis, which grew out of environmental sciences and agroecology, has pointed to the ways that distancing producers from consumers can create power inequalities and push the external costs of food production toward marginalized populations and regions.[7] Urban geographers and planners have analyzed most fully the role of infrastructure both in provisioning cities and in perpetuating inequalities.[8]

Notwithstanding these efforts to include infrastructure as an element within various studies of industrial foodways, there is analytical value in examining infrastructure holistically on its own terms. An innovative issue of the design magazine *Limn* recently proposed the concept of "food infrastructures" as a way to "move beyond the tendency towards simple producer 'push' or consumer 'pull' accounts of the food system, focusing instead on the work that connects producers and consumers."[9] The contributors to the current issue of *Global Food History* agree wholeheartedly, but we want to expand the perspective even further. Reaching beyond traditional conceptions of food systems, these essays probe fundamental divisions within the interdisciplinary field of food studies between economic and ecological dimensions of food supply and the social and cultural meanings within which they are embedded. In seeking to connect these too often disparate scholarly literatures, we have purposely chosen the term "culinary infrastructure" because it expresses the tension between avowedly subjective symbols and meanings of culinary cultures and seemingly more objective, indeed concrete, physical infrastructure.

The term infrastructure has been assigned diverse meanings within wide-ranging contexts, and therefore it is necessary to begin by offering a definition of culinary infrastructure. We intend it not simply as a substitute for food systems, a term that has been widely adopted for its implied scientific rigor (as distinct from, say, foodways) but that has seldom been defined beyond a rather amorphous sense of encompassing everything involved in the production and consumption of food.[10] We adopt a more restricted definition of culinary infrastructure as those artifacts, institutions, and media that are used to mobilize and organize food or to convey knowledge about food, thereby facilitating the production and consumption of food, but without having those transformations as a direct goal. The transformative power of infrastructure is nonetheless powerful for its indirect approach; the grain elevator inspired fundamentally new ways of using and conceptualizing grain without actually affecting its material nature. Of course, food often undergoes changes, generally unintended and undesirable, in transit and storage. Food may also be produced as a consequence of culinary infrastructure, for example, during a cooking demonstration intended primarily to convey knowledge. Infrastructure is also analytically distinct from commodity chains, with their linear nature, because of the multiplicity of uses for infrastructural components such as transportation and communication networks, port and market facilities, and even dedicated technologies such as grain elevators. Whereas the central question for a chain is generally distance, albeit measured in distinct ways, the most relevant attributes of infrastructural systems are the complexity and resilience of their networks.[11] Moreover, the infrastructure for moving food is largely invisible to the final consumers, involving linkages from business to business, although these are increasingly contained within vertically integrated corporate "value chains," which have their own political consequences. Therefore, it is important to keep in mind the users or "operators," as the historian JoAnne Yates has termed them, of infrastructural technologies and systems.[12] Indeed, humans are critical components of infrastructural systems, particularly systems for conveying knowledge.

As engineers readily appreciate, infrastructure exists constantly poised on the brink of collapse, and it therefore requires historical analysis encompassing both its initial design and construction as well as its ongoing maintenance and reinvention. Considering upkeep and renewal can help avoid the temptation to view industrial food production in a deterministic fashion. Such determinism need not assume the inevitability of any particular design, but may simply recognize the legacy entailed by infrastructural investments, or to use the language of the historian Thomas P. Hughes, the momentum of large technological systems which channel goods in particular ways.[13] Nevertheless, the perspective of the history of technology and of science and technology studies draws attention to the contingency and malleability of technological systems in response to unanticipated problems and human usages, as the grain elevator shows once again. Mixing grain within the elevator led at first to a downward spiral in quality, as farmers were no longer rewarded for cleaning the dirt and chaff from their harvest. The Chicago Board of Trade responded by imposing uniform grading standards to protect the reputation of the city's grain trade. This standardization allowed elevators to function as banks, whose receipts could be traded like currency across space and time – by way of the telegraph and contracts for future delivery – without inspecting individual lots of grain. Merchants, in turn, used these new financial, legal, and communication systems alternately to integrate global markets and to corner local ones, which could moderate the price effects of weather or cause wild speculative swings.[14] Historical perspective on decay and renewal and consideration of the inventive ways that humans navigate and repurpose works can therefore help take the structuralism out of infrastructure.[15]

Broad context is also needed in the study of culinary infrastructure as a collective of many subordinate undertakings, some of which may appear to

CULINARY INFRASTRUCTURE

be only tangentially related to food. Sewage systems carrying waste out of a city are as important as freight haulage bringing food in; both are needed to complete ecological circuits, and considerable work is required to keep the two streams separate and thereby ensure public health. Likewise, efforts to replace infrastructure often involve the construction of parallel systems, for example, modern supermarket supply chains were purposely developed to circumvent and displace public markets; as a result, the two must be viewed together to appreciate the politics of food distribution. This essay offers a brief survey of the development of culinary infrastructure over time, examining the knowledge infrastructure of media and social networks that create and transfer cultural meanings about food as well as the physical facilities that serve to transport it. The organization into two sections – the first on physical infrastructure and industrial production, and the second on knowledge infrastructure and culinary cultures – is convenient but artificial since industrial production depends on various organizational and media knowledge, just as restaurants and home kitchens require physical facilities. By moving across global, national, and local scales, the essay seeks to highlight the balance of public and private control over critical nodes of material provisioning and cultural knowledge, which have contributed to the rise of modern industrial food production and are also essential to potential alternatives to conventional industrial foods.

Physical Infrastructure

The long age of European empire, from fifteenth-century voyages of exploration to anti-colonial movements around World War II, was largely intended to provide European populations and settler colonists with foods that were once reserved for the aristocracy. Portuguese and Dutch spice traders, Newfoundland cod fisheries, tropical sugar, coffee, tea, and fruit plantations worked by African slaves and indentured servants, and temperate wheat fields and cattle ranges of North and South America, Siberia, and Australia – all formed part of what may be called an "extensive" global food system. By contrast, the industrial diet of fats and sugars did not spread globally until the postwar consolidation of an "intensive" food system of animal feedlots, industrial fisheries, farmyard chemicals, and radical food processing. While reaching fruition in the postcolonial era, the modern industrial diet was made possible by an infrastructure of empire comprising transportation and communication networks as well as technologies of military provisioning and labor discipline. Moreover, these early modern mercantilist empires, which employed the powers of the state to serve the interests of merchants, had already begun to tilt the balance of public–private control over the economy toward business, even during the so-called "age of absolutism."[16]

The first culinary infrastructure was constructed thousands of years ago by pioneering urban dwellers to obtain food supplies from the countryside. Early city builders often located marketplaces alongside monumental architecture, as if to establish a spatial supervision by gods and kings over everyday acts of provisioning. These linkages ran in both directions; widespread scatter patterns of debris outside early cities have been interpreted as fragments from pots used to carry human waste to fertilize surrounding fields.[17] Maritime archaeologists have likewise uncovered evidence of vast ancient trade networks using earthenware amphora to convey wine, olive oil, and other commodities. One of Rome's more obscure monuments, "Monte Testaccio," was the giant garbage dump of an imperial customs house containing the shattered remains of an estimated 50 million amphorae.[18] Distinctive Maya chocolate pots have been found among Ancestral Pueblo sites in what is now the Southwestern United States, testifying to the long-distance trade in Mesoamerica's most valuable foodstuff.[19] Imperial China built vast infrastructural systems, including markets, granaries, and a Grand Canal, to convey food from the agricultural heartland in the center and south to population centers of the north.[20] The meaning of pre-modern culinary infrastructure, like the existence of capital cities that it enabled, was foremost a statement of power by rulers capable of commanding resources to support populations that did not grow food for themselves. Because the breakdown of infrastructure could directly challenge that authority through food riots and revolutions, regimes were often deeply suspicious of mercantile interests and sought direct control over provisioning systems.[21]

Europe's early modern empires expanded regional networks of provisioning to a global scale, while still maintaining their circularity, as ships on outward voyages carried prepared food for overseas workers before returning loaded with colonial harvests to feed the metropolis. The anthropologist Richard Wilk has done much to further our understanding of this "extractive economy," noting first its origins in the logistical machinery of military provisioning. Naval ports depended on industrial complexes of butchering, milling, baking, brewing, and coopering, not to mention the construction and maintenance of the ships themselves. These industries were, of course, devoted to food production, but the sailors, slaves, indentured servants, privateers, and company factors who consumed hardtack, salt fish and meat, and other preserved foods were themselves components of a larger colonial enterprise dedicated to supplying food to home populations.[22] The instrumental nature of these diverse workers was also apparent from military systems of labor discipline deployed by colonial rulers to maximize their productivity.[23] In places where direct supervision was difficult, the carrot of preserved luxury foods and distilled alcohol often replaced the stick as a means to motivate workers and maintain their affiliations with Europe. Over the eighteenth and nineteenth centuries, imperial bureaucracies gradually clawed back mercantile companies' trade monopolies and military autonomy, in part to consolidate power in the face of threats from imperial rivals, pirates, and rebels. Customs houses were crucial facilities for centralizing power within this infrastructure of food trade by imposing uniform standards

CULINARY INFRASTRUCTURE

of weight, measure, and quality on the emerging commodity chains of the early modern Atlantic world. As Wilk observed, these regulatory nodes of imperial infrastructure, originally intended to ensure revenue for the crown, contributed to the eventual growth of branding and labeling, which like the grain elevator served to obscure knowledge of foods' geographic origins, replacing it in the market with a manufactured identity crafted for advertising purposes.[24]

Nineteenth-century industrialization magnified the scope of these networks of culinary infrastructure, while still preserving the extensive food system's basic goal of extracting resources from far-flung imperial domains and transferring them to the metropolis. Regional food markets in Europe and many of its colonies had become increasingly integrated by the late eighteenth century through the expansion of paved roads and canals, and the subsequent introduction of railroads, steamships, grain elevators, and other infrastructure, which facilitated intercontinental trade in bulky, relatively low-value goods such as staple grains.[25] Knowledge as well as physical infrastructure was crucial to these commodity markets as price information made available by telegraph and postal systems heightened efficiency and reduced transaction costs. The increasing sophistication of financial infrastructure, such as futures trading systems pioneered by Osaka's Dojima rice exchange and the Chicago Board of Trade, mobilized capital to exploit these far-flung resources. But even as the flow of food accelerated through these systems and as supplies became generally more secure for metropolitan consumers, food riots recurred at moments of disruption during war and economic crisis, and they continued to target infrastructural nodes and linkages of transport, storage, and retail.[26]

The balance between public and private control over this basic infrastructure was a point of ideological conflict in the nineteenth century, as free-market liberals placed increasing trust in private enterprise to distribute food efficiently, while populist movements and many government officials insisted on regulating railroads, grain elevators, and the like as public utilities.[27] Moreover, the power of emerging food systems to commodify and standardize products from around the world was often contested, usually through the lens of racialization. The Japanese, for example, insisted that local rice was superior to supplies from China or California that became available following the opening of trade in the mid-nineteenth century. The regulatory grading of foods, often carried out at customs houses, was likewise matched by parallel, albeit less scientific, classifications emerging from popular culture. Consumers in the United States, for example, came to imagine gradations between beet and cane sugar, which were virtually indistinguishable at a chemical level, but nevertheless produced alternately by white, domestic farm families or by racialized, tropical plantation workers.[28]

Some of the most important infrastructure of the modern food system has been dedicated to the cold chain, a system for conveying chilled food from producer to consumer, and a crucial component in the contemporary, intensive food system designed, at least in theory, to provide an animal protein-based diet to global populations. The metaphor of a chain effectively conveys the system's goal of extending the distances that commodities could travel without deteriorating, as well as the potentially disastrous consequences of a breakdown in any link along the way. Nevertheless, the cold chain actually consists of interlocking systems of refrigeration and transport that have been employed for an increasingly varied range of products. Although humans have used ice to preserve food for tens of thousands of years, the industrial commodification of cold began in the early nineteenth century with Frederick Tudor's efforts to harvest ice from New England lakes for sale to consumers in the tropics. The cold storage network had expanded by the 1880s, led by meatpackers from the Midwestern United States, through the creation of refrigerated railroad cars, steamships, and distribution centers to deliver frozen or chilled meat from factories in livestock-growing regions of the west to urban consumers along the east coast of North America and in Europe.[29] The variety of perishable foods shipped under refrigeration quickly grew to include dairy, oysters, bottled beer, iceberg lettuce, and other sturdy produce. By the mid-twentieth century, portable flash chillers and affordable domestic refrigerators had extended the North American cold chain from the field to the home.[30] Postwar European efforts to supply protein-rich food to hungry populations through cross-border integration of the cold chain marked an important step in the construction of the Common Market.[31] By the 1980s, air transport allowed a counter-seasonal trade in fruits and vegetables, supplying consumers in the Global North with year-round access to fresh produce from South America, Africa, and Australasia. These supply networks perpetuated a form of extractive neo-colonialism, but unlike earlier export enclaves, the growing middle classes of the Global South took advantage of them as well.[32]

As with other infrastructure, refrigerated transportation systems affected the economic values, social meanings, and sensory experiences of foods that traveled through them. Economists have credited the greater availability of protein from refrigeration as a major factor in turn-of-the-century health improvements among the working classes of Europe and North America.[33] But even if refrigeration ensured the healthiness of food by limiting bacterial contamination, the nature of those foods changed significantly over the days and weeks spent in transit. Aging gave ordinary meats the distinctive character of "high game," an acquired taste of the aristocracy that at first conveyed disgust rather than status to middle-class consumers. When buyers shunned these unfamiliar meats, Chicago packers resorted to monopolistic tactics, systematically dumping their products below cost to bankrupt merchants operating competing supply systems of livestock and local slaughter, thereby ensuring that chilled meats were the only ones available in markets. In cities such as London, where North American packers could not control the infrastructure of supply, two-tiered markets sold premium, freshly slaughtered Scottish beef and lamb to the rich while delivering chilled or frozen products from overseas to the

CULINARY INFRASTRUCTURE

poor. Tastes changed over time, and "dry-aged" steaks became a luxury item, just as consumers grew accustomed to iceberg lettuce, supermarket tomatoes, and other fruits and produce that were bred not for taste but to survive the rigors of transportation.[34]

Infrastructure also undergirded the modern shift in control over food retailing from public markets to corporate supermarkets. This transformation took place within new regulatory environments occasioned by changing notions of public health, from an Old Regime concern for order to a Pasteurian focus on bacterial contamination. Kyri Claflin has examined the power struggles over market inspection and new technologies within the Paris meat trades around the turn of the twentieth century.[35] More broadly, the proliferation of new industrial food processing methods with unknown health consequences led to widespread debates in Europe and North America between newly professionalized public health officials, scientific experts working for industry, and a nascent consumer movement.[36] As Greg Donofrio has shown, older ideas about public order remained a central concern for urban planners well into the twentieth century, a focus that did not help municipal officials adapt their regulatory apparatus to the rapidly changing nature of modern food supplies.[37] Indeed, the global reach of supply chains and the supposed inability of national regulators to efficiently manage or even comprehend these sprawling networks have been used to justify the privatization of supply chains in the postwar era.[38]

Just as important for the rise of supermarkets was an infrastructure of presentation and packaging to help overcome consumer resistance both to novel industrial foods and to the changing social experiences of self-service shopping. Although self-service spread across retail sectors from department stores to cafeterias, grocery shopping posed special problems. Clarence Saunders, who in 1916 founded the highly successful Piggly Wiggly supermarket chain in the southern United States, recognized the need to create an orderly, modern environment that would appeal to white, middle-class housewives who formerly employed servants to do the shopping. Saunders' answer was to use gates and aisles to channel customers efficiently through the store, thereby limiting potentially awkward social interactions. The shopping cart, invented a few decades later, enabled customers to move ever greater volumes of food through the store and out to waiting automobiles.[39] Packaging materials also helped retailers to display individual portions of food conveniently on shelves. After considerable experimentation, the Dupont Corporation developed a clear, plastic material called cellophane that delayed the onset of discoloration in meat. Another transformational technology was TetraPak, geometric-shaped, plastic-coated, paper cartons used for milk and other liquids. Inspired by efficiency studies at the Stockholm School of Economics, it facilitated Sweden's shift to self-service shopping in the 1950s, leading the way for the rest of Europe. This packaging infrastructure reduced retailers' costs by allowing them to pre-process food and to convey information about it with minimal human interactions.[40]

13

The historical development of corporate supermarket chains, from nineteenth-century pioneers Lipton and A & P to the contemporary global reach of Walmart and Auchon, was not the inevitable outcome of technological and managerial efficiency. These private supply chains have developed alongside and often in competition with alternative systems run by governments and migrant entrepreneurs. Countering claims that public bodies could not facilitate complex systems of international trade, the historian James Murton has documented the effectiveness of the British Empire Marketing Board in providing public infrastructure for global food trade in the interwar period.[41] Political factors such as anti-Communist propaganda contributed to the failure of food cooperatives to pose a significant challenge to supermarket chains in the postwar United States. Yet, at the same time, the Fascist regime of Francisco Franco continued to invest in public markets, helping them remain central to Spanish shopping cultures.[42] Donna Gabaccia, Valerie Imbruce, Elizabeth Zanoni, and others have demonstrated the ability of migrant networks to supply ethnic consumers with specialty items such as Italian olive oil, Chinese vegetables, and halal meats, although corporations have a long history of buying out the most successful of these specialty firms.[43]

The physical infrastructure of the modern food system has emerged through the conjuncture of alternately competing and cooperating investments by diverse public and private interests. Empires of the early modern era used military coercion to extract resources from subject peoples, while in the twentieth century they served at times to facilitate trade between commonwealth partners. Equally wide variations have arisen in the organization and practices of private enterprise, from corporate entities to family businesses. The contemporary triumph of private supply chains owes much to state disinvestment in public alternatives, and as a result, the most marginal groups living in so-called "food deserts" have been disadvantaged in access to healthy foods. These inequities in resource usage have been particularly unfortunate because of the clear social gains, or in the language of economics, positive externalities, of infrastructure as "shared means to multiple ends."[44] Moreover, attempts to create alternatives to industrial supply chains require further infrastructural investments, ironically recreating past systems such as farmers' markets and small-scale facilities for humane slaughter. Such physical infrastructure also depends on social networks, which both facilitate supply and create meaning around food.

Knowledge Infrastructure

The rise of new digital media and the dramatic recent transformations in universities, libraries, publishing, and intellectual property have focused scholarly attention on knowledge infrastructure, which has been defined by the historian Paul Edwards as "networks of people, artifacts, and institutions that

CULINARY INFRASTRUCTURE

generate, share, and maintain specific knowledge about the human and natural worlds."[45] Culinary cultures have likewise been profoundly affected not only by contemporary changes but also by historical shifts in these mechanisms of creating, sharing, and disputing knowledge.[46] In pre-modern societies, culinary knowledge infrastructure was largely human – the transmission of farming, processing, and cooking practices from one generation to the next as part of the labor of social reproduction. Although such societies were scarcely lacking in culinary innovation and exchange, the growing commercialization of societies at different times and places led to the creation of less immediate forms of cultural transmission through cookbooks and other media, new institutional authorities such as universities and trade unions, and the rise of notions of intellectual property.[47] This distancing of cultural knowledge in the modern world, running parallel to the physical distancing of commodity chains, has likewise brought political struggles over the boundaries of public and private enterprise. This section examines such transformations in the infrastructure of culinary knowledge, with particular attention to the restaurant as a site of innovation and cultural exchange.

The modern infrastructure of culinary knowledge has arguably been concerned less with the transmission of existing practices than with the pursuit of novelty and innovation. Both old and new media clamor for attention by constantly repackaging culinary instruction, criticism, and entertainment. Restaurants likewise pursue customers by promising the unique creations of artistic chefs or the untrammeled authenticity of ethnic cuisines. Even the traditional, artisanal, and authentic must now be painstakingly reconstructed by experts using ethnography and experimentation, and then marketed in a way that denies its commercialism. This denial is not new; the influential nineteenth-century French chef Antonin Carême fashioned himself as a romantic poet in the kitchen.[48] Nevertheless, the artistic independence of the "top chef" has always depended on a battery of trained subordinates recruited through professional training and labor markets, as well as raw materials bearing indicators of quality, critics and promotional media, and urban and touristic infrastructure, all financed by capital markets. Control over these nodes of culinary infrastructure has become a site of fierce international competition because of its power to determine value and maximize profits throughout the food industry.

As a culinary infrastructure of knowledge, cookbooks and the wider publishing industry have encouraged innovation and complexity in the kitchen. The anthropologist Jack Goody first observed the contribution of written recipes to culinary hierarchies, although critics have rejected his inverse logic that cooks without books are inherently unrefined. Like the physical infrastructure of urban provisioning, this knowledge infrastructure dates back to ancient times; cuneiform recipes document the presence of professional kitchens and elaborate cuisines in Mesopotamia.[49] The rise of publishing industries in early modern Europe and Japan disseminated the secrets of master chefs to emerging middle-class audiences, who may or may not have actually prepared any of the recipes, but nevertheless gained some satisfaction or status from possessing them, as with present-day coffee table cookbooks. At least some of these recipes facilitated actual work in the kitchen, judging by cookbooks' insistent claims about the impracticality of competing volumes. Authors followed various strategies for success in the literary marketplace, alternately using tones of authority and intimacy, novelty and familiarity, again like the modern publishing industry. The emphasis on innovation came through in cookbook titles such as *Nouvelle Cuisine*, a term used as early as 1742, and by the inclusion of recipes from foreign lands; in Japan, cookbooks provided a vehicle for introducing such novelties as tempura, originally a Portuguese dish.[50] Recent scholarship on cookbooks, which has moved beyond the culinary historian's genealogies of recipes to include the history of the book and of publishing, further supports the value of research on infrastructure.[51]

The restaurant, another important site of culinary innovation, depended on an elaborate infrastructure of knowledge and training. Indeed, the historian Rebecca Spang has shown that the modern French restaurant was a product of an eighteenth-century knowledge economy. Enlightenment philosophes sought out restorative broths (the original meaning of the word *restaurant*), and proprietors offered menus of different bouillons to match their customers' individual sensibilities, unlike the *table d'hôte* of the guest house, which served the same meal to all. After the Revolution of 1789, the menu format proved ideal for translating the haute cuisine of the Old Regime for a new bourgeois audience. The semi-public space of the restaurant, including its private banquet halls, thereby replaced the court as a space for elite socializing, competition, and advancement. Industrialists and professionals could demonstrate that they belonged alongside the old aristocracy by way of their manners at the table and sophistication in selecting a tasteful meal from a bewildering menu. In turn, the first-class restaurant chef's ability to prepare on demand any one of hundreds of different dishes required elaborate organizational systems including teams of cooks and waiters, utensils and appliances, supplies of perishable ingredients, and work processes allowing a few basic "mother" sauces to be augmented and garnished in countless ways.[52]

The professionalization of culinary labor came to depend on facilities and networks for creating and transmitting knowledge and for placing workers within labor markets. Even before the formal restaurant, the early modern apprenticeship system for training cooks inculcated the skills of large-scale cooking alongside a growing sense of professional consciousness. Cooks claimed occupational status to raise their position from mere domestic servants to the aristocracy, although the most skilled chefs, Italians and Frenchmen in particular, already had considerable autonomy and could find employment or commercial opportunities across the continent.[53] The nineteenth-century

CULINARY INFRASTRUCTURE

spread of restaurants increasingly moved cooks out of domestic service into the professional workplace, but they remained under the control of the restaurant owner and *maître d'hotel*, while employment agencies largely controlled hiring. To gain greater autonomy, cooks began forming mutual aid societies such as the *Societé des Cuisiniers Français* around midcentury. These organizations later established schools, trade journals, and culinary exhibitions and competitions, which were formalized in the 1920s by the official *meilleur ouvrier de France* system intended to promote excellence in crafts. Even as mobility increased for cooks moving between jobs, the restaurant workplace became more regimented, as the influential chef Auguste Escoffier organized his subordinates into a military-style *brigade de cuisine*.[54]

By the late nineteenth century, the culinary infrastructure of knowledge and labor markets had become thoroughly internationalized. Both employment agencies and mutual aid societies operated across borders, and Escoffier claimed to have placed more than 5000 French chefs abroad in professional kitchens and private service. The historian Peter Scholliers, in describing restaurant workers' proclivity to travel for status, professionalism, and identity, concluded that "cooks, eaters, and culinary writers 'forged' Europe long before this happened in an economic or political way."[55] Nevertheless, these international linkages were not limited to Europe; chefs and waiters served continental cuisine in cities throughout the Americas, in parts of Asia and Africa, and aboard luxury railroad cars and steamships traveling between them. Nor were all itinerant workers trained in European methods. The Chinese have a far older restaurant tradition than the French, dating back a thousand years to the Song dynasty. The age of proletarian migration sent millions of Chinese traveling around the world, but the historical contexts of this migration were far different from those of French chefs, both because the Qing dynasty discouraged foreign travel by its subjects, particularly skilled professionals, and because of racialized resistance to considering Chinese cuisine as appropriate for fine dining. The historian Heather Lee has shown that Chinese restaurant businesses in the United States during the first half of the twentieth century were organized primarily to facilitate the movement of family members under restrictive immigration laws rather than to promote Chinese cuisine and culture.[56]

An increasingly complex and globalized infrastructure of publishing encouraged the growth of restaurants and culinary innovation. The sociologist Priscilla Ferguson has described the range of literary genres involved in translating the noble cuisine of the Old Regime into the modern cultural field of gastronomy. In addition to the cookbooks of Carême and Escoffier, novelists, social commentators, philosophers, and especially journalistic critics served to instruct newcomers in the etiquette and aesthetics of the restaurant, thereby setting models for culinary authority.[57] With this heavy emphasis on culinary literature, the French publishing industry helped establish the nation as an international arbiter of culture; for example, Parisian houses dominated the publishing of culinary literature in Latin America throughout the nineteenth century.[58] Infrastructure also contributed to the spread of restaurants beyond Paris and other large urban centers in the early twentieth century; the tire company Michelin began publishing its influential critical restaurant guides to encourage people to drive.[59] Similar commercial patterns emerged in culinary education; gas companies sponsored home economists in the hopes of increasing sales of new technologies. Although an increasingly important sector of the media industry in the twentieth century, modern culinary instruction has faced a double bind for entrepreneurial women advocating domesticity such as Julia Child and her international counterparts, such as Doña Petrona de Gandulfo of Argentina.[60] Both new and old media have contributed to the dissemination of culinary knowledge and the establishment of brands, often using discourses of authenticity and exoticism that perpetuate social inequalities. New media such as blogging may have upended traditional notions of authority around reviewing, but without necessarily challenging the social distinction or gendered dilemmas conveyed by such claims.[61]

In addition to this knowledge infrastructure, the restaurant industry also depended on an elaborate physical infrastructure of real estate, transportation, and markets. Location was crucial as a mark of status, and early restaurants tended to cluster in central locations of cities such as Paris, London, Brussels, and New York. With the rise of railroad, steamships, and automobiles in the late nineteenth and early twentieth centuries, culinary entrepreneurs such as Escoffier and his partner Cesar Ritz established luxury hotels and spas for an increasingly mobile elite clientele. The Harvey House and Howard Johnson's chains offered reliable dining options for railroad and automobile travelers in North America. Postwar suburbanization made the car an increasingly important determinant of how people interacted with food in restaurants, not just in fast food restaurants, but also with the movement of immigrants out of old "Chinatowns" and "Little Italies."[62] The historian Camille Bégin has examined racial tensions over parking in the 1980s as Chinese malls proliferated in formerly white ethnic suburbs of Toronto. Meanwhile, as the sociologist Sharon Zukin observed, the gentrification of former ethnic enclaves has provided a fertile environment for new restaurants that capitalize on the authenticity attributed to former residents of these downtown neighborhoods in order to charge extravagant prices to tourists and those who can afford the inflated rents.[63]

The commercialization of authenticity has also extended to certification regimes, an infrastructure of knowledge and trust that has become important in determining the value of commodified foods. As industrial infrastructure has rendered the origins of food opaque and distant, consumers have been increasingly willing to pay a premium for products whose sources are guaranteed. These legal regimes were first codified to protect the French wine industry in the early twentieth century from competitors seeking to counterfeit valuable place names. Winemakers insisted that "champagne" referred not to just any

CULINARY INFRASTRUCTURE

sparkling wine but to the unique products of a particular soil or *terroir*. Over time, protected indicators have been enshrined in international treaties and extended to a wide range of goods. Complex regulations, overseen by national bureaucracies and certification agencies, now determine when foods can carry particular geographic names or labels such as "organic," "fair trade," and "fresh." In 2010, UNESCO even began to declare particular national cuisines as the intangible patrimony of humanity; two of the first recipients, the French gastronomical meal and Mexican peasant cooking, illustrated the cultural hierarchies conveyed by such designations. More generally, the terms of certification are subject to intense political negotiation, and often have precise legal meanings that differ from most consumers' understanding of particular words. The geographer Julie Guthman, for example, showed how "organic" was transformed from a countercultural method of farming into big business, abandoning along the way commitments to small-scale production, agro-ecological methods, sustainability, or social justice. In a similar fashion, the cultural studies scholar Fabio Parasecoli observed the ways that certification regimes work to the disadvantage of women and other marginalized populations, particularly in the Global South, precisely those groups whom conscientious consumers in the Global North profess to support.[64]

Culinary infrastructure has proliferated with the growing international competition for culinary tourism and high-value agricultural exports. When the grand cuisine lost relevance to modern life and rising labor costs made Escoffier's business model unsustainable following World War II, French restaurateurs sought to revitalize their industry with a *nouvelle cuisine* inspired by Japanese aesthetics, produced with industrial technologies, and promoted by a new guide from the critics Henri Gault and Christian Millau. Yet, postwar rivals were increasingly prepared to challenge French culinary hegemony. The United States was undergoing a restaurant revolution led by chefs trained at the Culinary Institute of America, founded in 1946, sourcing premium ingredients from a new generation of artisanal farmers, and guided by media critics at the *New York Times* and *Gourmet*. This infrastructure, in turn, created the basis for a regional hegemony within North America; Mexico and Canada eventually sought to build their own facilities and media to avoid reliance on cross-border critics and culinary schools, thereby hoping to free themselves from taco shell and donut stereotypes. Around the turn of the twenty-first century, the Catalan chef Ferran Adrià pioneered a new style of "molecular gastronomy" or "modernist" restaurant cuisine, building his own laboratory and equipment to create flavored foams and other concoctions. His restaurant, El Bulli, was quickly enshrined as the world's best by a new critical authority, the San Pellegrino Top 50 Restaurant List compiled by the British magazine *Restaurant*.[65]

Culinary competition now takes place at every level from geopolitical diplomacy to virtual blogs. Countries such as South Korea, Thailand, and Peru have created explicit policies of "gastrodiplomacy" to boost the perception of their food industries, often in more or less direct competition with perceived rivals. While UNESCO certification has become the Holy Grail of diplomatic lobbying, these governments are also intent on preserving the authenticity of iconic national dishes as well as promoting expatriate chefs and agricultural exports.[66] Street food has become an unlikely rival to the traditional restaurant, while nevertheless depending on its own infrastructure. With government support, such as in the case of Singapore's hawker courts, small vendors can provide the lynchpin for a healthful and flavorful urban provisioning system, but in many North American cities, overregulation has made street carts a site of culinary tourism for the elite rather than a democratic source of sustenance. In Los Angeles, Roy Choi used Twitter posts to attract customers to his Kogi Korean barbecue taco trucks, using new media to bypass critics and take control of his image.[67] Different forms of media have become a particularly intense site of international competition. Chefs and critics in the United States bemoaned the 2006 arrival in New York City of the Michelin guide, which they considered to be conservative and unable to comprehend the vibrancy of the city's culinary culture. In a further irony, the French Ministry of Culture has supported critics of the San Pellegrino Top 50 Restaurant list because it is seen as inimical to their culinary sovereignty by favoring rival, modernist-style restaurants.[68]

By considering disparate media, restaurants, professional societies, cooking schools, and certification regimes as a culinary infrastructure of knowledge and trust, we can better understand international competition for the profits of culinary tourism and agricultural exports. As first movers in the field of gastronomy, the French constructed a far-reaching culinary infrastructure that still commands prestige and determines value, not only in exclusive restaurants, but for wider food markets as well. Escoffier explicitly described the chefs he placed in foreign kitchens as both ambassadors of French civilization and salesmen of agricultural products like champagne and truffles. Attempts by international rivals to tilt the playing field in a more favorable direction have had to start literally from the ground up: New World winemakers challenging narratives of terroir that privilege growing grapes in a particular location for a thousand years, or Chinese and Mexican chefs questioning European aesthetics and basic knife skills. While the days of a single gastronomic hegemon may have passed, success in future competitions will still depend on critical nodes of culinary infrastructure.

Conclusion

The field of food studies has often separated analysis of the service sectors of restaurants and culinary tourism from agriculture and manufacturing, but both rely on elaborate infrastructural systems that cut across the entire food industry. This essay has sought to suggest productive linkages between humanistic and quantitative methodologies by showing how physical and knowledge infrastructure create value and meaning around food. Facilities and technologies such as grain elevators and refrigeration help determine the varieties and even the physical nature of foods that are available for sale in the marketplace, but the value of those foods are equally subject to distinctions and stereotypes fostered by media, culinary tourism, and systems of certification. The concept of culinary infrastructure connects these topics and scholarly methodologies in ways that hold great potential for advancing our understanding of food and society.

Although culinary infrastructure is diverse and pervasive, this special issue has focused on those facilities and technologies intended to move food at multiple scales, from global trade to urban transit and even digestion within the body, as seen in the essay by Sebastián Gil-Riaño and Sarah Tracy. Specialized infrastructure may be dedicated to a single purpose, such as the grain elevator, but railroads, ports, media, and similar systems are intended more often to serve multiple users. The study of infrastructure must consider perhaps unintentional but nevertheless significant connections between the mobility of goods, people, and ideas. Under nineteenth-century liberalism, migrants traveled with relatively few restrictions, bringing culinary knowledge along with trade goods, whereas contemporary neoliberalism has segmented the infrastructure of mobility into specialized containers, airliners, and media, thereby seeking to control more precisely what can and cannot move.[69] The consequences of this transformation are of deep concern not only for the field of food studies, but for any who would understand the modern world. And although agrarian and especially pastoral societies have their own forms of culinary mobility, cities are a particular locus of infrastructure because of their vast appetite for both staples to feed the masses and luxury goods to satisfy the elite. For this reason, city foods provide a valuable focus for studying cross-cultural encounters as social and sensory intersections of labor, commerce, and consumption.[70]

Identifying crucial nodes and linkages of culinary infrastructure will expand our understanding of what counts for food and who profits from it. The list of potential sites and institutions is expansive and often unexpected, as with Irina Mihalache's study of the museum as a point of culinary knowledge production and transfer. Historical perspective is also essential for understanding the changing nature of this infrastructure over time and the ways that availability can shape social distinction. Once refrigerated transport facilitated the supply of abundant fast-food hamburgers, the culinary elite sought out microgreens; both depended on the "cold chain" but they required very different technological systems to function effectively. These systems can also have profound health consequences, and not only because of the contamination that may result from failures in the cold chain or in sterile packaging. The essay by Nicole Tarulevicz demonstrates that these systems themselves often serve to constitute notions of proper health, albeit in dialog with popular beliefs. Finally, infrastructure is important as a site for political control over our basic subsistence. Seed companies, grain traders, and supermarket chains have invested huge sums in private infrastructure to move food efficiently around the world. Those who would seek alternatives to the conventional food industry will likewise need to start from the ground up.

Acknowledgments

I received valuable feedback on this essay from Dan Bender, Kyri Claflin, Donna Gabaccia, Irina Mihalache, Jo Sharma, Sarah Tracy, Elizabeth Zanoni, and other participants in the University of Toronto's 2016 Connaught Cross-Cultural/Cross-Divisional Seminar. Roger Horowitz, Tracey Deutsch, and Krishnendu Ray also provided very useful suggestions, as did Sarah Portnoy, my co-author on a previous article examining culinary infrastructure, and two anonymous readers for the journal.

Notes

1. Cronon, *Nature's Metropolis*, 97–147.
2. My thanks to Kyri Claflin for this reference.
3. *Oxford English Dictionary Online*.
4. Wallerstein, *The Modern World System*; Gereffi and Korzeniewicz, *Commodity Chains*; Belasco and Horowitz, *Food Chains*.
5. Mintz, *Sweetness and Power*; and Appadurai, *The Social Life of Things*.
6. Friedmann, "International Regimes of Food"; and McMichael, *Global Restructuring*.
7. Princen, "Distancing"; and Blay-Palmer, *Food Scares*.
8. Parham, *Food and Urbanism*; Donofrio, "Feeding the City"; Vitiello and Brinkley, "Hidden History of Food System Planning"; and Graham and Marvin, *Splintering Urbanism*.
9. Frohlich, Jauho, Penders, and Schleifer, "Preface: Food Infrastructures."
10. For an acknowledgment of the lack of a clear definition of the term food systems by senior scholars in the field, see Julier and Gillespie, "Encountering Food Systems," 359–60.
11. On distance in commodity chains, see Princen, "Distancing." On systems complexity, see Barabási, *Linked*; and Watts, *Six Degrees*.
12. On the diverse nature of technological users, see Yates, *Structuring the Information Age*.
13. Hughes, "Evolution of Technological Systems," 70–3.

CULINARY INFRASTRUCTURE

14. Cronon, *Nature's Metropolis*, 116–32.
15. On infrastructural systems and technological determinism, see van der Vleuten, "Infrastructures and Societal Change."
16. Merchants were often allies of the Crown in struggles against the landed nobility, and in turn, monarchs were leading investors in overseas ventures, at least since Prince Henry the Navigator and Isabella of Castile.
17. Ur and Colantoni, "Production and Consumption in a Mesopotamian City," 64.
18. Robinson and Wilson, *Maritime Archaeology*; McGovern, *Ancient Wine*; Hamilakis, "Food Technologies"; Garnsey, *Food and Society in Classical Antiquity*; and Morley, *Metropolis and Hinterland*.
19. Crown and Hurst, "Evidence of Cacao Use."
20. Chang, *Food in Chinese Culture*; Pee, "Purchase on Power"; Will and Wong, *Nourish the People*.
21. Braudel, *Structures of Everyday Life*; Wong, "Food Riots in the Qing Dynasty"; Kaplan, *Provisioning Paris*; and Bohstedt, *The Politics of Provisions*.
22. Wilk, "The Extractive Economy"; and Mott, "The Best Manned Fleet."
23. Wolf, *Europe and the People Without History*; and Mintz, *Sweetness and Power*.
24. Wilk, "Anchovy Sauce and Pickled Tripe"; and Roberts, "The Death of the Sensuous Chemist."
25. Nützenadel and Trentmann, "Mapping Food and Globalization"; Segers et al., *Exploring the Food Chain*; and Jacks, "Commodity Market Integration."
26. Brueghel, "Food Politics."
27. Miller, *Mastering the Market*; and Horowitz et al., "Meat for the Multitudes."
28. Ohnuki-Tierney, *Rice as Self*; and Merleaux, *Sugar and Civilization*.
29. Rees, *Refrigeration Nation*.
30. Petrick, "Like Ribbons of Green and Gold"; and Freidberg, *Fresh*.
31. van der Vleuten, "Feeding the Peoples of Europe."
32. Friedland, "The New Globalization"; and Freidberg, *French Beans and Food Scares*.
33. Craig et al., "The Effect of Mechanical Refrigeration."
34. Claflin, "Les Halles and the Moral Market"; Pilcher, "Empire of the 'Jungle'"; and Stovall, *Paris and the Spirit of 1919*.
35. Horowitz et al., "Meat for the Multitudes"; and Pilcher, *The Sausage Rebellion*.
36. Hierzholer, "Searching for the Best Standard"; and Hierzholer, "Food Security and Safety."
37. Donofrio, "Feeding the City."
38. Konefal et al., "Governance in the Global Agro-Food System."
39. Tolbert, "The Aristocracy of the Market Basket"; and Grandclément, "Wheeling One's Groceries around the Store."
40. Horowitz, *Putting Meat on the American Table*; Lee and Torell, "Promoting Packaging and Selling Self-Service."
41. Murton, "John Bull and Sons."
42. Tracey Deutsch, *Building a Housewife's Paradise*; and Miller, *Feeding Barcelona*.
43. Gabaccia, *We Are What We Eat*; Imbruce, "From the Bottom Up"; Zanoni, *Migrant Marketplaces of the Americas*; and Belasco, *Appetite for Change*.
44. Frischmann, *Infrastructure*, 5.
45. Edwards, *A Vast Machine*, 17.
46. Edwards et al., *Knowledge Infrastructures*, 1.
47. See, for example, the rise of "innovation intermediaries" in the Netherlands as a response to the privatization of agricultural research in Klerkx and Leeuwis, "Matching Demand and Supply."

CULINARY INFRASTRUCTURE

48. Ferguson, *Accounting for Taste*.
49. Goody, *Cooking, Cuisine, and Class*; MacLean and Insoll, "Archaeology, Luxury and the Exotic"; McCann, *Stirring the Pot*; and Bottéro, *The Oldest Cuisine in the World*.
50. Mennell, *All Manners of Food*; Flandrin and Montanari, *Food*; Capatti and Montanari, *Italian Cuisine*; Rath, *Food and Fantasy in Japan*; and Pennell, "Professional Cooking, Kitchens, and Service Work."
51. For exemplary works, see Spiller, "Recipes for Knowledge"; Sherman, *Invention of the Modern Cookbook*; Gabaccia and Aldrich, "Recipes in Context."
52. Spang, *The Invention of the Restaurant*; Ferguson, *Accounting for Taste*; and Trubek, *Haute Cuisine*.
53. Davis, *Defining Culinary Authority*; and Takats, *The Expert Cook*.
54. Drouard, "Escoffier, Bocuse et (surtout) les autres …"; Trubek, *Haute Cuisine*; and Ferguson, "The French Invention of Modern Cuisine," 244.
55. Scholliers, "Anonymous Cooks and Waiters," 164; and Trubek, *Haute Cuisine*, 47.
56. Lee, "Entrepreneurs in the Age of Exclusion"; Chen, *Chop Suey USA*; Liu, *From Canton Restaurant to Panda Express*; and Ray, *The Ethnic Restaurateur*.
57. Ferguson, *Accounting for Taste*.
58. Bak-Geller Corona, "Los recetarios 'afrancesados.'"
59. Ferguson, "Michelin in America," 51.
60. Rebekah Pite, *Creating a Common Table*; Polan, *Julia Child's The French Chef*; Tracey Deutsch.
61. Johnston and Bauman, *Foodies*; Rousseau, *Food Media*; Wang, "Learning from Los Kogi Angeles"; and de Solier, *Food and the Self*.
62. Belasco, "Toward a Culinary Common Denominator"; Jakle and Sculle, *Fast Food*; and Penfold, *The Donut*.
63. Bégin, "Mapping 'Scarborough Chinatown'"; and Zukin, *Naked City*.
64. Guy, *When Champagne Became French*; Guthman, *Agrarian Dreams*; Friedberg, *Fresh*; Paxson, *The Life of Cheese*; Trubek, *Taste of Place*; and Parasecoli, "The Gender of Geographical Indications."
65. Freedman, "Restaurants," 267–71; and Pilcher, *Planet Taco*, 199–201.
66. Kim, "From Kimchi to Infinity"; and August, "The Refugee Aesthetic."
67. Tarulevicz, *Eating Her Curries and Kway*; Duruz and Khoo, *Eating Together*; Portnoy and Pilcher, "Roy Choi and Pacific Fusion."
68. Ferguson, "Michelin in America," 52–3; and Collins, "Who's to Judge," 75.
69. Gabaccia, *Foreign Relations*.
70. "City Food."

Bibliography

Appadurai, Arjun, ed. *The Social Life of Things: Commodities in Cultural Perspective*. Cambridge: Cambridge University Press, 1986.

August, Timothy. "The Refugee Aesthetic: Relocating Southeast Asian American Literature." Unpublished manuscript.

Baker, Lauren E. "Tending Cultural Landscapes and Food Citizenship in Toronto's Community Gardens." *Geographical Review* 94, no. 3 (Jul. 1, 2004): 305–325.

Bak-Geller Corona, Sarah. "Los recetarios 'afrancesados' del siglo XIX en México: La construcción de la nación Mexicana y de un modelo culinario nacional," *Anthropology of Food* S6 (Dec., 2009): 3, 9. Accessed December 7, 2010. http://aof.revues.org/index6464.html

CULINARY INFRASTRUCTURE

Barabási, Albert-Lazlo. *Linked: The New Science of Networks*. New York: Perseus, 2002.

Bégin, Camille. "Mapping 'Scarborough Chinatown.'" 2014. Accessed March 2, 2016. http://www.utsc.utoronto.ca/culinaria/mapping-scarborough-chinatown

Belasco, Warren J. "Toward a Culinary Common Denominator: The Rise of Howard Johnson's, 1925–1940." *The Journal of American Culture* 2, no. 3 (Fall 1979): 503–518.

Belasco, Warren. *Appetite for Change: How the Counterculture Took on the Food Industry*. Ithaca, NY: Cornell University Press, 1993.

Belasco, Warren, and Roger Horowitz, eds. *Food Chains: From Farmyard to Shopping Cart*. Philadelphia, PA: University of Pennsylvania Press, 2009.

Blay-Palmer, Alison. *Food Scares: From Industrial to Sustainable Food Systems*. Aldershot: Ashgate, 2008.

Bohstedt, John. *The Politics of Provisions: Food Riots, Moral Economy, and Market Transition in England, c. 1550–1850*. Burlington, VT: Ashgate, 2010.

Bottéro, Jean. *The Oldest Cuisine in the World: Cooking in Mesopotamia*. Translated by Teresa Lavender Fagan. Chicago, IL: University of Chicago Press, 2004.

Braudel, Fernand. *The Structures of Everyday Life: The Limits of the Possible*. Vol. 1 of *Civilization and Capitalism, 15th-18th Century*. Translated by Siân Reynolds. New York: Harper & Row, 1979.

Bruegel, Martin. "How the French Learned to Eat Canned Food, 1809–1930s." In *Food Nations: Selling Taste in Consumer Societies*, edited by Warren Belasco and Philip Scranton, 113–130. New York: Routledge, 2002.

Brueghel, Martin. "Food Politics: Policing the Street, Regulating the Market." In *In the Age of Empire*, edited by Martin Bruegel, 87–105. Vol. 5 of *A Cultural History of Food*, edited by Fabio Parasecoli and Peter Scholliers. London: Berg, 2012.

Capatti, Alberto, and Massimo Montanari. *Italian Cuisine: A Cultural History*. Translated by Aine O'Healy. New York: Columbia University Press, 1999.

Chang, K. C., ed. *Food in Chinese Culture: Anthropological and Historical Perspectives*. New Haven, CT: Yale University Press, 1977.

Chen, Yong. *Chop Suey, USA*. New York: Columbia University Press, 2014.

"City Food." Accessed March 14, 2016. http://www.utsc.utoronto.ca/culinaria/city-food

Claflin, Kyri W. "Les Halles and the Moral Market: Frigophobia Strikes in the Belly of Paris." In *Food and Morality: Proceedings of the Oxford Symposium on Food and Cooking 2007*, edited by Susan R. Friedland, 82–92. Oxford: Prospect Books, 2008.

Collins, Lauren. "Who's to Judge? How the World's 50 Best Restaurants are Chosen." *The New Yorker*, November 2, 2015.

Craig, Lee A., Barry Goodwin, and Thomas Grennes. "The Effect of Mechanical Refrigeration on Nutrition in the United States." *Social Science History* 28, no. 2 (Summer 2004): 325–336.

Cronon, William. *Nature's Metropolis: Chicago and the Great West*. New York: Norton, 1991.

Crown, Patricia L., and W. Jeffrey Hurst. "Evidence of Cacao Use in the Prehispanic American Southwest." *Proceedings of the National Academy of Sciences* 106, no. 7 (Feb. 17, 2009): 2110–2113.

Davis, Jennifer J. *Defining Culinary Authority: The Transformation of Cooking in France, 1650–1830*. Baton Rouge: Louisiana State University Press, 2013.

Deutsch, Tracey. *Building a Housewife's Paradise: Gender, Politics, and American Grocery Stores in the Twentieth Century*. Chapel Hill: University of North Carolina Press, 2010.

Donofrio, Gregory Alexander. "Feeding the City." *Gastronomica* 7, no. 4 (2007): 30–41.

Drouard, Alain. "Escoffier, Bocuse et (surtout) les autres...: Towards a History of Cooks in France in the Nineteenth and Twentieth Centuries." In *Eating out in Europe:*

Picnics, Gourmet Dining, and Snacks Since the Late Eighteenth Century, edited by Marc Jacobs and Peter Scholliers, 215–228. Oxford: Berg, 2003.

Duruz, Jean, and Gaik Cheng Khoo. *Eating Together: Food, Space, and Identity in Malaysia and Singapore*. Lanham, MD: Rowman and Littlefield, 2015.

Edwards, Paul N. *A Vast Machine: Computer Models, Climate Data, and the Politics of Global Warming*. Cambridge, MA: MIT Press, 2010.

Edwards, P. N., S. J. Jackson, M. K. Chalmers, G. C Bowker, C. L. Borgman, D. Ribest, M. Burton, and S. Calvert. *Knowledge Infrastructures: Intellectual Frameworks and Research Challenges*. Ann Arbor, MI: Deep Blue, 2013. Accessed June 20, 2016. https://deepblue.lib.umich.edu/handle/2027.42/97552

Ferguson, Priscilla Parkhurst. *Accounting for Taste: The Triumph of French Cuisine*. Chicago, IL: University of Chicago Press, 2004.

Ferguson, Priscilla Parkhurst. "The French Invention of Modern Cuisine." In *Food in Time and Place: The American Historical Association Companion to Food History*, edited by Paul Freedman, Joyce E. Chaplin, and Ken Albala, 233–252. Berkeley: University of California Press, 2014.

Ferguson, Priscilla Parkhurst. "Michelin in America." *Gastronomica* 8, no. 1 (Winter 2008): 49–55.

Flandrin, Jean-Louis, and Massimo Montanari, eds. *Food: A Culinary History*. Translated by Albert Sonnenfeld. New York: Columbia University Press, 1999.

Freedman, Paul. "Restaurants." In *Food in Time and Place: The American Historical Association Companion to Food History*, edited by Paul Freedman, Joyce E. Chaplin, and Ken Albala, 253–275. Berkeley: University of California Press, 2014.

Freidberg, Susanne. *French Beans and Food Scares: Culture and Commerce in an Anxious Age*. New York: Oxford University Press, 2004.

Freidberg, Susanne. *Fresh: A Perishable History*. Cambridge: Harvard University Press, 2009.

Friedland, William H. "The New Globalization: The Case of Fresh Produce." In *From Columbus to ConAgra: The Globalization of Agriculture and Food*, edited by Alessandro Bonnanno, Laurence Busch, William H. Friedland, Lourdes Gouveia, and Enzo Mingione, 210–231. Lawrence: University of Kansas Press, 1994.

Friedmann, Harriet. "International Regimes of Food and Agriculture since 1870." In *Peasants and Peasant Societies*, edited by Theodor Shanin, 258–276. Oxford: Basil Blackwell, 1987.

Frischmann, Brett M. *Infrastructure: The Social Value of Shared Resources*. New York: Oxford University Press, 2012.

Frohlich, Xaq, Mikko Jauho, Bart Penders, and David Schleifer. "Preface: Food Infrastructures." *Limn* 4 (May, 2014). Accessed January 24, 2016. http://limn.it/preface-food-infrastructures/

Gabaccia, Donna R. *Foreign Relations: American Immigration in Global Perspective*. Princeton, NJ: Princeton University Press, 2012.

Gabaccia, Donna R. *We Are What We Eat: Ethnic Food and the Making of Americans*. Cambridge, MA: Harvard University Press, 1998.

Gabaccia, Donna R., and Jane Aldrich. "Recipes in Context: Solving a Small Mystery in Charleston's Culinary History." *Food, Culture & Society* 15, no. 2 (Jun., 2012): 197–221.

Garnsey, Peter. *Food and Society in Classical Antiquity*. Cambridge: Cambridge University Press, 1999.

Gereffi, G., and M. Korzeniewicz, eds. *Commodity Chains and Global Capitalism*. Westport, CT: Greenwood Press, 1994.

Goody, Jack. *Cooking, Cuisine, and Class: A Study in Comparative Sociology*. Cambridge: Cambridge University Press, 1982.

Graham, Stephen, and Simon Marvin. *Splintering Urbanism: Networked Infrastructures, Technological Mobilities and the Urban Condition*. New York: Routledge, 2001.

Grandclément, Catherine. "Wheeling One's Groceries around the Store: The Invention of the Shopping Cart, 1936–1953." In *Food Chains: From Farmyard to Shopping Cart*, edited by Warren Belasco and Roger Horowitz, 233–251. Philadelphia, PA: University of Pennsylvania Press, 2009.

Guthman, Julie. *Agrarian Dreams: The Paradox of Organic Farming in California*. Berkeley: University of California Press, 2004.

Guy, Kolleen M. *When Champagne Became French: Wine and the Making of a National Identity*. Baltimore, MD: Johns Hopkins University Press, 2003.

Hamilakis, Yannis. "Food Technologies/Technologies of the Body: The Social Context of Wine and Oil Production and Consumption in Bronze Age Crete." *World Archaeology* 31, no. 1 (Jun., 1999): 38–54.

Hierzholer, Vera. "Food Security and Safety." In *In the Age of Empire*, edited by Martin Bruegel, 67–86. Vol. 5 of *A Cultural History of Food*, edited by Fabio Parasecoli and Peter Scholliers. London: Berg, 2012.

Hierzholer, Vera. "Searching for the Best Standard: Different Strategies of Food Regulation during German Industrialization." *Food and History* 5, no. 2 (2007): 295–318.

Horowitz, Roger. *Putting Meat on the American Table: Taste, Technology, Transformation*. Baltimore, MD: Johns Hopkins University Press, 2006.

Horowitz, Roger, Jeffrey M. Pilcher, and Sydney Watts. "Meat for the Multitudes: Market Culture in Paris, New York City, and Mexico City over the Long Nineteenth Century." *The American Historical Review* 109, no. 4 (Oct., 2004): 1055–1083.

Hughes, Thomas P. "The Evolution of Large Technological Systems." In *The Social Construction of Technological Systems: New Directions in the Sociology and History of Technology*, edited by Wiebe E. Bijker, Thomas P. Hughes, and Trevor Pinch, 45–76. Cambridge, MA: MIT Press, 1987.

Imbruce, Valerie. "From the Bottom Up: The Global Expansion of Chinese Vegetable Trade for New York City Markets." In *Fast Food/Slow Food: The Cultural Economy of the Global Food System*, edited by Richard Wilk, 163–179. Lanham: Altamira Press, 2006.

Jacks, D. S. "Intra and International Commodity Market Integration in the Atlantic Economy, 1800–1913." *Explorations in Economic History* 42 (2008): 381–413.

Jakle, John A., and Keith A. Sculle. *Fast Food: Roadside Restaurants in the Automobile Age*. Baltimore, MD: Johns Hopkins University Press, 1999.

Johnston, Josée, and Shyon Baumann. *Foodies: Democracy and Distinction in the Gourmet Foodscape*. New York: Routledge, 2010.

Julier, Alice, and Gilbert W. Gillespie, Jr. "Encountering Food Systems: A Conversation About Thinking, Teaching, and Social Change." *Food, Culture & Society* 15, no. 3 (2012): 359–373.

Kaplan, Steven Laurence. *Provisioning Paris: Merchants and Millers in the Grain and Flour Trade during the Eighteenth Century*. Ithaca, NY: Cornell University Press, 1984.

Kim, Chi-Hoon. "From Kimchi to Infinity: The Spicy Fermented Cabbage Prepares for its Moment in the Spotlight." *Hyphen: Asian American Unabridged* 25 (Spring 2012). Accessed March 25, 2016. http://hyphenmagazine.com/magazine/issue-25-generation-spring-2012/kimchi-infinity

Klerkx, Laurens, and Cees Leeuwis. "Matching Demand and Supply in the Agricultural Knowledge Infrastructure: Experiences with Innovation Intermediaries." *Food Policy* 33 (2008): 260–276.

Konefal, Jason, Michael Mascarenhas, and Maki Hatanaka. "Governance in the Global Agro-Food System: Backlighting the Role of Transnational Supermarket Chains." *Agriculture and Human Values* 22 (2005): 291–302.

Lee, Heather. "Entrepreneurs in the Age of Chinese Exclusion: Transnational Capital, Migrant Labor, and Chinese Restaurants in New York City, 1850–1943." PhD diss., Brown University, 2014.

Lee, Jenny, and Ulrika Torell. "Promoting Packaging and Selling Self-Service: The Rapid Modernization of the Swedish Food Retail Trade." In *The Food Industries of Europe in the Nineteenth and Twentieth Centuries*, edited by Derek J. Oddy and Alain Drouard, 181–197. Farnham: Ashgate, 2013.

Liu, Haiming. *From Canton Restaurant to Panda Express: A History of Chinese Food in the United States*. New Brunswick, NJ: Rutgers University Press, 2015.

MacLean, Rachel, and Timothy Insoll. "Archaeology, Luxury and the Exotic: The Examples of Islamic Gao (Mali) and Bahrain." *World Archaeology* 34, no. 3 (Feb., 2003): 558–570.

Margulis, Stephen T., Jaideep Motwani, and Ashok Kumar. "The Tiffin Carriers of Bombay, India: An Organizational And Logistical Analysis." *International Journal of Commerce and Management* 7, no. 3/4 (1997): 120–140.

McCann, James. *Stirring the Pot: A History of African Cuisine*. Athens: Ohio University Press, 2009.

McGovern, Patrick E., and Ancient Wine. *The Search for the Origins of Viniculture*. Princeton, NJ: Princeton University Press, 2003.

McMichael, Philip, ed. *The Global Restructuring of Agro-Food Systems*. Ithaca, NY: Cornell University Press, 1994.

Mennell, Stephen. *All Manners of Food: Eating and Taste in England and France from the Middle Ages to the Present*. Oxford: Basil Blackwell, 1985.

Merleaux, April. *Sugar and Civilization: American Empire and the Cultural Politics of Sweetness*. Chapel Hill: University of North Carolina Press, 2015.

Miller, Montserrat. *Feeding Barcelona, 1714–1975: Public Market Halls, Social Networks, and Consumer Culture*. Baton Rouge: Louisiana State University Press, 2015.

Miller, Judith A. *Mastering the Market: The State and the Grain Trade in Northern France, 1700–1860*. Cambridge: Cambridge University Press, 1999.

Mintz, Sidney W. *Sweetness and Power: The Place of Sugar in Modern History*. New York: Viking Press, 1985.

Morley, Neville. *Metropolis and Hinterland: The City of Rome and the Italian Economy, 200 B.C.– A.D. 200*. Cambridge: Cambridge University Press, 1996.

Mott, Lawrence. "The Best Manned Fleet Ever Beheld: The Catalan-Aragonese Fleet in Sicily during the War of the Sicilian Vespers, AD 1282–1295." PhD diss., University of Minnesota, 1999.

Murton, John. "John Bull and Sons: The Empire Marketing Board and the Creation of a British Imperial Food System." In *Edible Histories, Cultural Politics: Towards a Canadian Food History*, edited by Franca Iacovetta, Valerie J. Korinek, and Marlene Epp, 225–248. Toronto: University of Toronto Press, 2012.

Nützenadel, Alexander, and Frank Trentmann. "Mapping Food and Globalization." In *Food and Globalization: Consumption, Markets, and Politics in the Modern World*, edited by Alexander Nützenadel and Frank Trentmann, 1–20. New York: Berg, 2008.

Ohnuki-Tierney, Emiko. *Rice as Self: Japanese Identities Through Time*. Princeton, NJ: Princeton University Press, 1993.

Oxford English Dictionary Online. Accessed January 24, 2016. http://www.oed.com.myaccess.library.utoronto.ca/view/Entry/95624

Parasecoli, Fabio. "The Gender of Geographical Indications: Women, Place, and the Marketing of Identities." *Cultural Studies – Critical Methodologies* 10, no. 6 (2010): 467–478.

Parham, Susan. *Food and Urbanism: The Convival City and a Sustainable Future*. London: Bloomsbury, 2015.

Paxson, Heather. *The Life of Cheese: Creating Food and Value in America*. Berkeley: University of California Press, 2012.

Pee, Christian de. "Purchase on Power: Imperial Space and Commercial Space in Song-Dynasty Kaifeng, 960–1127." *Journal of the Economic and Social History of the Orient* 53 (2010): 149–184.

Penfold, Steve. *The Donut: A Canadian History*. Toronto: University of Toronto Press, 2008.

Pennell, Sara. "Professional Cooking, Kitchens, and Service Work: *Accomplisht* Cookery." In *In the Early Modern Age*, edited by Beat Kümin, 103–121. Vol. 4 of *A Cultural History of Food*, edited by Fabio Parasecoli and Peter Scholliers. London: Berg, 2012.

Petrick, Gabriella. "'Like Ribbons of Green and Gold': Industrializing Lettuce and the Quest for Quality in the Salinas Valley, 1920–1965." *Agricultural History* 80 (Summer 2006): 269–295.

Pilcher, Jeffrey M. "Empire of the 'Jungle': The Rise of an Atlantic Refrigerated Beef Industry, 1880–1920." *Food, Culture & Society* 7, no. 1 (Fall 2004): 63–78.

Pilcher, Jeffrey M. *Planet Taco: A Global History of Mexican Food*. New York: Oxford University Press, 2012.

Pilcher, Jeffrey M. *The Sausage Rebellion: Public Health, Private Enterprise, and Meat in Mexico City, 1890–1917*. Albuquerque: University of New Mexico Press, 2006.

Pite, Rebekah E. *Creating a Common Table in Twentieth-Century Argentina: Doña Petrona, Women, and Food*. Chapel Hill: University of North Carolina Press, 2013.

Polan, Dana. *Julia Child's The French Chef*. Durham: Duke University Press, 2011.

Portnoy, Sarah, and Jeffrey M. Pilcher. "Roy Choi, Ricardo Zárate, and Pacific Fusion Cuisine in Los Angeles." In *Global Latin America*, edited by Matthew Gutmann and Jeffrey Lesser, 146–162. Berkeley: University of California Press, 2016.

Princen, Thomas. "Distancing: Consumption and the Severing of Feedback." In *Confronting Consumption*, edited by Thomas Princen, Michael Maniates, and Ken Conca, 103–132. Cambridge: MIT Press, 2002.

Rath, Eric C. *Food and Fantasy in Early Modern Japan*. Berkeley: University of California Press, 2010.

Ray, Krishnendu. *The Ethnic Restaurateur*. London: Bloomsbury, 2016.

Rees, Jonathan. *Refrigeration Nation: A History of Ice, Appliances, and Enterprise in America*. Baltimore, MD: Johns Hopkins University Press, 2013.

Roberts, Lissa. "The Death of the Sensuous Chemist: The 'New' Chemistry and the Transformation of Sensuous Technology." In *Empire of the Senses: The Sensual Culture Reader*, edited by David Howes, 106–139. Oxford: Berg, 2005.

Robinson, Damian, and Andrew Wilson, eds. *Maritime Archaeology and Ancient Trade in the Mediterranean*. Oxford: Oxbow Books, 2011.

Rousseau, Signe. *Food Media: Celebrity Chefs and the Politics of Everyday Interference*. London: Berg, 2012.

Scholliers, Peter. "Anonymous Cooks and Waiters: Labour Markets and the Professional Status of Restaurant, Café and Hotel Personnel in Brussels, 1840s–1900s." *Food and History* 2, no. 1 (2004): 137–166.

CULINARY INFRASTRUCTURE

Segers, Yves, Jan Bieleman, and Erik Huyst. *Exploring the Food Chain: Food Production and Food Processing in Western Europe, 1850–1990*. Turnhout: Brepols, 2009.

Sherman, Sandra. *The Invention of the Modern Cookbook*. Santa Barbara, CA: Greenwood, 2010.

Smith, Colin. "The Wholesale and Retail Markets of London, 1660–1840." *Economic History Review* 55, no. 1 (2002): 31–50.

de Solier, Isabelle. *Food and the Self: Consumption, Production, and Material Culture*. London: Berg, 2013.

Spang, Rebecca L. *The Invention of the Restaurant: Paris and Modern Gastronomic Culture*. Cambridge: Harvard University Press, 2000.

Spiller, Elizabeth. "Recipes for Knowledge: Maker's Knowledge Traditions, Paracelsian Recipes, and the Invention of the Cookbook, 1600–1660." In *Renaissance Food from Rabelais to Shakespeare: Culinary Readings and Culinary Histories*, edited by Joan Fitzpatrick, 55–72. Farnham: Ashgate, 2010.

Stovall, Tyler. *Paris and the Spirit of 1919: Consumer Struggles, Transnationalism, and Revolution*. Cambridge: Cambridge University Press, 2012.

Takats, Sean. *The Expert Cook in Enlightenment France*. Baltimore, MD: Johns Hopkins University Press, 2011.

Tarulevicz, Nicole. *Eating Her Curries and Kway: A Cultural History of Food in Singapore*. Urbana: University of Illinois Press, 2013.

Tolbert, Lisa C. "The Aristocracy of the Market Basket: Self-Service Shopping in the New South." In *Food Chains: From Farmyard to Shopping Cart*, edited by Warren Belasco and Roger Horowitz, 179–195. Philadelphia: University of Pennsylvania Press, 2009.

Trubek, Amy. *Haute Cuisine: How the French Invented the Culinary Profession*. Philadelphia: University of Pennsylvania Press, 2000.

Trubek, Amy. *The Taste of Place: A Cultural Journey into Terroir*. Berkeley: University of California Press, 2009.

Ur, Jason A., and Carlo Colantoni. "The Cycle of Production, Preparation, and Consumption in a Northern Mesopotamian City." In *Inside Ancient Kitchens: New Directions in the Study of Daily Meals and Feasts*, edited by Elizabeth A. Klarich, 55–82. Boulder: University of Colorado Press, 2010.

van der Vleuten, Erik. "Feeding the Peoples of Europe: Transport Infrastructures and the Building of Transnational Cooling Chains in the Early Cold War, 1947-1960." In *Materializing Europe: Transnational Infrastructures and the Project of Europe*, edited by Andreas Fickers and Alexander Badenoch, 148–177. London: Palgrave Macmillan, 2010.

van de Vleuten, Erik. "Infrastructures and Societal Change: A View from the Large Technical Systems Field." *Technology Analysis and Strategic Management* 16, no. 3 (Sep., 2004): 395–414.

Vitiello, Domenic, and Catherine Brinkley. "The Hidden History of Food System Planning." *Journal of Planning History* 13, no. 2 (2014): 91–112.

Wallerstein, Immanuel. *The Modern World System: Capitalist Agriculture and the Origins of the European World Economy in the Sixteenth Century*. New York: Academic Press, 1974.

Wang, Oliver S. "Learning from Los Kogi Angeles: A Taco Truck and its City." In *Eating Asian America. A Food Studies Reader*, edited by Robert Ji-Song Ku, Martin F. Manalasan IV, and Anita Mannur, 78–97. New York: New York University Press, 2013.

Watts, Duncan. *Six Degrees: The Science of a Connected Age*. New York: Gardner's Books, 2003.

Welsh, Jennifer, and Rod MacRae. "Food Citizenship and Community Food Security: Lessons from Toronto, Canada." *Canadian Journal of Development Studies* 19 (1998): 237–255.

Wilk, Richard R. "Anchovy Sauce and Pickled Tripe: Exporting Civilized Food in the Colinal Atlantic World." In *Food Chains: From Farmyard to Shopping Cart*, edited by Warren Belasco and Roger Horowitz, 87–107. Philadelphia: University of Pennsylvania Press, 2009.

Wilk, Richard R. "The Extractive Economy: An Early Phase of the Globalization of Diet and its Environmental Consequences." In *World System History and Global Environmental Change*, edited by Alf Hornborg, J. R. McNeill, and Joan Martinez-Alier, 179–198. Lanham, MD: Altamira, 2007.

Will, Pierre-Étienne, and R. Bin Wong. *Nourish the People: The State Civilian Granary System in China, 1650-1850*. Ann Arbor: University of Michigan, Center for Chinese Studies, 1991.

Wolf, Eric R. *Europe and the People without History*. Berkeley: University of California Press, 1982.

Wong, R. Bin. "Food Riots in the Qing Dynasty." *The Journal of Asian Studies* 41, no. 4 (Aug., 1982): 767–788.

Yates, Jo Anne. *Structuring the Information Age: Life Insurance and Technology in the Twentieth Century*. Baltimore, MD: Johns Hopkins University Press, 2005.

Zanoni, Elizabeth. *Migrant Marketplaces of the Americas*. Urbana: University of Illinois Press, forthcoming.

Zukin, Sharon. *Naked City: The Death and Life of Authentic Urban Places*. New York: Oxford University Press, 2009.

Frozen Food and National Socialist Expansionism

Julia S. Torrie

ABSTRACT

Fast freezing, developed from the 1920s, preserved food quality, taste, and appearance better than earlier techniques. After 1933, the National Socialists encouraged fast freezing in Germany because it promised to solve wartime supply problems and aligned with their ideas about modernity, efficiency, and centralization. During World War II, they used freezing to integrate the agricultural products of occupied and allied areas into a continental European economy (Grossraumwirtschaft) under German control. Although occupied populations might have been expected to reject the German-led spread of fast freezing, French responses to these initiatives suggest that some occupied people interpreted them more positively. French experts saw German fast freezing as a continuation of pre-war projects and an investment for the post-war, when they hoped to see France use new infrastructures to gain a pivotal position in a broader European food economy. After surveying alignments between National Socialist expansionism and fast freezing, this article examines reactions to German initiatives in the La Rochelle area on the western coast of France. The French case suggests that local reactions to German involvement in fast freezing were more complex than simple collaboration or, alternately, a juxtaposition of expansionist ambition and local resentment. Wartime formed part of longer patterns of transnational development, transfer, and exchange, and interactions during World War II may have opened the door for the spread of freezing in subsequent years.

Frozen food, though commonplace today, was a seldom-used commodity in the early twentieth century. Especially meat and fish had been frozen since the later nineteenth century, but were considered poor-quality substitutes for fresh. Fast freezing, developed in the United States, replaced earlier methods in the 1920s. After 1933, the National Socialists in Germany found fast freezing attractive because it maintained food quality and texture. They supported domestic research in this area and in 1939, to make large-scale freezing feasible quickly, purchased the rights to the industrial process developed by American Charles Birdseye.[1]

CULINARY INFRASTRUCTURE

Although not the only European country interested in frozen food, Germany was the first to implement fast freezing extensively. Why? Fast freezing promised to solve problems and aligned well with National Socialist ideas about modernity, efficiency, and centralization. Initially, fast freezing supported the desire for autarchy stemming from the experience of blockade and hunger during World War I. With the renewed outbreak of war in 1939, the appeal of such freezing grew, for it seemed an ideal tool to exploit the agricultural resources of newly occupied lands. Fast freezing offered a way to bridge gaps between excess and shortage across time and space, making summer's vitamin-rich foods available in winter, and enabling the surplus products of one European region to be enjoyed in others where they were scarce.[2] By removing a bottleneck in the process of exploitation and domination, it opened up the possibility of supplying soldiers and civilians with limitless, year-round abundance.

Freezing was desirable to the Third Reich not only because of pre-war preparations and the conditions of war itself, including increased demand for collective meals and the risk of food shortages, but also due to the expansionist thrust of National Socialist war specifically. Its development was partly predicated on the fact that Germany now occupied vast swaths of European agricultural land. To realize the full potential of these areas, occupying authorities believed that intervention in food production and conservation was essential. Fast freezing would integrate agricultural products from far-flung occupied and allied areas into a continental European economy (Grossraumwirtschaft) under German control.

Given the connection between this new technology and National Socialist domination, one might have expected occupied populations to reject the introduction of fast freezing. Indeed, insofar as they have written about this subject, historians have suggested that local people resented German involvement in frozen food production and that wartime experiences contributed to giving such food a poor reputation. In Norway, for instance, Terje Finstad argues that poor wartime quality and negative associations with the occupation made it difficult for frozen fish to gain traction with consumers in the post-war years.[3] Alongside Norway, France was the foremost testing ground for German freezing outside the Reich.[4] Experts' reactions to new facilities there suggest that responses to German initiatives were complex, and that some occupied people saw them in a more positive light.

After surveying alignments between National Socialist expansionism and fast freezing, this article examines reactions to German initiatives in the La Rochelle area on the western coast of France. Prominent representatives of the French meat processing industry and the health and safety inspection were surprisingly open to German projects. These specialists tended to view German involvement in food preservation as a necessary evil, a way to ensure supplies for both occupying and occupied populations. As nationalists who subscribed at least partly to Maréchal Philippe Pétain's plans for national renewal along

33

Hitlerian lines, they viewed German innovations as potentially beneficial for France, embracing them as part of a longer drive to bring refrigeration to the French meat business, in particular.[5] At the same time, French observers sought recognition for French contributions to freezing. They interpreted the occupation as part of a longer continuum of scientific and technical interchange in which France played as important a role as its neighbor to the East. Finally, although they did not like the fact that the occupiers were expanding French freezing capacities to their own ends in wartime, French experts looked to the longer term. They viewed wartime growth as a continuation of pre-war projects and an investment for the post-war, when they hoped to see France use new infrastructures to gain a pivotal position in a broader European food economy.

The French case suggests that local reactions to German involvement in frozen food were more complex than simple collaboration or, alternately, a juxtaposition of expansionist ambition and local resentment. Food experts' attitudes underline the fact that wartime forms part of longer patterns of transnational development, transfer, and exchange. Even if associations with war and occupation gave specific frozen foods, like fish, a bad reputation, wartime interactions may have opened the door for the spread of freezing in the postwar years.

Historians have already begun to explore the connections between wartime and food innovations such as freezing. Like the history of food more generally, freezing may be approached from a variety of angles, including the history of science and technology, of consumerism, or of specific enterprises, individuals, or associations.[6] The foremost expert on war and freezing in Germany, Ulrike Thoms, has written a series of insightful essays that show how wartime furthered German food and nutrition science and the use of specific foods and processes such freezing, dehydration, and soybean cultivation.[7] In a global context, Lizzie Collingham has addressed freezing as one of a number of tools used to safeguard wartime food supplies. Like Thoms, she has pointed to the war as a key moment for the introduction of new technologies that became popularized after 1945.[8]

Other scholars have looked specifically at freezing in German-occupied territories. In Norway, they have shown how advances in freezing enabled the export of fish to address the perceived "protein gap" in German nutrition.[9] They have also traced the implications of German involvement for the post-war acceptance of frozen fish by Norwegians.[10] Although these works raise important questions, they are limited by their focus on fish, and on the Norwegian situation, specifically. In France, Kyri Claflin has examined meat processing and uncovered controversies over the use of refrigeration at the Paris abattoir La Villette in the late nineteenth and early twentieth centuries.[11] We also know a great deal about the overall food situation during the German occupation, and about the black market, but freezing has not yet drawn historians' attention nor has Franco–German interaction in this domain.[12] Looking

CULINARY INFRASTRUCTURE

at freezing beyond occupied Norway brings to light both concrete connections between German expansionism and increased use of freezing, and "symbolic" links between this technology and the thorough-going exploitation of occupied lands. Moreover, freezing in the La Rochelle area offers insight into local responses to German initiatives, and helps fit wartime experiences into longer term patterns of exchange in Europe.

National Socialists took up fast freezing enthusiastically, for it aligned with their goals in important ways. Compared to earlier preservation techniques, like canning, fast freezing seemed practical, innovative, and modern. In the years before the war, it promised to make Germany less reliant on imported goods, fostering self-sufficiency. Once war began, it seemed a perfect tool to further the exploitation of occupied Europe.

Although industrial canning factories existed in Germany from the 1870s, Uwe Spiekermann points out that canned goods were slow to catch on.[13] Canned food became popular in the USA and Britain, but in Germany, it "symbolize[d] artificial and unhealthy fare."[14] Contemporaries worried about cans' nutritional value, and had doubts about additives used in production.[15] While canning, doubtless, accustomed Germans to industrially processed food, the bad reputation of canned goods may have helped encourage, or at least removed an impediment to, the adoption of frozen foods. In contrast to canned goods, frozen foods "were high in vitamins, contained no preservatives, and produced no poisoning incidents."[16] Whereas can-making required imported tinplate, which used up foreign currency and was difficult to obtain after 1939; frozen goods could be packed in paper, cardboard, or increasingly commonly in plastic film.[17] They were lighter to transport for the same amount of edible weight, and did not leave empty cans behind. Freezing and storing frozen foods required electricity, but such foods could be transported over long distances in insulated rather than actively cooled trains and trucks. Thawed products did, however, need to be cooked upon arrival, which was not the case with canned goods.

For the National Socialists, the potential to retain vitamins was another part of freezing's appeal. They believed that vitamins, "would improve the physical performance of workers and soldiers."[18] According to Thoms, the high vitamin content of frozen foods was the prerequisite for their use by the SS.[19] Contemporaries also understood that taste was important and saw frozen fruit, for example, as a way to add interest to a military diet. The introduction to the 1941 Field Cookbook reminded army cooks that, "You boost the mood and capabilities of your comrades if you provide them with food that tastes good."[20]

Military food expert Wilhelm Ziegelmayer emerged as a key proponent of frozen food.[21] In 1940, he argued that, "frozen foods offer considerable advantages for military provisioning," among which was the fact that such foods were "equivalent to fresh" (frischwertig), maintained vitamin content, and could be stored over long periods of time without alteration.[22] Properly warehoused, they were relatively impervious to rot, pests, and such war-specific threats as "poison gases."[23] Moreover, freezing offered "the advantage of convenience, cleanliness and central waste processing."[24] Since most of the work preparing frozen food was undertaken at the production point, the packets were practical and easy to use. Cans had to be round because of pressure that arose during the heat preservation process, but frozen food could be made in any shape.[25] In contrast to earlier freezing efforts that used whole sides of beef, pork, or mutton, fast freezing introduced smaller rectangular blocks that were easy to transport and store. These frozen "bricks" of meat saved valuable time in field kitchens and other collective feeding establishments. Central preparation also meant that food waste was efficiently gathered for recycling, a particular advantage in wartime.[26]

Quite apart from the practical advantages and potential military applications of freezing, National Socialists were also drawn to it because it implied a broader kind of superiority. Access to cold in warm seasons had long been an elite privilege, and the ability to freeze goods and keep them frozen for transport over long distances was an impressive technological achievement.[27] Freezing added value to food not only because it limited spoilage, but also because frozen products demonstrated German industrial and technological strength. Through freezing, foods became imbued with an aura of modernity. If Europeans seemed a little behind Americans in food processing generally and the adoption of fast freezing specifically, Germany wanted to show itself to be the exception to this rule. Frozen foods were important "for the self-staging of the National Socialist state as a modern state that [was] able to solve its problems by techno-scientific solutions."[28] Moreover, Germany could not afford to be left behind if, as Ziegelmayer argued, "it is already clear today that the planned activation of the fast freezing process will play an outstanding role in the provisioning of modern armies."[29]

Along with its practicality, potential health benefits, and modernity, freezing also appealed to the National Socialists for political reasons. A technique that enabled summer's harvests to be used year round fostered self-sufficiency, an important priority of the pre-war and wartime years. Having no desire to repeat experiences of hunger during World War I, the National Socialists prepared for a possible blockade by exploiting existing agricultural land fully and finding substitutes for foreign goods. Refrigeration researcher Rudolf Plank had been commissioned to study meat and fish freezing in World War I, but Germany's blockaded situation did not allow for large facilities to be established.[30] Now, although demand for canned food also increased, the drawbacks of canned goods meant that the "four-year plan of 1936 incorporated the goal of establishing a new freezing industry."[31]

Freezing was developed despite objections from both canning and tin-plate industries, which feared the potential loss of market share.[32] In 1937, researchers at the Reich Institute for Food Conservation (Reichsinstitut für Lebensmittelfrischhaltung) in Karlsruhe carried out fast freezing experiments

CULINARY INFRASTRUCTURE

in cooperation with Nordsee, a fish processing company.[33] The state also helped found Solo-Feinfrost, which focused on freezing for the army.[34] Alongside meat and fish, state intervention added freezing capabilities to fruit and vegetable canning plants. Four-Year Plan proponent Hans Mosolff reported that, "the result of this work was that now a few preserving factories also found the courage to begin producing frozen products independently."[35] By 1940, some 22,000 tons of frozen food were being made, of which fish represented 7,000–8,000 tons and fruits and vegetables 14,000 tons.[36] The desire for autarchy fostered through the Four-Year Plan thus strongly motivated the development of freezing in Germany.

Notwithstanding National Socialist enthusiasm for freezing, it should be emphasized that freezers did not become standard household equipment in Germany until well after the war. The freezer's sibling, the home refrigerator, which sometimes included a compartment to make ice, had been advertised as a luxury product in the 1930s. National Socialists took up refrigeration, like freezing, because it aligned with notions of modernity and with their goal of exploiting food resources fully. They argued that home refrigerators would limit food wastage, and the Four-Year Plan included preparations for an affordable "People's Refrigerator" (Volkskühlschrank).[37] These plans never moved beyond the prototype stage, but a contemporary professional publication suggested that the number of refrigerators in Germany had nonetheless grown from 80,000 to 240,000 between 1936 and 1939.[38] By way of comparison, the American refrigeration industry produced some 850,000 refrigerators annually at this time, and nine million refrigerators had already been sold in the USA by 1936.[39] War and post-war shortages put a stop to the spread of home refrigerators in Germany, and refrigerators, let alone freezers, were owned by less than half of German households before the early 1960's.[40]

The fact that individual households rarely owned electric refrigerators, let alone freezers, did not prevent a remarkable expansion of freezing during the war years.[41] Military and civilian collective kitchens were the direct beneficiaries of most of this activity, for military supply lines and large-scale deliveries to factory canteens could be more easily adapted to frozen foodstuffs than the networks that supplied private households. Wartime helped accustom Germans to the idea of frozen food, and encouraged canteen chefs to learn how to cook it.

The long-term intention behind developing freezing was to improve German food supplies, a nationalist project that was intimately linked to war.[42] Ensuring better food supplies was an oft-cited justification for Hitler's expansionism. Four months before the invasion of Poland, the Führer informed his highest commanders that the problem was not Danzig, but rather, "For us it is a matter of expanding our living space in the East and making food supplies secure."[43] While overseas colonies might provide food for the British who, as Chris Otter has put it, "outsourced" their food production from the beginning of the industrial revolution, from Hitler's perspective colonies represented "no solution to the food problem" due to the danger of "blockade."[44] Instead, occupied lands in Europe offered the best potential sources of plant and animal foods. Yet, even with canning and increasingly common dehydration technologies, the perishable nature of fresh foods had hitherto limited the extent to which they could be harvested and stored for later use. Freezing promised to furnish soldiers and civilians with "fresh" produce year round. As Dr. Wirz of the Reich Main office for People's Health (Hauptamt für Volksgesundheit) put it, through freezing,

> A people can become healthier and more physically capable than its living space [Lebensraum] would otherwise allow, because it has the opportunity of using more of the highest quality and most vitamin-rich fruit and vegetables from neighbouring lands with more favourable climates.[45]

To increase their freezing capacity, German innovators turned to mobile freezing equipment, which was attractive for several reasons. Mobile equipment could preserve the freshest produce by processing fruits and vegetables in the growing regions immediately after harvest. More flexible than conventional fixed freezing facilities, mobile freezers could be added as an accessory to existing fruit processing plants. Moreover, at least theoretically, mobile equipment could be stationed in one agricultural area in summer to preserve fruits and vegetables, then moved to the coast in winter to freeze fish. Refrigeration expert Plank explained that, "The cost effectiveness of these facilities is thereby significantly increased."[46] Plank did not mention perhaps the greatest advantage of mobile equipment – potentially it gave the German freezing industry a greater reach outside the Reich heartland. It could be deployed outside Germany during the growing season, and returned home for safekeeping at other times of the year. In a military emergency, such equipment was easily evacuated from endangered zones. Once the war had begun, the concept of German autarchy stretched to include the Reich's occupied territories. Although portable equipment was never built extensively, fast freezing became a key component of efforts to develop European "Grossraumwirtschaft," a tool to facilitate the exploitation of occupied Europe.

First, however, frozen food was used to support the military while campaigning. During the invasion of France in 1940, for example, blocks of frozen meat were sent to the Front in insulated containers. Even on a standard army supply train without special freezing equipment, the shipment arrived "without showing significant changes within 18 days."[47] Still, since most frozen foods needed to be cooked before they could be eaten, they were probably served mainly to men in fixed positions. The two-week standard menu for troops in Berlin in late June 1942 showed that they ate a frozen fish filet for lunch once in a two-week period.[48] The widely used 1941 military *Field Cookbook* (*Feldkochbuch*) included an appendix with "Guidelines for the handling of frozen meat and deep-frozen foods."[49] Readers learned that frozen halves of pork needed three to four days' refrigerated thawing and quarters of beef four to five. An extra day to hang thawed meat was recommended, after which it was to be used "as soon as possible."[50] Chefs in a hurry were advised to saw frozen meat into manageable pieces, add it to boiling liquid, and wait until the liquid boiled again before proceeding with their recipes. The book also included information about fast-frozen "bricks" of meat that could be thawed at room temperature and added directly to recipes if time were short. Finally, there were instructions for dealing with cellophane-packed frozen fish, vegetables, and fruit.

It is difficult to tell how much cooking practices actually changed, but Germans learned about frozen foods on home as well as war fronts. The Reich's food authorities were at pains to connect military and civilian eating, insisting that recipes developed for military use could also be applied in home front kitchens. Linking domestic and military cooking was the specified objective of *Field Kitchen Recipes,* a cookbook for factory canteens and collective kitchens that reproduced the 1941 field cookbook with military references removed.[51] Sharing field kitchen-style food allowed Germans to perform the unity of home and front, and indeed the unity of the *Volksgemeinschaft* more broadly. Since connecting home and war fronts also meant sharing new frozen foods, *Field Kitchen Recipes* included precisely the same instructions about how to use them as its parent text.[52] In concrete ways, therefore, as well as rather abstract ones, war and National Socialist expansionism fostered the development and popularization of frozen food.[53]

As German-held territory grew, Hitler's planners increasingly viewed Europe as a single economic zone to be led and managed by the Reich. Initially, they had hoped to make Germany itself independent of outside imports. Now, with the help of freezing, Europe as a whole could develop "sustenance freedom."[54] Refrigeration engineer Eduard Emblik saw freezing as a way to even out disparities between European regions of shortage and abundance. Making more goods available in areas of scarcity would benefit producers, who could obtain higher prices for their wares, and consumers, who would enjoy a greater range of food choices. In the past, Emblik claimed, fish export prices had been so low that, for example, the Norwegian government had had to offer subsidies to fishermen. Now, the opening of the German market had solved this problem, and Norway produced some 60,000 tons of frozen fish fillets in 1940.[55]

Alongside fish, Emblik included examples of other "surplus" foods in German-allied or occupied areas that could be brought to broader markets through freezing. The wealth of Italian growing areas, for instance, was said to rival that of California, and there were important fruit and vegetable-growing regions in Bulgaria, France, Holland, Romania, Hungary, and Croatia. The Ukraine, "was already famous as a fruit-producing land; in the future it will be accorded an important role in fruit provisioning."[56] Freezing would be particularly beneficial for vitamin-rich foods like spinach or tomatoes, or tasty ones like berries, which fared poorly in conventional cold storage facilities.[57] German intervention was justified because "lands that are provided with fresh fruits and vegetables during a long growing season have little interest in building freezing facilities for their own use."[58] For Emblik, opening up Europe's resources required the "involvement of the freezing industry in the right place, that is to say in production areas."[59] Since there was little point in developing frozen products without appropriate ways to distribute them, he also argued for German-sponsored expansion and coordination of railway networks and the development of freezer cars.[60]

The greater European economy that Emblik and his contemporaries envisioned was not an exchange of equals, but a hierarchy with Germany at the top. The strengths of different countries should complement each other "such that a turn away from excessive industrialization follows for the agrarian lands."[61] In these "agrarian lands," Germans might establish modern food preservation facilities while local people continued to work the farms.

These ideas were ambitious, but how did German initiatives actually play out in occupied lands? France was among the countries National Socialists believed had a strong future in agriculture, rather than industry. Within a few months of the armistice, in October 1940, German freezing experts were asked to study how the army might exploit French food.[62] Occupiers' projects in the La Rochelle area shed light on the installations they developed, and on how occupied countries responded to these initiatives. Rather than rejection, German ideas met with interest and even support from local specialists, who viewed them as technologically advanced compliments to their own plans. French experts interpreted German initiatives as potentially beneficial in the longer term, part of an ongoing Franco–German exchange that pre-dated and would outlast the war.

Since Germans were well aware of French farming potential, economic historian Alan Milward has argued, "Germany came increasingly to use French agriculture as a substitute for the great agricultural empire in the east of which she had dreamed."[63] To ensure that France continued to produce, Germany provided allotments of raw materials like fuel, seed, and fertilizer in exchange for agricultural products, including frozen foods. In 1941, an agreement with the French authorities allowed for an "annual delivery of 12,000 tons of vegetables frozen at low temperatures, the buyers according to French producers the necessary fertilizers and ... seeds."[64]

German intervention in agriculture and food processing in France, like other occupied areas, rested on a strong conviction that the existing resources of these areas were not being exploited properly.[65] The French agricultural situation is illuminated by an early post-war study of occupiers' agricultural practices undertaken by German exile Karl Brandt for the Food Research Institute at Stanford University.[66] According to Brandt, at the beginning of the occupation, "yields per hectare of the most important crops, with the exception of sugar beets, were from 30 to 40 percent below comparable German yields."[67] French livestock density was 25 percent lower than in Germany, and average output per animal was also lower.[68] Failing to take manpower shortages

CULINARY INFRASTRUCTURE

sufficiently into account, "German specialists believed ... that it was possible to mobilize [French] resources quickly, particularly under German occupation."[69] Increasing production was simply a matter of putting more land into cultivation, and working the land and people harder.

Lest there be any misunderstanding, Brandt clarified that French resources were not intended for the French, but were "expected to feed a large part of the Wehrmacht ... and to have enough left to feed French industrial workers employed in German armament factories and to improve the supply situation in Germany."[70] German authorities set about reforming French agriculture, including through the deployment of hundreds of *Landwirtschaftsführer*, agricultural specialists of whom there were 788 in France in early April 1944.[71]

Brandt pointed out that Hitler saw himself as having won the war in France, and this longer term perspective meant that, "The military government ... emphasized all sorts of measures by which the French could ... orient agriculture toward coordination with the unified Continental European economy and give French agriculture a secure position within it."[72] At first reading, the notion that occupation might "orient" agriculture in France toward "coordination" with a broader European economy seems redolent of the propaganda the occupiers themselves used to justify their actions on behalf of a greater European "good." Indeed, on one level, talk of unified European projects during the occupation was simply propagandistic sleight of hand intended to make a difficult situation palatable to subject populations. On another level, however, the notion of sharing in larger European projects was attractive to some occupied people, including those French who subscribed to Pétain's "Révolution nationale" and saw an important place for France in Europe's German-led future.[73] Brandt noted that the German view that "France had large dormant production resources in agriculture.... was shared by many French experts and statesmen."[74] A closer look at freezing capabilities, specifically, shows that French and Germans alike viewed expansion in this area as a key to bringing agricultural resources to market.

France had long looked to Germany alongside other countries, especially the United States, for inspiration in modernizing food preservation and distribution systems. The interwar drive for rationalization in the French fishing industry, for example, took developments in Germany, including the role of the Nordsee enterprise, as a model.[75] The French continued to watch their neighbor closely through the 1930s, growing increasingly anxious as the decade advanced.

With war looming in 1938, the French government initiated a program to develop reserves of frozen domestic meat for military use.[76] Seeking to avoid the supply problems of World War I, the Minister of Agriculture argued that it was essential even in peacetime "for the army supply corps to have at its disposal refrigeration facilities to produce frozen meat."[77] A year later, the departmental council of central French Allier wrote to the same Minister to say that the measure had had a positive effect on the price of meat, and to request that more

41

refrigeration and freezing facilities be built across France "as soon as possible."[78] After the German invasion, Allier's chief veterinarian noted that the opening of cooling facilities at the industrial abattoir at Villefranche-d'Allier was likely to be delayed because the equipment was being made in the zone now occupied by the Germans. He added that, "it would also be useful to provide all the public abattoirs with adequate refrigeration facilities including compartments specifically equipped for freezing."[79] Both before the war, and once it had begun, many in France argued in favor of expanding freezing capacity, particularly for meat.

One of the strongest proponents of freezing was Maurice Piettre, Chief veterinary health inspector for the Department of the Seine and a member of the French Agricultural Academy (Académie de l'Agriculture). Having served as veterinary liaison for the French army supply corps in Latin America from 1915–9, Piettre was an authority on meat production and war. Moreover, although he would not voluntarily have given the Germans the dominance they enjoyed in his country after 1940, he rather admired German methods, and saw a future for France as a major exporter of food to "central and northern Europe" in exchange for raw materials like coal.[80] Indeed, Piettre claimed to have suggested this very thing during a 1934 visit to Berlin, when, as director of the International Refrigeration Institute, he had attended the 25th anniversary celebrations of the German Refrigeration Association (Deutsche Kaelteverein).[81] Piettre not only argued in favor of refrigeration and freezing alongside his contemporaries; he saw food preservation by cooling as a way to bring French products to wider European and global markets.

A few weeks before the German invasion, Piettre had suggested that to avoid a diminution of its cattle reserves comparable to World War I, France should add another five or six refrigerator ships to its existing fleet of seven, and purchase frozen meat particularly from Argentina.[82] Rather than freezing more domestic meat following the program mentioned above, Piettre preferred to focus on importing, storing, and redistributing products from overseas.[83]

In early 1940, France had the capacity to store 75–80,000 tons of frozen food, which Piettre claimed was largely unused in peacetime. Space to store 40–45,000 tons could be turned over to the military without much difficulty, which he thought made it unnecessary to build new freezing facilities.[84] At the same time, Piettre conceded that if a new facility were to be built, it would make sense "to devote it most especially to the study of fast freezing, American 'quick freezing.'"[85] Fast freezing was important for the future of freezing in general and French freezing more specifically, and Piettre argued that "It was, in fact, French engineers who blazed the trail with regard to rapid freezing of large pieces of meat, quarters of beef, veal carcasses, pigs, sheep."[86] In 1937, Frenchman Charles Hovemann had used a salt solution to freeze quarters of beef vacuum-packed in latex, reducing their temperature to $-26\,°C$ within less than 20 h. Piettre reported that this technique had been adopted for smaller livestock and fowl in the United States as well.[87]

CULINARY INFRASTRUCTURE

Prior to the German invasion, therefore, Piettre was conscious of France's connection to global frozen food networks and saw his country as a leader in this domain. He spoke against hasty expansion of facilities, and favored fast freezing using French technology. Once occupied, however, France was no longer a dominant player able to set agendas and import foods advantageously from less powerful parts of the world. Instead, it found itself weakened, open to such exploitation itself.

The impact of this change became apparent by 1941 at the latest. In June of that year, again representing the International Refrigeration Institute, Piettre was invited to attend the inauguration of a large freezer warehouse at the port of La Rochelle-La Pallice. He noted that this warehouse, which could stock 4,500 tons of food, was ideally situated for the import trade from the Americas, as well as for foods from La Rochelle's own rich hinterland, including the regions of Poitou and Vendée.[88] His eye firmly trained on French interests, Piettre failed to mention, if he knew, that the German 3rd U-boat flotilla was soon to be stationed at La Pallice, and that construction of a large protective bunker had already begun.[89] Instead of commenting on the potential convenience of a freezer warehouse for supplying submarines, Piettre noted that French plans for a cold storage facility at La Pallice actually dated from World War I. A Franco–Argentinian project started in 1916 had been completed the following year by the American forces fortuitously arriving under the leadership of a certain Colonel Evans, chief engineer of the Chicago meat-packing firm Armour & Company and an expert in refrigeration.[90] In the interwar years, the facility had fallen into disuse until restoration began in October 1940.[91] Now, in June 1941, the warehouse was again fully functional, dedicated to Pétain, and it was being inaugurated in the presence of local French dignitaries and "the commanding colonel of the occupying army, accompanied by his aides-de-camp."[92]

Whether Piettre admitted it or not, even at this early phase, when relations between occupiers and occupied people remained relatively cordial, the hierarchy of power between them was clear. Indeed, it was inscribed in the use of space and temperature inside the new freezer warehouse at La Pallice. Of the five floors visited, Piettre explained that the top three were used for meats from the municipal abattoir at La Rochelle, and the refrigerated industrial abattoirs at nearby Bressuire, Pouzauges, and La Roche-sur-Yon. These three floors were kept at $-15\,°C$, while the next lowest floor, at $-21\,°C$, was "reserved entirely for the Berlin Low Temperature Syndicate."[93] Though Piettre did not explain this to his French listeners, this organization, actually called the German Syndicate of Freezing Companies for France (Syndicat deutscher Tiefkühlgesellschaften für Frankreich), had been founded in 1940 to bring together German freezing concerns with an interest in exploiting French produce.[94] In an article for a German military administrators' magazine, food expert Ziegelmayer clarified that French companies provided the Syndicate with raw and processed foods in return for "suitable compensation" while "the freezing, storage and marketing of the frozen products [remained] the exclusive affair of German industry."[95] The Syndicate's role was to facilitate the exploitation of French agriculture for the German war effort, and the goods on its floor of the La Pallice facility were French foods bound for Germany.

Like the floor above it, the ground floor of the La Pallice freezer warehouse was also reserved for German interests. Convenient for loading and unloading, it benefited from cooled air descending from above, and was likely to have been more consistently cold than other areas. Piettre described "a vast chamber at -21 °C containing 50 tons of butter and 150 tons of vegetables and fruit prepared according to the American technique of fast freezing."[96] Remarkably, these goods had been brought to La Pallice from Hamburg "in road trains composed of a tractor and three heavily insulated trailers.... During transportation, cold was obtained using solid carbonic acid."[97]

The new freezer warehouse made power relations between occupiers and occupied population clear. Not only were the less convenient top floors reserved for the French, but since these were also the warmest, they were not ideal for long-term stockpiling. Sensitive to his French audience, Piettre glossed over the activities of the German Syndicate on the floor below. On the ground floor, underlining the fact that cold equated with power, the German army stored foods from the Reich to supply occupying troops and the soon-to-arrive U-boats. Germans' ability to transfer frozen products over long distances surely impressed those French who knew of it. Over the longer term, this cost-intensive procedure was likely abandoned, and the ground floor of the La Pallice facility turned over to local fruits and vegetables, furnished willingly or less willingly by French producers for German use.

In 1943, after three years of occupation, Piettre again spoke to the French Agricultural Academy about freezing in the La Rochelle area. In 1941, he had welcomed the freezer warehouse at La Pallice with grudging admiration, focusing on its French origins, and turning a blind eye to its less palatable uses. Two years later, he was part of a mission sponsored by the French Ministry of Education and Scientific Research Center (Centre de la Recherche Scientifique) that visited several abattoirs and a new freezing center (Centre de Congélation) northwest of La Rochelle at La Roche-sur-Yon. Here, Piettre highlighted construction delays and a budget overrun of 5 million francs that meant the facility had cost 7 million francs for a capacity of just 200 tons of food.[98] Worse, the developers (who remained unnamed in the report) had failed to integrate the new freezing center into the city's preexisting industrial meat processing facility. Somewhat obliquely, Piettre criticized the constructors for having ignored French expertise, arguing that contracts for such an important edifice should have been "given to qualified French refrigeration engineers ... following the usual administrative procedure but accelerated due to wartime.[99]" In early 1940, Piettre had insisted that any new freezing facility "be very closely inspired by the techniques and equipment" already developed in France, rather than

CULINARY INFRASTRUCTURE

"venturing into the unknown with the pretext of originality."[100] His advice had not been heeded, and instead, the new center at La Roche-sur-Yon had been built without connection to French methods, or to the city's existing industrial meat processing and refrigeration plant.

How had this come to pass? Although Piettre did not point a finger specifically at the Germans, it is likely that they or their closest collaborators were behind the new construction. Piettre's complaints that French procedures and expertise had been ignored were likely a code his listeners would have understood as a reference to German involvement. A 1945 report by Henri Monthulet, scion of an important family of food entrepreneurs and the wartime director of the meat processing plant at La Roche-sur-Yon, confirms this suspicion.[101] Piettre recounted that Monthulet's plant had been taken over by the French army at the opening of hostilities, then handed on to the Germans in 1940 without any recognition of its status as a private company called *Les Eleveurs Vendéens*.[102] During the occupation, the Germans made full use of the *Les Eleveurs Vendéens* abattoir, and Monthulet stayed on as manager, insisting in his 1945 report that he had continued to work even without pay simply to fulfill his contract and to ensure the survival of the business.

Monthulet's report also discussed the new freezing center at La Roche-sur-Yon. In contrast to Piettre's 1943 view that the center had been built without connection to the industrial abattoir, in 1945, Monthulet described the two as intimately linked. He explained that he had approached the French government in the mid-1930s about building a freezing center. This made sense, given Monthulet's own training as a refrigeration engineer and his family's longstanding interest in supplying the military with meat and other foods.[103] Representatives of the French army and Ministry of Agriculture had visited, and decided "that the first big facility for fast freezing [in France] should be built at La Roche."[104] The decision to begin building the facility was made in November 1939, presumably as part of the larger development of frozen meat reserves for military use. After that, reported Monthulet, "its completion was due in large measure to my initiatives at the Majestic and with the [German] Chief Veterinarian at La Roche, without which it would probably never have come to fruition."[105] Monthulet claimed that his constant presence had kept the Germans from carrying off abattoir equipment for facilities in La Rochelle, and that, in late August 1944, he had not only prevented the abattoir from being dynamited as the Germans retreated, but also assisted an Allied representative in acquiring remaining German food stocks.[106]

Monthulet's report reveals both his post-war desire to justify his occupation-era actions, and the importance he saw in ensuring the ongoing function of *Les Eleveurs Vendéens*. Like Piettre with regard to the freezer storage facility at La Pallice in 1941, four years later, Monthulet chose to describe the center at La Roche as the completion of a longstanding French project. The variance between Monthulet's depiction of the center as closely related to his company's abattoir and Piettre's depiction of its separation may have been the result of Piettre's desire not to paint Monthulet as a collaborator in 1943, and later, Monthulet's own desire to retain control over the new freezing infrastructure for his business in 1945. Monthulet also mentioned that he had been involved in construction at the abattoir in 1944, which may have had the goal of linking the two facilities more closely.[107]

Modern freezing and cold storage facilities outlasted the war, and both men were clearly making arguments not only about the past, but also the future. If Monthulet had worked so hard to save *Les Eleveurs Vendéens*, it was because like Piettre, he knew that wars might come and go, but France would maintain its place as a European agricultural producer. The question of who owned a freezer facility at the end of the occupation, like the question of who had built it a few years earlier, was not just about who controlled production and distribution of frozen foods during the war years. For both the French and their occupiers, these questions were also about who would emerge as the foremost post-war producer and distributor of frozen food in Europe. As early as the beginning of World War I, according to Piettre, the economist André Lebon, "had imagined that the creation of warehouses in French ports would give our country a monopoly on refrigerated storage for the whole of continental Europe, with very favourable consequences for our credit and our influence."[108] Thirty years later, both Piettre and Monthulet understood that France and Germany were still jockeying for position, military occupation causing a shift more than an interruption in longer patterns of exchange and trade. In the same speech in which Piettre criticized the new freezing center at La Roche-sur-Yon, he reiterated his view that France had much to contribute to Europe's economy, commenting that:

> if a common economic agreement were brought in in Europe following a doctrine circulating these last three years, there is no doubt that France would have a significant role to play. An essentially agricultural country, alone and with its colonies, it has the capacity … to supply its neighbours abundantly with both animal and vegetable foods.[109]

Piettre foresaw that if infrastructures were developed taking international norms and standards into account, France would be in an excellent position to provide for a hungry post-war Europe.

For both Piettre and Monthulet, the war and occupation years constituted a deviation, rather than a rupture, in longer term projects to modernize French food preservation through cold. For better or for worse, the development of freezing and refrigeration across France continued during this time. An Organisational Committee for Refrigeration Enterprises (Comité d'organisation des exploitations frigorifiques) was created in 1941, as part of the larger drive to centralize and manage French industry.[110] Its head, cold-chain transportation expert Jean Bernard Verlot reported that France's freezing capacity had risen from 90 tons per day in 1939 to 400 tons per day in 1942, while storage

CULINARY INFRASTRUCTURE

capacities rose from 40,000 to 97,000 tons.[111] A journalist who interviewed him in 1943 described Verlot as a firm proponent of fast freezing, a "convinced partisan of the new method that is beginning to be applied in France."[112] Not only did fast freezing promise to improve the French diet in the short term, but, "above all," Verlot argued, "it is important think of post-war markets and there is no doubt that many possibilities will open up for French enterprises."[113] This prominent representative of the French refrigeration business, like Piettre and Monthlet, spoke in favor of fast freezing not only to solve present-day problems, but also as a key to developing export markets in the post-war era.

In the hungry years just after the war, material conditions were so poor in many parts of Europe that freezing did not offer a viable remedy for food shortages. By the 1950s, however, freezing was once again high on European and even global agendas. In Germany, Thoms has emphasized continuities across 1945, arguing that, "Though under very different political circumstances, the actors followed up the very same vision that had formerly been supported by the state for the sake of autarchy and *Volksgesundheit* [the people's health]."[114] She also argues that, "This view was shared by international institutions, which now stressed the role of deep freezing as a means to solve the problem of hunger in Europe."[115]

In France, it is difficult to know exactly how much the experience of occupation influenced the post-war development of freezing. Regarding agricultural products generally, Milward has suggested that Germany's failed war in the East and the occupation of France together "broke the established pattern of German trade and created a pattern much more akin to that which emerged after the war in western Europe."[116] Franco–German trade increased, and although "French agricultural exports to Germany … diminished in the immediate aftermath of the German collapse; by 1950 they were responsible for 41 percent of all French exports to Germany by value."[117] The war clearly led to an increase in French agricultural products being sent to Germany, though the exact role of frozen food in this trade remains to be explored.

A history of German wartime fast freezing that takes France into account suggests that National Socialist expansionism both fed the growth of freezing in Germany and had longer term impacts on food production and exchange Europe-wide. The potential to exploit occupied European food resources was clearly an important driver of National Socialist interest in freezing. Since frozen food did not go bad, was vitamin rich, and convenient, it overcame seasonality and removed a barrier to fuller exploitation of agricultural land. Collective feeding in the army, factory canteens, and other communal settings provided suitable frameworks within which to experiment with frozen foodstuffs, and occupied areas offered favorable conditions for testing new facilities.

For a short time, fast freezing supported occupiers' exploitation of the territories they controlled. The attitudes of Piettre, Monthlet, Verlot, and their contemporaries suggest that occupied populations saw advantages as well as disadvantages in the German presence. In the longer term, the facilities Germans built may have given France and other occupied nations the infrastructures they required to bring food products to broader European markets.[118] Further research would be necessary to trace the post-war history of these facilities more fully, but at the very least, it is evident that occupied people saw such facilities as foundations for a European food economy in which frozen goods would play a central role.

On the face of it, wartime freezing reinforced longstanding patterns in which central, powerful regions exploit and preserve the food resources of peripheral, less powerful ones. French responses to German freezing initiatives in the La Rochelle area add complexity to the picture by underscoring the point that not everyone in the subject populations is hostile to such developments, particularly when they are expected to be short-lived and promise long-term gain. Recognition of the role freezing might play in long-distance supply chains was not new and the full potential of the technology was never realized in wartime; however, despite unequal and exploitative circumstances, both Germans and occupied populations like the French gained experience in freezing that fostered its spread in the post-war world.

Acknowledgements

Research for this article was supported by the German Academic Exchange Service (DAAD). The author would also like to thank the *Global Food History* peer reviewers for their most insightful comments.

Notes

1. Such a purchase was somewhat surprising for Hitler's nationalist regime. Thoms, "The Innovative Power of War: The Army, Food Sciences and the Food Industry in Germany in the Twentieth Century," 256 and Thoms, "The Introduction of Frozen Foods in West Germany and Its Integration into the Daily Diet," 205–6.
2. Emblik, "Die Bedeutung der Gefrierkonserve", 89.
3. Finstad, "Familiarizing Food", 28–9.
4. Ziegelmayer, "Praktische Grossraumwirtschaft der deutschen Heeresverwaltung," 66–8.
5. See Claflin, "Les Halles and the Moral Market", 82–92.

CULINARY INFRASTRUCTURE

6. Thoms, "Introduction," 201–2. On the historiography of food, see e.g. Claflin and Scholliers, *Writing Food History: A Global Perspective* and Pilcher, "Introduction," In *The Oxford Handbook of Food History*, xvii–xxviii.
7. Thoms, "'Ernährung ist so wichtig wie Munition.'", 207–30; Thoms, "Innovative Power"; Thoms, "Introduction" and Thoms, "Zum Konzept der Ernährung", 89–112.
8. Collingham, *The Taste of War*, 492. On National Socialist food policy beyond freezing, see Corni, *Hitler and the Peasants* and Gerhard, *Nazi Hunger Politics*.
9. Pelzer-Reith and Reith, "Fischkonsum und „Eiweisslücke" im Nationalsozialismus," 4–26.
10. Finstad, "Familiarizing Food," 22–45.
11. Claflin, "Les Halles" and Claflin, "La Villette, la viande" 53–79.
12. Milward, *The New Order and the French Economy*, chap. 11; Mouré, "Food Rationing and the Black Market, 262–82; Mouré and Schwartz, "On vit mal", 261–95 and Veillon, *Vivre et survivre en France*.
13. Spiekermann, "Twentieth-Century Product Innovations, 305.
14. Ibid., 306.
15. Ibid., 307.
16. Ibid., 311.
17. Ibid., 310 and Thoms, "Innovative Power," 256. Such film was called "Cellophan" (Oberkommando des Heeres, *Zubereitung der Kost*, iv.i.) or "Viskosefolie" (Verein Deutscher Ingenieure, *Gefrier-Taschenbuch*, 62).
18. Thoms, "Introduction," 204.
19. Ibid.
20. Oberkommando des Heeres, *Feldkochbuch*, 7. Cf. Thoms, "Ernährung," 210.
21. On Ziegelmayer, see Thoms, "Ernährung," 212 and Thoms, "Konzept," 90–1.
22. Ziegelmayer, *Unsere Lebensmittel und ihre Veränderungen*, 155.
23. Ibid.
24. Ziegelmayer, *Rohstoff-Fragen der deutschen Volksernährung*, 242.
25. The square box was part of the innovation. Kurlansky, *Birdseye: The Adventures of a Curious Man*, 145–6.
26. Ziegelmayer, *Lebensmittel*, 155.
27. Plank, "Die Frischhaltung von Lebensmitteln durch Kälte," 139–41 and Wilson, *Consider the Fork*, 224.
28. Thoms, "Introduction," 208.
29. Ziegelmayer, *Rohstoff-Fragen*, 242. Cf. Ziegelmayer, "Die Entwicklung industriell zubereiteter Lebensmittel", 1–4.
30. Thoms, "Introduction," 204.
31. Spiekermann, "Innovations," 310–11.
32. Mosolff, "Der Aufbau der deutschen Gefrierindustrie,": 596. Cf. Kurlansky, *Birdseye*, 161.
33. Pelzer-Reith and Reith, "Fischkonsum," 13.
34. Thoms, "Introduction," 205. Solo-Feinfrost was a German affiliate of Unilever. Pelzer-Reith and Reith, "Fischkonsum," 13. On Unilever in the Third Reich, see Forbes, "Multinational Enterprise, 'Corporate Responsibility'", 149–67 and Wubs, "Unilever's Struggle for Control", 57–84.
35. Mosolff, "Aufbau," 597.
36. Ibid.; Pelzer-Reith and Reith, "Fischkonsum," 13 and Thoms, "Introduction," 207.
37. Hellmann, *Künstliche Kälte*, 109–18 and Heßler, "*Mrs. Modern*", 373–79.
38. *Werbeleiter*, vol. 4–5 (1939): 62 cited in Heßler, *Mrs. Modern*, 379.

39. Hellmann, *Künstliche*, 117.
40. Heßler, *Mrs. Modern*, 187, 366.
41. Hellmann notes that there was more freezing activity undertaken in this era than there would be again until the 1970s. *Künstliche*, 116.
42. On connections between food, hunger, war, and the Holocaust, see Gerhard, *Nazi Hunger Politics*.
43. Adolf Hitler, Speech of May 23 1939, document 539, Noakes and Pridham, eds., *Foreign Policy, War and Racial Extermination*, 737.
44. Ibid.; Chris Otter, "The British Nutrition Transition", 815.
45. Mosolff, ed., *Tiefkühl-ABC*, 4. Also cited in Thoms, "Introduction," 204.
46. Plank, "Frischhaltung," 161.
47. Ziegelmayer, *Rohstoff-Fragen*, 314.
48. "6. Tagungsbericht der Arbeitsgemeinschaft 'Ernährung der Wehrmacht'," August 21 1942 (Bundesarchiv-Militärchiv Freiburg, RH 9/11).
49. Oberkommando des Heeres, *Feldkochbuch*, 103.
50. Ibid., 104.
51. Ziegelmayer, *Die Feldküchengerichte*.
52. Ibid., 97.
53. Freezing information was also published in e.g. Verein Deutscher Ingenieure, *Gefrier-Taschenbuch*; Mosolff, *Tiefkühl-ABC*.
54. Emblik, "Gefrierkonserve," 89, 93.
55. Ibid., 89. Under German control, the frozen portion of Norwegian fish exports increased from 10 to 65 percent between 1940 and 1943. Pelzer-Reith and Reith, "Fischkonsum," 20.
56. Emblik, "Gefrierkonserve," 90.
57. Ibid.
58. Ibid., 92.
59. Ibid.
60. Ibid., 93. Developing refrigerated and frozen food transportation and distribution networks was a renewed priority after 1945. Thoms, "Introduction," 208–9.
61. Emblik, "Gefrierkonserve," 89.
62. Ziegelmayer, "Grossraumwirtschaft," 66.
63. Milward, *New Order*, 255.
64. Piettre, "Inauguration des entrepôts frigorifiques", 773.
65. A full account of German involvement in French agriculture is beyond the scope of this article. See Brandt, Schiller, and Ahlgrimm, *Management of Agriculture and Food* and Milward, *New Order*, chap. 9.
66. Brandt was a University of Berlin professor of agriculture who left for the USA in 1933. In 1945/46, he became the economic adviser to the Chief of Food and Agriculture of the US Military Government in Germany. Though he displayed keen insight into agricultural conditions, Brandt's report tended to view German policies in France as relatively benign or comprehensible. He based his conclusions on "eyewitnesses to the agricultural and food administration of the occupied territories willing to co-operate." Brandt, Schiller, and Ahlgrimm, *Management*, xxv.
67. Ibid., 514.
68. Ibid., 515.
69. Ibid., 520. On rural labour, see Milward, *New Order*, 259–60.
70. Brandt, Schiller, and Ahlgrimm, *Management*, 520.
71. Ibid., 521.
72. Ibid., 511.

CULINARY INFRASTRUCTURE

73. Radtke-Delacor, "Produire pour le Reich", 112.
74. Brandt, Schiller, and Ahlgrimm, *Management*, 520.
75. Bloch, "La crise de la pêche maritime (I)", 234–59 and Bloch, "La crise de la pêche maritime (II)", 396–419.
76. "Décret relatif à l'encouragement de la congélation des viandes métropolitaines," 1 July 1938, *Journal officiel de l'état français*, 2 July 1938, 7739.
77. "Crise du troupeau national: organisation de l'élevage," *Journal officiel de la République française*, parliamentary debates, senate (1938): 631.
78. Maurice, "Mesures pour l'intensification", 214.
79. Jouve, "Services vétérinaires sanitaires", 152–3.
80. Piettre, "Organisation de la production agricole", 677.
81. Ibid., 678. Franco–German exchange in refrigeration and freezing also involved German Carl Linde, who had started a refrigeration equipment company in 1879. Founder of the German Refrigeration Association, he was a driving force behind the International Refrigeration Institute, founded in Paris in 1908. Thoms, "Introduction," 203.
82. Piettre, "Ravitaillement complémentaire" 335–6. Argentina provided meat to France from the later nineteenth century. See Arnoux, "Le rôle des Français", 92–3.
83. Piettre, "Ravitaillement," 335.
84. Ibid., 337–8.
85. Ibid., 338.
86. Ibid.
87. Ibid.
88. Piettre, "Inauguration," 765.
89. The first U-boat arrived in November 1941. Hellwinkel, *Hitlers Tor zum Atlantik*, 60–1.
90. Piettre, "Inauguration," 767.
91. Ibid., 766.
92. Ibid., 769.
93. Ibid., 771.
94. Ziegelmayer, "Grossraumwirtschaft," 66. Cf. Ziegelmayer, *Rohstoff-Fragen*, 314.
95. Ziegelmayer, "Grossraumwirtschaft," 67.
96. Piettre, "Inauguration," 771.
97. Ibid. Apparently, the absence of a ventilation system meant rather inconsistent shipment temperatures.
98. Piettre, "Technique et hygiène", 47.
99. Ibid.
100. Piettre, "Ravitaillement," note 1, 338.
101. "Rôle d'Henri Monthulet pour maintenir la société en activité pendant la guerre 1939–1945," report, [1945] (Archives de la Vendee [henceforth ADV]: 97J/182).
102. Piettre, "Technique," 46.
103. Monthulet represented the third generation of a family that began in grain and later provided refrigerated meat for the army during World War I. In the interwar, they developed fish and vegetable canning interests, and the company became *Les Eleveurs Vendéens* in 1937. See introduction to the Monthulet family papers (ADV, series 97J).
104. Monthulet, "Rôle d'Henri Monthulet," 2 (ADV: 97J/182).
105. Ibid., 1. The Majestic Hotel housed the German military administration headquarters in Paris.
106. Ibid., 2.

107. The previous year, Piettre had suggested that modifications would make the abattoir more efficient. Ibid., 1 and Piettre, "Technique," 46–7.
108. Piettre, "Ravitaillement," 337.
109. Piettre, "Technique," 54.
110. It should be noted that "frigorifique" could refer to either refrigeration or freezing, or both. The decree creating this committee on 15 July 1941 is cited in "Exploitations frigorifiques," *Journal official de l'Etat français* (1942): 1754.
111. Bouny, "Voyage au pays du froid artificiel".
112. Ibid.
113. Ibid., 3.
114. Thoms, "Introduction," 208.
115. Ibid.
116. Milward, *New Order*, 255–6.
117. Ibid., 256.
118. This process could be indirect. In Norway, for instance, large German plants were disassembled and the equipment spread among smaller freezing facilities. Finstad, "Familiarizing Food," 24.

Bibliography

Arnoux, Henri. "Le rôle des Français dans la fondation de l'industrie argentine à la fin du XIXe et au début du XXe siècle." *Cahiers des Amériques Latines* 17 (1994): 79–104.

Bloch, Richard. "La crise de la pêche maritime de marée fraîche (I)." *Revue politique et parlementaire* 38, no. 435 (Feb 10, 1931): 234–259.

Bloch, Richard. "La crise de la pêche maritime de marée fraîche (II)." *Revue politique et parlementaire* 38, no. 436 (Mar 10, 1931): 396–419.

Bouny, Henry. 1943. "Voyage au pays du froid artificiel : des fraises et des framboises en plein hiver, voilà ce que nous vaudra le système de la 'congélation-choc'." *Le Journal*, May 4; May 5; May 6.

Brandt, Karl, Otto Schiller, and Franz Ahlgrimm. *Management of Agriculture and Food in the German-Occupied and Other Areas of Fortress Europe: A Study in Military Government.* Stanford, CA: Stanford University Press, 1953.

Claflin, Kyri W. "La Villette, la viande – 'enseigne et marchandise' (1867–1914)." *Food & History* 3, no. 2 (Sep 2005): 53–79.

Claflin, Kyri W."Les Halles and the Moral Market: Frigophobia Strikes in the Belly of Paris." In *Food and Morality: Proceedings of the Oxford Symposium on Food and Cookery 2007*, edited by Susan R. Friedland, 82–92. Totnes, Devon: Prospect Books., 2008.

Claflin, Kyri W., and Peter Scholliers. *Writing Food History: A Global Perspective.* London: Berg, 2013.

Collingham, Lizzie. *The Taste of War.* London: Penguin, 2012.

Corni, Gustavo. *Hitler and the Peasants: Agrarian Policy of the Third Reich, 1930–1939.* New York: Berg, 1990.

Emblik, Eduard. "Die Bedeutung der Gefrierkonserve in der europäischen Großraumwirtschaft, ihre Herstellung und ihr Transport." *Zeitschrift für die gesamte Kälte-Industrie* 50, no. 7/8 (Aug 1943): 89–93.

Finstad, Terje. "Familiarizing Food: Frozen Food Chains, Technology, and Consumer Trust, Norway 1940–1970." *Food and Foodways* 21, no. 1 (2013): 22–45.

Forbes, Neil. "Multinational Enterprise, 'Corporate Responsibility' and the Nazi Dictatorship: The Case of Unilever and Germany in the 1930s." *Contemporary European History* 16, no. 02 (May 2007): 149–167.

Gerhard, Gesine. *Nazi Hunger Politics: A History of Food in the Third Reich.* Rowman & Littlefield Studies in Food and Gastronomy. Lanham, MD: Rowman & Littlefield, 2015.

Heßler, Martina *"Mrs. Modern Woman". Zur Sozial- und Kulturgeschichte der Haushaltstechnisierung.* Campus Forschung 827. Frankfurt: Campus-Verl, 2001.

Hellmann, Ullrich. *Künstliche Kälte. Die Geschichte der Kühlung im Haushalt.* Werkbund-Archiv. Gießen: Anabas-Verlag, 1990.

Hellwinkel, Lars. *Hitlers Tor zum Atlantik. Die deutschen Marinestützpunkte in Frankreich 1940–1945.* Berlin: Ch. Links Verlag, 2012.

Jouve, F. "Services vétérinaires sanitaires, rapport du directeur par intérim (année 1940)." *Allier, Conseil général, rapports et délibérations* (1941): 128–159.

Kurlansky, Mark. *Birdseye: The Adventures of a Curious Man.* New York: Doubleday, 2012.

Maurice, M. "Mesures pour l'intensification de la consommation de la viande indigène." *Allier, Conseil général, rapports et délibérations* (1939): 214.

Milward, Alan S. *The New Order and the French Economy.* Oxford: Clarendon P., 1970.

Mosolff, Hans. "Der Aufbau der deutschen Gefrierindustrie." *Der Vierjahresplan* 5 (1941): 596–600.

Mosolff, Hans, ed. *Tiefkühl-ABC.* Hamburg: Hans A. Keune Verlag, 1941.

Mouré, Kenneth. "Food Rationing and the Black Market in France (1940–1944)." *French History* 24, no. 2 (Jun 1, 2010): 262–282.

Mouré, Kenneth. and Paula Schwartz. "On vit mal." *Food, Culture & Society* 10, no. 2 (Summer 2007): 261–295.

Noakes, Jeremy, and Geoffrey Pridham (eds.). *Foreign Policy, War and Racial Extermination: A Documentary Reader.* Nazism 1919–1945. 3 vols. Exeter: University of Exeter Press, 1995.

Oberkommando des Heeres. *Feldkochbuch.* Berlin: Erich Zander, 1941.

Oberkommando des Heeres. *Zubereitung der Kost.* Berlin: Mittler und Sohn, 1941.

Otter, Chris. "The British Nutrition Transition and Its Histories." *History Compass* 10, no. 11 (2012): 812–825.

Pelzer-Reith, Birgit, and Reinhold Reith. "Fischkonsum und „Eiweisslücke" im Nationalsozialismus." *Vierteljahrschrift für Sozial und Wirtschaftsgeschichte* 96, no. 1 (Mar 2009): 4–26.

Piettre, Maurice. "Inauguration des entrepôts frigorifiques et maritimes de La Rochelle-Pallice." *Comptes rendus des séances de l'Académie d'agriculture de France,* July 9, 1941, 765–778.

Piettre, Maurice. "Organisation de la production agricole au cours de la crise actuelle: Restauration du cheptel national [Organisation of agricultural production during the current crisis: restoring the national livestock herd]." *CRSAA,* September 18, 1940, 668–684.

Piettre, Maurice. "Ravitaillement complémentaire de l'armée en viandes congelées d'importation." *CRSAA,* April 13, 1940, 328–346.

Piettre, Maurice. "Technique et hygiène dans les abattoirs: Mission du centre national de la recherche scientifique (Ministère de l'Education Nationale)." *CRSAA,* January 20, 1943, 45–54.

Pilcher, Jeffrey M. "Introduction." In *The Oxford Handbook of Food History,* edited by Jeffrey M. Pilcher, xvii–xxviii. New York: Oxford University Press, 2012.

Plank, Rudolf. "Die Frischhaltung von Lebensmitteln durch Kälte." Edited by Deutsches Museum. *Abhandlungen und Berichte* 12, no. 5 (1940): 139–176.

Radtke-Delacor, Arne. "Produire pour le Reich: Les commandes allemandes à l'industrie française (1940–1944)." *Vingtième Siècle* 70 (Apr 2001): 99–115.

Spiekermann, Uwe. "Twentieth-Century Product Innovations in the German Food Industry." *Business History Review* 83, no. 2 (Summer 2009): 291–315.

Thoms, Ulrike. "'Ernährung ist so wichtig wie Munition.' Die Verpflegung der deutschen Wehrmacht 1933–1945." In *Medizin im Zweiten Weltkrieg. Militärmedizinische Praxis und medizinische Wissenschaft im "Totalen Krieg"*, edited by U. Wolfgang Eckart and Alexander Neumann, 207–230. Paderborn: Schöningh, 2006.

Thoms, Ulrike. "The Innovative Power of War: The Army, Food Sciences and the Food Industry in Germany in the Twentieth Century." In *Food and War in Twentieth Century Europe*, edited by Ina Zweiniger-Bargielowska, Rachel Duffett, and Alain Drouard, 247–262. Burlington, VT: Ashgate, 2011.

Thoms, Ulrike. "The Introduction of Frozen Foods in West Germany and Its Integration into the Daily Diet." In *History of Artificial Cold, Scientific, Technological and Cultural Issues*, edited by Kostas Gavroglou, 201–229. Dordrecht: Springer, 2014.

Thoms, Ulrike. "Zum Konzept der Ernährung am Deutschen Institut für Ernährungsforschung und seinen Vorläufern 1946–1989." In *Essen in Europa. Kulturelle "Rückstände" in Nahrung und Körper*, edited by Susanne Bauer, 89–112. Bielefeld: Transcript, 2010.

Veillon, Dominique. *Vivre et survivre en France, 1939–1947*. Paris: Editions Payot & Rivages, 1995.

Verein Deutscher Ingenieure. *Gefrier-Taschenbuch. Herstellung, Bewirtschaftung und Verbrauch schnell gefrorener Lebensmittel*. Berlin: VDI-Verl, 1940.

Wilson, Bee. *Consider the Fork: A History of How We Cook and Eat*. New York: Basic Books, 2013.

Wubs, Ben. "Unilever's Struggle for Control: An Anglo-Dutch Multinational under German Occupation." *Zeitschrift für Unternehmensgeschichte* [Journal of Business History] 52, no. 1 (Jan 1, 2007): 57–84.

Ziegelmayer, Wilhelm. "Die Entwicklung industriell zubereiteter Lebensmittel durch die deutsche Wehrmacht in Europa und ihr Einfluss auf England und Amerika. Aus der Gruppe Entwicklung im Oberkommando des Heeres." *Angewandte Kochwissenschaft* 2, no. 1 (1943): 1–4.

Ziegelmayer, Wilhelm. *Die Feldküchengerichte. Nach dem Original-Feldkochbuch des OKW 1941*. 2nd ed. Berlin: Alfred H. Linde, 1943.

Ziegelmayer, Wilhelm. *Rohstoff-Fragen der deutschen Volksernährung. Eine Darstellung der ernährungswirtschaftlichen und ernährungswissenschaftlichen Aufgaben unserer Zeit, mit einem Ausblick auf die Grossraumwirtschaft*. Dresden: T. Steinkopff, 1941.

Ziegelmayer, Wilhelm. "Praktische Grossraumwirtschaft der deutschen Heeresverwaltung." *Die Heeresverwaltung* 7, no. 3 (Mar 1942): 61–68.

Ziegelmayer, Wilhelm. *Unsere Lebensmittel und ihre Veränderungen*. Dresden: Steinkopff, 1940.

Food Safety as Culinary Infrastructure in Singapore, 1920–1990

Nicole Tarulevicz

ABSTRACT

A nuanced understanding of food safety encompasses how people think about food threats and safety and the interwoven institutions, regulations, and technologies that create the related knowledge. Using examples drawn from Singapore, this article shows that the less structured, more informal body of popular knowledge about food safety can be understood as a kind of culinary infrastructure. In a nation that has always relied on imported food, a contextual and contingent historical approach demonstrates elements of continuity and change in popular food safety knowledge, across colonial and postcolonial moments. A complex tripartite arrangement among the main local players – the state, merchants, and the consumers – was established which emphasized local responsibility for food safety. This is illustrated by the commercial and information functions of the local English-language press, where articles, advertising campaigns for products such as refrigerators and insecticide, public campaigns, and consumer advocates helped shape knowledge of food safety as a shared responsibility. Singapore's experience highlights popular knowledge as culinary infrastructure and is relevant for a globalized world, demonstrating a food safety regime geographically distant from food production and simultaneously highly reliant on effective local actors. In so doing, Singapore suggests a potential alternative way to engage with globalized food – via a popular focus on shared local responsibilities.

Introduction

Food safety is a historically constructed body of knowledge intersecting technology, regulation, and practice. Systematized or formalized bodies of specialist knowledge constitute one form of infrastructure: what in this volume Jeffery Pilcher describes as the "knowledge infrastructure of media and social networks that create and transfer cultural meanings about food as well as the physical facilities that serve to transport it."[1] Using examples drawn from

Singapore, I argue in this article that the less structured, more informal, body of popular knowledge about food safety is also infrastructure. That is, for many Singaporean consumers, the popular is the lived experience site where food safety knowledge is constructed, disseminated, and practiced. Framing food safety knowledge(s) with the popular, usefully illustrates questions about these knowledges and how they form. In the case of Singapore, historical elements of popular food safety include knowledges about bugs, germs, adulteration, disease, filth, fraud, and greed. The creation and propagation of these knowledges is part of the cultural work done by advertising, news, and folk narratives.

For food scholars, Singapore offers many delicious advantages. In the colonial era, Singapore was a British East India Company territory, founded in 1819 and run by the British as an entrepôt port within Malaya, allowing large shipments of goods in transit to be stored and/or processed before continuing to other destinations. Because of its tax-free status and trade-strategic Southeast Asian location – where the Straits of Malacca meet the South China Sea – Singapore quickly became one of the largest ports in the world, emerging as a center of exchange where different cultures, as well as goods, met. Singapore's small size, 704 km^2, has always belied its economic importance, and its focus on free trade has remained a defining characteristic.

Historically, most food was imported into Singapore. Anticipating contemporary globalization, the conditions of the production of food were generally invisible, hidden behind long supply chains. Responding to this opacity, public campaigns and consumer advocates gradually established a complex tripartite arrangement among the state, merchants, and consumer that emphasized local food safety knowledge, action, and practices. In emphasizing the popular aspects, maintaining a sense of historical chronology illustrates the continuities in popular constructions of food safety knowledge from the colonial era (1819–1959) to the postcolonial (1959 onwards).

Although issues of poor food quality were experienced privately at the gustatory and gastrointestinal levels, they were also understood as matters of public concern and public health, and this is one of the reasons they played out in the public forum of newspapers. Elements of this are exemplified by the advertising of international products such as Flit insecticides that taught consumers to fear pests and vermin; in the advertising of food safety technology such as refrigeration; in the folk narratives about food scares such as the 1958 "bad beer" incident; in letters to the editor about public health and space and their replies; in editorials about profiteering; and in coverage of consumer advocacy. These exemplars present issues of concern for each decade (1920s–1980s) in this period, highlighting the continuity between colonial and postcolonial in popular constructions of food safety knowledge, as well as between the colonial and postcolonial administrations and their attitudes to food safety.

Food Safety and Newspapers

This article relies on newspaper sources for unpacking popular knowledge of food safety, especially the *Straits Times*. The importance of newspapers, described by Jürgen Habermas as the "public sphere's preeminent institution," is firmly established.[2] Likewise, print capitalism in the service of emergent nationalism is well-trod ground.[3] In the colonial context, newspapers have been understood as playing a particular role in the ferment of nationalism, as opposed to regionalism.[4] Recognition of the role of newspapers in colonial environments in shaping less explicitly political ideologies has been slower to emerge.

Established in 1854, the *Straits Times* started as a newspaper for the European community in Singapore and consequently had a small readership. During the time span examined in this article, it became Singapore's newspaper of record. Editor George Seabridge (1928–1946) transformed the *Straits Times* into the "common man's paper." Circulation increased fivefold, and shared within households and workplaces; readership presumably increased proportionately.[5] Renamed during the Japanese occupation, the paper kept publishing, but as C. M. Turnbull notes, "on the eve of Second World War, the *Straits Times* claimed more Asian than European readers."[6] In the postcolonial era, the *Straits Times* dominated the market: by the election of the People's Action Party in 1959, daily circulation was over 100,000.[7] The 1970s and 1980s in Singapore were marked by increases in population (by 25%), literacy (from 72 to 90%), by circulation of English-language newspapers (by 105%), and of readership of English-language newspapers (of which the *Straits Times* is the most significant) by a massive 144%.[8] In this context and time period, tracing the construction of popular food safety knowledge via the English language press is quite revealing, even in a Southeast Asian city state.

Like Singapore itself, the newspaper became "regulated." After more than 125 years of independent ownership, the publishing company was split in two in 1972 and the *Straits Times* soon came under government directorship, where it remains. Compared to earlier years, the changes of the 1970s did not cause any apparent differences in the newspaper's coverage of, or attitude to, food.[9] In considering popular constructions of food safety in early and mid-twentieth-century Singapore, it was the press, especially the English-language newspapers, which were central to prompting anxiety about food quality. Singaporeans read about food poisoning, food adulteration, fake food, and a wide range of food safety issues. Newspapers also advertised protective products and were the site of more contemporary food safety campaigns.

Scholarly Connections

State intervention as food regulation is always multi-layered. Writing about food regulation in Britain between 1875 and 1938, Michael French and Jim Phillips revealed that while an idealized market may operate in the minds of regulators, "the actual operation of markets is characterised by uncertainties, limited information and effects that generate 'public-interest'-based calls for government intervention."[10] Legislation was not always effective and the pursuit of safe food in Singapore relied on a raft of actors, pursuing private, public, and mercantile interests.

Food adulteration and misrepresentation were so common everywhere in the nineteenth century, and even earlier, that the claim of "purity" provided an obvious basis for advertising in the twentieth century, attempting to deflect anxieties, real and imagined, and develop confidence in the food system. Writing about the centrality of purity to the Heinz Company advertising in America, and drawing on the work of Miles Orvell, Gabriella M. Petrick argued for a connection between industrialized food production and consumer concern about food purity and safety. She suggested "when strangers manufactured and sold products to unknown masses" this "intensified the public's resolve to determine the real from the fake, or in the food industry, what was pure from what was poisoned."[11] For Keir Waddington, writing about food and fear in Victorian and Edwardian Britain, it was less the rise of industrialization and more the accompanying regulatory culture and apparatus that heightened anxiety about food quality.[12]

For Singapore, both the distance of consumers from producers (even greater than in the American example) and the ensuing regulatory culture drew attention to issues of food quality. The challenge of feeding a nation from the pantries of other places seems like a phenomenon of our postmodernist time, but it was Singapore's reality. Singapore's port was both the engine of the economy and the source of its food. Policing the quality of that food was a challenge. In the early twentieth century, distance from the primary producers reflected both the industrialization of food production and an economy of Empire, meaning the port provided access to products from global networks of trade with long supply chains.

Issues of food quality, its adulteration, contamination, and corruption, have sustained continued interest in Singapore for consumers and regulators. For more than a century, newspaper readers encountered articles, editorials, and letters detailing milk adulteration, the sale of illegally slaughtered animals, maize sold as coffee, and so forth.[13] It is not just the fact of their reportage but the often sensationalist and moralizing style that is of interest. The inclusion of details was a common feature and functioned to assist the reader in identifying fraud and unsafe food and, in the process, constructed educated consumers. As Stephanie Newell cautioned us in the context of newspapers in colonial West Africa, we "should look not simply at what people were reading, but also for the ways local consumers responded to printed material."[14] In the *Straits Times*, "letters to the editor" reveal a little of that dialog, but consumer responses to advertising, for example, are much more opaque. Taken as a whole, the press constructs food safety as an integral element of civil society.

CULINARY INFRASTRUCTURE

Advertising's deep connection to the imperial project, what Anne McClintock referred to as the "mass marketing of empire as an organized system of images and attitudes," also reveals the way that commodities inhabited and mediated "the uncertain threshold zones between domesticity and industry, metropolis and empire."[15] The advertisements in Singaporean newspapers amply illustrate these uncertain and unstable thresholds. As historian Kristin L. Hoganson reminds us, these intersections of metropolis and empire go beyond centre and periphery, and in her study of the global production of American domesticity, she notes that "the attractions of secondhand empire can be found not only in household furnishings but also in Orientalist fashions, curried eggs, lectures on the Taj Mahal, and native arts displays."[16] Food, its packaging, storage, and, of course, its contamination, draw our attention to the intersection of domesticity and industry, metropolis and empire, and the multiple actors in this space.

Discourses of public health and hygiene cannot be separated from modernity because, as Dipesh Charabarty cautioned, "it is the language not only of imperialist officials but of modernist nationalists as well." This is certainly true for Singapore, where both colonial and postcolonial officials have used regulation about public health and hygiene as a way of bringing order to disorder.[17] Waste, bodily and culinary, must be regulated for fear of disease and social contamination, and the city itself is subject to purification.[18] Regulation of bourgeoisie bodies has been bound historically with the regulation of the city and the body of the Other.[19] By extension, food – sorted, carried, cleaned, prepared, sold, and served by the Other – also needed to be regulated. In Singapore, food emerged as a site of extensive state interventions in the form of discourse and legislation regarding food purity.

Singapore was, and remains, a nation obsessed with food, where the pleasures of the plate do significant cultural and social work. These pleasures have received the greatest scholarly and popular attention, ranging from Lily Kong's study of street food[20] to Jean Duruz's work on culinary nostalgia.[21] The ways food helps form and reinforce ethnic and national identity has been of repeated interest for Singapore scholars.[22] Spatial reflections of identity, from street food[23] to coffeeshops,[24] have occupied scholars too. In these examples, food safety and quality are assumed, even celebrated. Harvey Neo provides a notable exception when his work on pig farming explicitly grapples with issues of food supply, quality, and purity as well as with the broader issues of the (un-)sustainability of agriculture in Singapore.[25] One of the goals of this article is to begin the work of mapping under-examined assumptions about food in Singapore, especially around constructions of safety, quality, opaque supply chains, and taken-for-granted infrastructure.

Historiographically, most Singapore food scholarship focuses on the post-independence era, but the colonial period has received some attention, most notably by Cecilia Leong-Salobir.[26] Looking to the period of the Japanese occupation, Wong Hong Suen's analysis of food culture emphasizes the common narrative of overcoming hardship.[27] But one remarkable characterizing of Singapore-specific historical food scholarship is how it tends to recast the period before the nation state as the history of the nation state. As I have, however, suggested elsewhere, the different patterns of continuity and change seen in lived food experiences suggest an alternative periodization of Singaporean history.[28]

1920s: Filthy Feet in Food

In the Singapore of the 1920s, bugs were important to popular constructions of food safety knowledge. For even if food started out pure and safe, it could be transformed by encounters with bugs and vermin. Flit, an American insecticide product of Standard Oil, exemplifies this. Flit advertised extensively in Singapore and used fear of contamination to promote their products. Their marketing also illustrates how non-food advertisers contributed to the development of food safety knowledge.

In a 1927 advertisement, a massive fly, twice the size of an infant, stretched four hands (complete with four fingers and opposable thumbs) over the body of a mother and toward her suckling infant. Below, in bold print, the words make clear the intentions of the fly: "Flies are Murderers." Showing little knowledge of the local vernacular or urban environment, the text of the advertisements described the journey of the fly: "Laden with disease, flies drag their dirty, filthy feet direct from the stable, garbage, and outhouses right into your home and table – depositing filth and disease germs on you and your food."[29] While "garbage" and "outhouses" do not quite fit in the Singaporean context (linguistically or architecturally), the sentiment was still clear.

The same oversized fly was shown in another advertisement drinking from a bowl of soup, legs entangled in toast, as a crying child sat in its highchair watching the corruption of its meal. These flies were not just killers, they were also deceptive: "Thieves and murderers swarm into your home everyday disguised as common houseflies." The flies come from their "dens of filth" with diseases "gathered from squalid refuse heaps and cesspools" to track their foul feet onto food.[30] Although children often were featured as the victims of bugs and vermin ("flies are children's deadliest enemies!"[31]), flies were also "a Menace to Man," as the shocked face of a middle-aged man watching the oversized flies drink from his soup bowl indicated. This was not the fly in the infamous waiter-there-is-a-fly-in-my-soup joke; this man understands the risks the soup-swilling fly posed. In case the reader needed reminding, they were told that these flies are "monsters eager to take your life."[32]

While some of the lack of local vernacular can be explained by the fact that Flit was marketed internationally, there was also market segmentation. In the United States, Flit cartoon advertisements were drawn by Theodore Geisel, who was soon to go on to fame and fortune under the name of "Dr. Seuss."[33] An interesting difference between the American Flit advertisements and the

Singaporean versions described here is an emphasis on keeping insects away from food in the Singapore marketing, as opposed to an emphasis on the annoyance of discomfort in the American versions.[34] There is, however, a clear visual similarity between the Flit advertisements in Singapore and those used in India, and some advertisements were used verbatim in both markets.[35] The menacing flies put in peril the very lives of readers in Singapore and India both pre- and post-date Geisel's tenure and it is reasonable to assume a different illustrator responsible for the Singaporean examples in which insects contaminated food and by extension home and bodies.

The process of contamination relied on an understanding of germ theory. Nancy Tomes noted that by virtue of their religious heritage, ordinary Americans were able to accept germ theory because they already believed "in an 'invisible world' dominated by unseen forces that held the power of life and death."[36] Although this could also be applied to miasma theory, contaminated air was, after all, also an unseen force. For Singaporeans, those with Christian views and those with Hindu, Buddhist, or Islamic views, unseen forces were also part of their world view. Flit advertisements explicitly connected flies to germs and germs to disease in ways that made sense: "Flies, with their foul-tainted bodies, drag the germs of typhoid, infantile paralysis, cholera, dysentery over your food." In a 1929 advertisement, a fly, its head replaced by a skull, flew across the page toward the words "Winged Death!"[37]

In another advertisement, two upright flies wore shoes (on two of their feet) and were shown walking at a great pace carrying suitcases, one of which contained cholera and typhoid, the other which contained diphtheria and tuberculosis (only the first two are actually transmitted by flies). Despite the shoes, the flies were described as having "filth-dragging feet."[38] A skeleton, as emblem of death, featured in another advertisement, riding the back of a fly bigger than the plate it feasted from. It was not just a single dish that was imperiled by flies, it is the whole community: "Whenever a fly enters your home, Disease rides in on its back. Your own health and the health of your community demands that you kill these arch enemies of Man."[39] Connecting personal responsibility to community responsibility resonated in Singapore, where ethnic identity historically stood for community and was the organizing principle for social support.[40]

The contamination of food was a persistent focus, addressed directly ("Danger from Fly-Touched Food") and through generalized fear ("Death may come into your home on the wings of flies.")[41] Having told readers that flies contaminate food, one advertisement posed the question: "Can you eat, with ease of mind, the food this germ-laden insect has polluted?"[42] In another advertisement, a mother buttered bread for her child while flies waited ready to pounce above the text: "Flies Poison Food." Poisoned food corrupts the body: "Health cannot abide in the house infected by flies. Make your choice – flies or health?"[43] Flies do pose a threat to health, but the threat these advertising flies pose was not just embodied and physical; although it is that, it is also ideological, creating both fear and a shared understanding of what poses a threat. Flies are now being farmed in South Africa, with the larvae used as fish food and heralded as a green solution for nutrient recycling in the future and as a strategy for saving fish populations.[44] The transformation of flies from foe to friend, as embryonic as it currently is, gives us a sense of the temporality of the technologies of food safety knowledges.

Flies, of course, were not the only culprits in the Flit world, and in one advertisement, a skeleton, again representing death, stood at the blackboard, "teaching" a range of insects – flies, mosquitoes, bedbugs, cockroaches, and "their loathsome allies." They were, according to the bolded text, being "Schooled in Spreading Disease."[45] That education was put to work in the kitchens, pantries, and plates of innocent victims. Insects emerged almost as characters in horror literature, feasting on human dishes and wreaking havoc on that food. Ants could have already tasted your meal, and readers were asked: "how can you eat when you know that creeping, crawling ants have already touched your food!"[46] With an almost Edgar Allan Poe style, the exploits of cockroaches were described:

> Cockroaches hold midnight revels in millions of homes – you pay the bills for these vile insects' feasts! It is your food on which these disgusting intruders glut themselves, your provisions that they contaminate and ruin, your dishes and crockery that they spoil ....[47]

Flit provided a clear solution – death to the insects. Although insecticides are not food safety products per se, it is clear that the advertising strategy of a leading multinational product such as Flit contributed to how food safety was understood; or, to put it another way, using fear of food contamination to sell insecticide also constructed popular knowledges about food safety in Singapore.

1930s and 1940s: Corporations and Technology to the Rescue

If food had to be kept free from vermin, it also had to be correctly stored, and from the 1930s onwards that meant perishables had to be refrigerated. Imported foods with long supply chains obscured food production, but also obscured the cold chain. That is, refrigeration as a safety mechanism only worked to keep food safe if the food was safe to begin with, and in Singapore, the ideological beginning was the point of purchase. Cultural geographer Susanne Friedberg makes the argument for the cultural, culinary, and economic importance of technology, such as refrigeration, in the construction and pursuit of the preservation of freshness. She notes, "the refrigerator stood out amongst appliances. It was part of a larger system that connected people and places in new ways, and by doing so it transformed what it meant to be a food consumer."[48] Refrigeration was transformative for Singapore. The establishment there of the Cold Storage Company in 1903 heralded significant change in culinary as well as economic terms. Cold storage – the ability to ship and store refrigerated and frozen goods – literally changed what was in the bowls of the nation, and the

CULINARY INFRASTRUCTURE

company with that decidedly utilitarian name became the iconic supermarket chain that is still in existence and a producer of major products such as Magnolia brand ice cream.[49]

Refrigeration also changed how people understood food safety. Appliance manufacturers advertised vigorously during the 1930s and 1940s, with some decline during the Japanese occupation in World War II. In a 1934 advertisement for Westinghouse refrigerators, a thermometer showed the "Danger Line" of 50°F (10 °C) and explained to readers:

> No form of refrigeration other than electric can offer you the absolute certainty of a maintained low temperature which defies the growth of micro-organisms causing food souring and decay. At 50°F. is the danger-line. Above this lurks the source of many human ills – below this is safety – crisp fruits and vegetables, fresh milk and meats, delicious ices.[50]

Safety was thus measurable – a specific temperature – but also sensuous and experiential through crisp vegetables and delicious ices. Safety could be verified by taste and experience. It was not only safe because you do not get sick (another form of verification), but the crispness of the vegetables and the coldness of the ice provided further evidence of safety.

Grunow Refrigerators also encouraged potential consumers to get to know the machine; in 1934, they chose not to focus on the condensing units but rather on the refrigerant. Readers were told that they owed it to themselves and their families to look inside the refrigerator to "examine the important thing, the refrigerant, which is responsible for freezing ice cubes and keeping the cabinet cold." They were "glad to show you 'what's inside' a Grunow" and "explain its amazing features" which would "positively interest and delight you." The refrigerant was Carrene, and Grunow was the only brand that used this substance. Its qualities of safety and visibility ("it can be poured in an open container before our eyes, like water") were stressed in advertising with slogans such as "Carrene for SAFETY." Carrene, indeed, is a liquid, not a gas; it is dichloromethane or methylene chloride (CH_2Cl_2), which, while it may look like water, is toxic and exposure can cause poisoning.[51]

The claim that Carrene was safe because the refrigerant was visible and secure, meaning the household would not be poisoned in case of leaks, had some truth, but it also made repairs difficult and production was short-lived. That said, the Carrene system proved quite reliable and there is a Grunow refrigerator at the Refrigeration Research Museum which has been operating efficiently for more than 60 years.[52] In combining Carrene and refrigeration, Grunow provided protection: "The HOME that has a GRUNOW REFRIGERATOR is a home that is Protected."[53] This combination, they claimed, was "A new page in refrigeration development," making the Grunow "revolutionary" for its combination of "safety, simplicity and efficiency," and with a protected home you had "super-safe refrigeration."[54]

A nearly universal advertising appeal relied on women's sense of household pride. A 1936 Westinghouse refrigerator advertisement, for example, asked "Are you a good housekeeper?" implying their product defined a good housekeeper. In this instance, it was not just safety that was being provided, it was also thrift, what we might understand as fiscal safety. The "good housekeeper" could save money through "quality buying" and by stocking up on "bargain days." Westinghouse suggested these savings were so great that in most cases, they would "cover the hire purchase payments."[55] Another advertisement showed that Westinghouse had troubled to localize their approach. "Three Wise Women!", shown reading a Malayan newspaper, were deemed wise because they had "studied all the advantages and conveniences of a Kitchen Proved Refrigerator and decided to install a Westinghouse without delay," a decision promising better food protection, greater convenience, faster freezing, and greater economy. By connecting safety, fear, and thrift, the advertisement covered the bases of marketing refrigeration to women:

> How many people in the tropics are "upset" and sometimes made seriously ill by food that is not quite fresh. This would never happen if every home possessed a Westinghouse Kitchen Proved Refrigerator. It's your safeguard – and you cannot afford to be without it. Be sure of Kitchen Proved Protection for your health and pocket. Install a Westinghouse.[56]

Westinghouse, of course, was not just selling refrigeration; it was selling Westinghouse-branded refrigeration. Readers were thus instructed to look over their methods of food preservation to "make sure that you are getting the fullest measure of protection." The connection between protection and health was stressed: "Every day you may be eating foods which are tainted, from your present refrigerator." That is, refrigeration per se was not adequate; it had to be Westinghouse refrigeration in order to ensure full protection. The advertisement reiterated the dangers of storing food above 50°F ("Remember that poisonous bacteria thrive in temperatures above 50°F") and suggested that "if you are not sure of your present protection," Westinghouse would make an obligation-free study of your food storage equipment.[57]

The threat of sickness was repeatedly explained in refrigeration advertisements. Food spoilage was expensive and one of the "greatest hazards to health in the home," the exact nature of that threat described as coming from "mould and bacteria that contaminate foods." General messages like this were complemented with detailed threats about specific products: "in a single drop of milk at 58°F ... bacteria increases to several millions in just a few hours." And most alarming was that the good housekeeper cannot detect this herself because "food may be contaminated hours before detection is possible through sight, taste or smell." The good housekeeper was assumed unable to apply acquired skills of observation to the matter of food safety; she had to rely instead on infallible technology. Here, technology was oppositional to nature, which is especially unreliable in tropical Singapore where: "Nature is totally unreliable for food preservation ... the outside temperature stays within safe food preservation limits only a few days in the entire year."[58]

CULINARY INFRASTRUCTURE

Given that Singapore is only 137 km north of the equator, has a tropical climate with no distinctive seasons, uniform temperature and pressure, with a range from 22 to 35 °C, it is hard to imagine that Singapore's outside temperature is *ever* safe for food preservation. An illusion of climatic variation was also present in earlier Westinghouse advertisements. One from 1934 showed a frazzled looking couple and their dog looking at the closed door of their Westinghouse refrigerator. The text reads: "This hot weather has defeated the ice box and most people, but it has not touched the contents of a Westinghouse Refrigerator."[59] So technology trumps nature, and what is normal (hot weather) becomes an adversary that can be defeated. In fact, just three decades later, air conditioning became the new normal.

All of these refrigerator brands were marketed globally, and the origins of their marketing strategies and advertising "art" are likely to have been in head offices in the United States or Europe, but the trade-savvy Singapore market would have been used to this. For consumers in a tropical climate, a company's emphasis on the dependability of the workings of their machine may well have been an effective pitch, and it certainly worked to construct popular knowledges of food safety as personal and as technological.

1950s: Bad Beer – A Newspaper Exemplar

In October 1951, the *Straits Times* reported that a "Government spokesman" had announced that the adulteration of beer and label-swapping were uncommon in Singapore. It was rare because there was sufficient supply of good beer, profit margins for beer were healthy, and beer drinkers were reputed to be frequent enough drinkers that they would recognize any change in the taste of their beverage.[60] Just seven years later, the two leading breweries in Singapore were actively voicing concerned about bad beer: "large-scale adulteration of beer and stout sold to the unsuspecting public in Singapore is causing grave concern to the two local breweries, beer importers and to the police."[61]

Close reading of this "bad beer" narrative reveals a template of how popular knowledges about food safety were constructed and contested, highlighting tension between the food safety roles of the state and of the consumer. One typical multi-column article under the headline "Steps taken to curb the sale of 'bad beer'" claimed the theft of 30,000 bottle tops a few weeks earlier (and 45,000 beer labels the year before) demonstrated how "racketeers have been able to flout the law with impunity." Exciting and colorful narrative details were reserved for the popular aspects, the adulteration and illicit consumption of beer:

> Those who frequent night eating stalls after midnight know that beer can be had although it is an offence to sell liquor after hours. There is always a boy ready to take your money, vanish up a side lane and return with a bottle of beer or stout which he places unopened before you.[62]

The food safety key to this urchin table service is the unopened bottle. The physical cues of opening a beer – the crack of the breaking seal or/and the hiss of exploding gas – are the popular guarantee of authentic product.

But other narrative details work to question the food safety knowledge of the unopened bottle. For it is reported that racketeers made their own brew "cheaply, if unhygienically" by mixing molasses, hops, and water over a charcoal fire. Purchasing 200 bottles of genuine beer (and carefully removing the caps in such a way as to avoid marking them), they will filter their foul fermented brew through a rag and mix it 1:2 with the genuine beer to produce 300 bottles of now unsafe beer, crowned with a mixture of stolen and reused caps. Narratively, this implausible recipe for criminality challenges the usual visual and auditory signs of food safety (sealed bottle, branded labels and cap, and/or the hiss of a pressured release), framing them as unreliable markers of food safety.

The challenge to popular knowledge is in further tension with recurring ambivalence about state regulation. On the one hand, this article touted for a new ordinance. On the other, problems with the law were identified – slow processes, difficulty of conviction, and ineffectual fines. During this period, concern over the effectiveness of state intervention recurred regularly. New laws and ordinances were repeatedly proposed, and repeatedly failed to live up to expectations. That is, stories of bad beer and narrative distrust of consumer food safety knowledge uneasily coexisted with criticism of the inability of the legal apparatus to stop the sale of impure and unsafe foods and was the view most commonly expressed in and by newspapers.

Taking a different approach to effective regulation, this particular newspaper article ends by quoting Max Lewis (general manager of beer distributor Fraser and Neave) on solving the problem of beer adulteration:

> But the only really effective way of stamping it out is to revert to the pre-war practice of permitting eating places to sell beer and stout without a licence and at any hour. Then these places would prefer to get it from reputable sources.

Mr. Lewis's commercial interests in increased beer consumption are more evident than his logic, but by ending thus, this bad beer narrative illustrates the tripartite nature of food safety regulation in Singapore. Much responsibility rests with the beer consumer. The scope and effectiveness of state regulation are an ongoing issue. The reliability of the seller (whether urchin, racketeer, or legitimate distributor) is of utmost importance. Yet, while the concern of the brewers is mentioned in passing, the producer and conditions of production remain largely invisible. The formula of this article was repeated in a myriad of others, showing Singaporeans how fraudulent and unsafe food practices took place. Milk adulteration, for example, was repeatedly detailed; there are literally thousands of articles in the newspapers of twentieth-century Singapore that do this work of constructing knowledge about the corruption of food.

CULINARY INFRASTRUCTURE

1960s: Hawkers, Hygiene, and Letters to the Editor

The popular tensions about state regulation of food safety illustrated by bad beer narratives were gradually and unevenly worked out in other sites, such as the regulation of hawkers. For much of Singapore's early history, colonial authorities made hawking illegal, and conducted regular raids. It was, however, very popular with consumers, despite being potentially unhealthy. The inevitable food waste that accompanied the practice attracted disease-carrying flies; the dispersion of dirty water carried diseases like typhoid; inadequately cleaned hands and utensils spread gastroenteritis, enteric fever (typhoid), dysentery, cholera, and parasitic infections like hookworm and roundworm. Hawking, then, became a matter of public health and needed to be cleaned up.

Long seen as a problem, itinerant food sellers or hawkers were the subjects of much commentary about food safety in the 1960s. In the decade of Singaporean independence, hawking transformed from chaotic to ordered and the itinerant sellers who walked the streets came under tight regulation in new air-conditioned indoor spaces. This transformation required a bureaucracy, most notably an army of inspectors, a legal apparatus (empowering police and inspectors), and a shift in popular knowledge, the last of which was facilitated by newspapers.

In Singaporean newspapers of the mid-1960s, particularly after independence in 1965, "Letters to the Editor" columns were used to explain shifts in food safety policy. As a city state, Singapore governance was (and is) very local as well as national, and these letters provide an insight into how polices were implemented, perceived, and negotiated during this critical period of development. Never strictly one-way communication, these spaces (predominantly in the *Straits Times*) functioned in ways akin to community service announcements, town hall meetings, or call-in talk radio. That is, they were a site of public dialog between citizens and the bureaucracy. A concerned citizen, for example, wrote a letter complaining about the state of hawkers in a specific location ("Will the Hawkers Department please look at the hazards created by hawkers at the junction of Kim Keat Road and Kim Keat Avenue?"[63]) A few days later, a department head replied: "My Department is taking actions in respect of streets and five footways. The writer ... will be aware that this is not an easy problem to overcome, but continued action is being taken."[64]

In 1965, a number of letters expressed dissatisfaction with how the government and/or police were cleaning up hawking. R. Wong, for example, wrote to the *Straits Times* to say: "I see the police are doing great work raiding brothels. I wish they would be equally enthusiastic and constant in tackling other evils, especially the traffic and hawker problems in Balestier Road."[65] M. Chong, a recent recipient of a parking fine, was disgruntled that he was fined for a first offence but hawkers were not.[66] Chong took special exception to an earlier exchange, where Dr. Thevathansan, Senior Health Officer in the Department of

Environmental Health, had replied to a string of letters in the preceding months by suggesting that the "education of hawkers is a slow process."[67] Chong noted that when it came to the parking fine, there was "no question of 'education' here," and went on to ask: "Which is the greater crime against public health and safety – the deliberate dumping of tons of waste food in drains, or illegal parking?" Chong was not arguing for lenience regarding his parking fine, but for harsher penalties for hawkers: "May I suggest to Dr. Thevathasan that hawkers and other could complete their 'education' quicker with fines and not words."[68] This public exchange was doing some of the work of publicizing food safety issues, legitimizing government actions, and providing evidence of community support for punishments. Singapore was slowly becoming a "fine" city.

Announcements of specific locations cleared of itinerant hawkers, the progress of licensing, and similar information featured regularly in newspapers of the 1960s. The division between news reporting and government communications (often unclear in Singapore, even when the *Straits Times* was independent) was especially unclear around the reporting of the hawking clean-up. No detail was too small to report, and these minutiae underlined for readers the type and scale of the hard work done by officials, thereby signaling bureaucratic competency. In one article, for example, the payment of a license fee by 681 hawkers on 19 and 20 April 1966, for "pitches" (delineated positions) on Scotts Road was detailed, as were the specifics of the licenses – how many were licensed for six days a week, how many for seven days, and the number of days remaining to pay for the May license fees.[69] The payment of fines, number of fines issued, amount of fine, and so forth were regularly published, and even the distribution of license forms was worthy of coverage.[70] This bureaucratization culminated in the introduction of a Hawker Code, which, among other things, prohibited street hawking and in so doing, profoundly changed both the public eating experience in Singapore and popular knowledge of food safety.[71] In practice, hawker food was safely contained in fixed, air-conditioned locations. Consumer and seller behaviors became regulated. These gustatory changes mirrored the scale of change taking place more broadly in the social and built environment.[72]

1970s: Fiscal Safety for the Developing Economy

Singapore experienced massive economic growth in the 1970s. According to the government, growing the economy was a matter for all citizens. Growth, however, had to be free from corrupt practices and be undertaken in terms that met with government approval. Stable food prices were understood to contribute to safety and profiteering (a recurrent threat) and seriously frowned on. Responding to greater demand by charging more for eggs and pork at Chinese New Year, for example, also worked to undermine the safety of food supply. Furthermore, silently omitting or substituting for an expensive ingredient was long established as a form of adulteration: "or if any valuable constituent has been abstracted wholly or in part from it."[73] That is, greed-driven ingredient substitution is not only fraud, but financialized food adulteration.

During the international oil crisis of 1974, the government made it clear that the very safety of the nation was imperiled by profiteering. What could happen, suggested Lim Kim San, then Minister for the Environment, was an inflationary spiral: if retailers made too much profit, then wholesalers would increase their prices, leading retailers to raise prices further, and "if shopkeepers and hawkers continue upping prices, wages and salaries will rise," which, in turn, would affect Singapore's competitiveness in the world market, with the nation unable to export sufficient goods to earn foreign exchange needed for food and oil. Lim feared it would lower the standard of living: "There will be more unemployment and our industrial progress will be checkered."[74]

A "checkered" industrial progress had to be avoided. In addition to the roles of the state, it was the responsibility of merchants not to profiteer, and it was the responsibility of consumers to avoid buying from people who overcharged them and to report if they were overcharged. Sabotage of the retail system by hoarding had to be avoided, and consumers had to "discard the bad habit of wasting food." The Ministry threatened bad publicity, consumer boycotts, and publication of the names of individuals and shops that profiteered. Lim said he would consider cancelling the licenses of repeat over-charging offenders. Public humiliation is a strategy the Singaporean state has used repeatedly and in other public hygiene contexts, most notably in the 1993 shaming of litterers,[75] but in 1974, it was quite novel. Regular reminders of stiff penalties appeared in newspapers along with news stories stressing legislative approaches and procedures. Popular knowledge about food safety connected with knowledge about law, regulation, and punishment.

In 1974, Prime Minister Lee Kuan Yew emphasized the role of the consumer, saying that if people were willing to allow themselves to be cheated and pay inflated prices, "there was little any Government or anybody else could do." He called on consumers to be "bloody-minded" and "willing to do without" in order to break the will of the profiteers. Making the connection between the government and media explicit, Lee was quoted (in the now government-controlled *Straits Times*) as saying: "with the co-operation of the newspapers, through radio and TV we can deter profiteering, especially of perishables – vegetables, fresh meat and eggs."[76] The Trade Department issued price lists of what essential items *should* cost, so that consumers knew what prices were considered reasonable. In this formulation, the state and the consumer stand together against the greed of the profiteering middleman. Greedy or not, production costs were again invisible.

Some citizens took a more balanced approach. Writing in 1977 about profiteering hawkers, Madalene Hee in a letter to the editor implicated everyone in the process and suggested the only solution was a joint effort by the community.[77] Many consumers, however, felt the responsibility lay with the government to deal with profiteering, and they were not afraid to say so, albeit under noms de plume. In a letter to the editor, "Fleeced" asked why the Singapore Tourist Promotion Board could not do something to ensure fair prices at hawker centers that were designed to attract foreign visitors, where not only was "Fleeced" charged more, but the portions were smaller.[78] Economic stresses and political change had made both the fiscal and literal safety of food the popular responsibility of the state.

1980s: From Consumer Advocacy to Consumer Responsibility

The decade of the 1980s amply illustrates the ongoing themes of popular food safety knowledge, illustrating continuity and connections between the colonial and postcolonial moments. The alliance between state and consumer continues, and is blurred by food safety interventions by non-governmental organizations. The shopkeeper was once again in the crosshairs. The 1980 controversy over the quality of spices encapsulates the tripartite merchant–consumer–state relationship in food safety knowledge-making. Producers are hidden in the mists of complex supply chains.

One newspaper article, for example, explicitly stated that the "responsibility of cleaning and ensuring that the spices are fit for consumption lies with the local factories or shops that sell them to the consumers." The nature of the problem was that "filth and impurities like excreta, hair, twigs and insects can be found in spices when they are imported here."[79] Spices of the Orient, a local firm, shared this view of merchant responsibility, and in newspaper articles (or what we would today classify as "advertorials") published across several days, described their processes of meeting this responsibility. With considerable narrative attention to science and technology, the spices were processed, "sterilised to kill off bacteria," hand cleaned to remove visible debris, mechanically screened, and then screened a second time with fine mesh before they were put in a "gravity separation machine which uses compressed air to remove the last traces of filth and impurities." The spices were then stacked in a sterilization chamber, air extracted from the chamber, and high-pressure ethylene oxide gas pumped in and left for 24 h to kill any remaining bacteria. The necessity, efficacy, and effect on flavor of these procedures were left unaddressed. Spices of the Orient also contrasted their elaborate procedures with the practices of other companies who "simply pour the raw materials into the grinding machine without even cleaning them." Or to put it more bluntly, Spices of the Orient's narrative of technology made everyone else's spices dirty and pre-modern.

Similar stories discussed adulteration of ground spices – using flour, brick powder, sawdust, or corn – that same year.[80] Again, the merchant was responsible for deploying technology, time, and investment to make processed food safe, and consumers taught that this took place mainly at the processing level, not the primary production level. The spice pattern was repeated: produce generally must be altered, cleaned, and processed to be fit for consumption (now and then). In Singapore, this responsibility lies with the companies that sell, not those that grow. The key food safety bottleneck was constructed as the point of sale, not production. And buying, not eating, was consumption.

The line between the consumer and the state blurred in this period. Throughout the 1980s, the Consumers Association of Singapore, a non-government lobby group, sustained an energetic food consumer advocacy role, sponsoring lab testing and spot-checks of nutritional value, potential adulteration, expiration dates, packing defects, and value-for-money. Echoing earlier links between food and profiteering, simple safety was not enough: "even if foods are found to be safe, the price will come under scrutiny."[81] They understood adulteration broadly, as a "social crime," concerned that producers could adhere to the letter of the law and create products that appear wholesome, yet were not. Information from their tests formed the basis for campaigns explaining food quality to the public.[82] In 1983, the Consumer Association began to target primary school children with a quarterly four-page bulletin to "help them grow up to be good consumers." Content included money management and issues around the safety of toys, food, and drinks.[83] Food safety knowledge was embedded in general consumer knowledge and wrapped with the formal institution of childhood.

But the state still had responsibilities, including food tests and maintaining consumer trust. To continue the spice example, only days after the *Straits Times* articles about spice quality, the Environment Ministry issued a statement assuring consumers that spices sold in Singapore were generally wholesome and fit for human consumption. The newspaper detailed the tests carried out by the Ministry, which showed fewer instances of spice adulteration than the Singapore Consumers Association tests had, but included some novel adulterations, including one with ash and a sample portentously described as "microbiologically unsatisfactory."[84] That the primary responsibility rested with sellers, not producers, remained uncontested and clear in newspaper coverage of the issues.

A 1983 article in the independent, but short-lived (1980–1985) *Singapore Monitor*, detailing consumer rights under the Sale of Food Act, focused clearly on merchants – and shows no difference from the *Straits Times* in treatment of the food safety topic. Having noted the nine ways a shopkeeper could commit an offense under the Act (from misleading descriptions to adulteration and poisoning), it was noted that there are circumstances in which a shopkeeper might purchase "foodstuffs in packages which have been adulterated and made impure by the exporter." In such a case, the shopkeeper could raise the defense that "he relied on the representation made by the exporter and believed them to be true." A shopkeeper who objected to the government's findings could also have the suspect sample tested by an independent analyst, and consumers could likewise take suspect samples for testing at both public and private facilities.[85]

These consumer rights, however, were not adequate for the Consumer Association of Singapore, which in 1989 called for a Bill of Rights for consumers. The Bill, while protecting consumers, would also re-inscribe the food safety responsibility of consumers. The Executive Secretary of the Association went so far as to say that "consumers were equally responsible in the fight for quality food." Wise shoppers needed to do six things: compare prices and quality; check product weight; avoid buying expired items; buy nothing with damaged wrapping; avoid dented cans; and "complain if they spot a malpractice."[86] This decade of information dissemination and sharpening of responsibility was hard work for both consumer advocate groups and consumers.

Food safety advice to consumers burgeoned in the 1980s. Newspaper articles offered advice on how to avoid exploding vacuum flasks, how to be a good host (go easy on the drinks), and how to get the most out of your kitchen aides. Readers of the *Singapore Monitor* were cautioned to place a rubber mat in front of their refrigerator "to minimize the possibility of suffering an electric shock if the wiring has become defective." A dishwasher was no reason to gloat because "there are many occasions when a piece of steel wool and a good scrub is still the best way to get things clean." Toasters may spell the end to burnt bread, but some take a long time to brown bread or pop the bread too vigorously, cook bread unevenly, and could "breakdown soon after purchase."[87] Technology – in actual use – required vigilance, and food safety meant practicing safety around food as well as with food.

The role of food inspectors, "today's version of royal food tasters," was explained across several newspaper articles, and their methods – sampling, inspecting, testing, date checking, fining, educating hawkers who had bad samples, and prosecution – described at length.[88] Another article strung together miscellaneous advice about the risk of incorrectly frozen vegetables, the need to cover food to prevent dehydration, and the physical risk of placing a cooker near a kitchen window or door.[89] The narrative form of newspaper food safety advice reflected attempts to (at least appear to be) fulfilling a responsible role in the food safety campaign. That is, structuring knowledge about food safety in a format reminiscent of an official public campaign had become a rhetorical means of claiming popular validity for that knowledge.

At the end of this decade, the state released *Food for Thought*, a handbook on food hygiene for the general public.[90] The declared intent was to get consumers to help the authorities, and for "consumers who come across food that they are suspicious of to pass on that information to the ministry."[91] Educated citizens could thus be deployed as an army of food inspectors. The site of food safety was commercial kitchens, not domestic kitchens, reflecting both that Singaporeans ate out more than in, but also the popular perception of risk.[92] Given the scale and scope of dining in Singapore, the reported risks were not particularly high. In 1988, there were 191 cases of food poisoning from commercial establishments, with 1145 people affected, and by December of the following year, although there was a slight decrease in cases (164), more people were affected by the cases (1551).[93] Now regulated and contained by air-conditioned hawker centers and tested by both state and non-governmental organizations, popular knowledge of food safety worries still about the heirs of bad beer as sites of special danger.

Food for Thought addressed some domestic food issues, especially consumer education around food purchases and storage, but the clear emphasis was on training the eating-out consumer. In the words of the Ministry of the Environment: "What we hope is for the public to be more discerning when they eat out." This was an issue explicitly affecting all Singaporeans: "Hygiene or the lack of it affects all and sundry. Bacteria and viruses make no distinction of who you are." *Straits Times* coverage of the new handbook included reproducing illustrations from *Food For Thought*. An undershirt-wearing, tattooed, overweight, smoker puffed over a cooked chicken. A coughing woman sprayed cakes with saliva, and the reader told: "Good hygiene is a must when handling food."[94] The images of food safety – bacteria, viruses, unsafe smoke, and/or the spray of saliva – repulse and stoke fears, and the popular knowledge of food safety echoes the colonial-era horror of Flit's flies.

Conclusion

Over the decades examined in this article, Singapore underwent an extraordinary transition, from steamy colonial port to wartime occupation, postwar boom, and independent, air-conditioned city state. Yet, since inception, Singapore has been overwhelmingly reliant on imported food, with almost no control over the conditions of production and little over the conditions of processing. For Singapore, food safety is a complicated business.

These decades saw rapid deployment of science and technology for domestic life across the developed world. As shown, for Singaporeans, this was accompanied by the development of a detailed understanding of food safety as a shared responsibility. Popular knowledge of food safety was constructed to understand food could be diseased, adulterated, contaminated, improperly stored, and sold by dirty hawkers or by profiteers. Food could be physically, fiscally, and nationally unsafe. These challenges to food safety were managed by a tripartite merchant–consumer–state relationship of food safety knowledge-making, focusing on local actions, good and bad. The beer adulterator, the merchant who sells dirty spices, the tuberculosis-infested hawker, the profiteering shop keeper who increases the price of eggs at Chinese New Year, the careless housewife who buys food with a damaged wrapping, can all be educated, disciplined and, if necessary, punished.

The construction of food safety, as seen in the varied pages of Singapore's twentieth-century newspapers, worked to frighten consumers, threaten merchants, and prompt the state into regulatory mode. Private and public, commercial and non-commercial, these interests worked both against each other and in collaboration across the Singaporean food system to create changing meanings of food safety – it was everyone's responsibility. Conflicted and contingent, encompassing both continuity and change, the resulting popular knowledges, I argue, illustrate one form of culinary infrastructure.

Finally, we must not overlook the practical results, for in a moment when the global trade in food and ingredients increasingly complicates the policing of food safety, Singapore anticipated contemporary issues by more than a century. Local production is impossible; the 100-mile diet an eccentric absurdity. Yet, for all the very real problems of food preparation, the near invisibility of the food producer, and long, obscures supply chains; Singapore is now a remarkably "safe" place to eat. As such, Singapore suggests a potential alternative way to engage with globalized food – instead of striving to make production more visible via shortened supply lines and/or technological surveillance, Singapore's remarkable food safety achievement was via a popular focus, not on local production, but on shared local responsibilities.

Acknowledgments

This article was supported by a Colonialism and its Aftermath Small Grant, from the University of Tasmania. Eric Anderson, Howard Gilbert, Martin Collins and Sheila Allison provided much appreciated critiques of drafts of this article. I would also like to thank the two anonymous reviewers and Jeffery Pilcher for constructive feedback.

Funding

This work was supported by the University of Tasmania.

Notes

1. Pilcher, "Culinary Infrastructure."
2. Habermas, *The Structural Transformation of the Public Sphere*, 181.
3. Anderson, *Imagined Communities*, 43.
4. Jeffrey, "Testing Concepts about Print," 485.
5. Kenley, *New Culture in a New World*, 100.
6. Turnbull, *A History of Modern Singapore*, 154.
7. Turnbull, *Dateline Singapore*, 246.

CULINARY INFRASTRUCTURE

8. Bokhorst-Heng, "Newspapers in Singapore," 563, 564.
9. A sometimes cautiously written history of the newspaper, published on its 150th anniversary, states that between 1908 and 1926, the paper became known as "the Thunderer of the East," that it "acted as watchdog and critic of the colonial administration." Cheah, "Review of *Dateline Singapore*," 116–119.
10. French and Philips, *Cheated Not Poisoned?* 3.
11. Petrick, "Purity as Life," 53.
12. Waddington, "We Don't Want Any German Sausages Here!" 1030.
13. Tarulevicz, "I Had No Time to Pick Out the Worms," 1–24.
14. Newell, "Articulating Empire," 39.
15. McClintock, *Imperial Leather*, 209–210.
16. Hoganson, *Consumers' Imperium*, 253.
17. Chakrabarty, *Habitations of Modernity*, 66.
18. Laporte, *A History of Shit*.
19. Stallybrass and White, *The Politics and Poetics of Transgression*, 126.
20. Kong, *Singapore Hawker Centres*.
21. Duruz, "The Taste of Retro," 133–158.
22. Duruz and Khoo, *Eating Together*.
23. Chua, "Taking the Street Out of Street Food," 23–40.
24. Lai, "The *Kopitiam* in Singapore," 103–132.
25. Neo, "Placing Pig Farming in Post-Independence Singapore," 83–102.
26. Leong-Salobir, *Food Culture in Colonial Asia*.
27. Wong, *Wartime Kitchen*.
28. Tarulevicz, *Eating Her Curries and Kway*.
29. *Singapore Free Press and Mercantile Advertiser*, January 20, 1927.
30. *Singapore Free Press and Mercantile Advertiser*, February 24, 1927.
31. *Singapore Free Press and Mercantile Advertiser*, July 2, 1926.
32. *Singapore Free Press and Mercantile Advertiser*, January 27, 1927.
33. Geisel drew Flit cartoons for over 15 years, beginning in 1927, and made the product wildly successful. In the United States, the catch-cry of one of his characters, "Quick, Henry, the Flit!" was popularized by the public. Allen, *The War on Bugs*, 110–114.
34. *Atlantic Constitution*, July 27, 1941.
35. *Times of India*, July 31, 1926. Flit also continued their advertising campaign for much longer in India than Singapore, with advertisements that highlighted the life-threatening nature of insects being used as late as 1966, the saliva of the mosquito "may contain dangerous germs which can cause malaria, yellow fever, dengue and filariasis." *Times of India*, 15 July 1966.
36. Tomes, *The Gospel of Germs*, 7.
37. *Singapore Free Press and Mercantile Advertiser*, September 2, 1929.
38. *Singapore Free Press and Mercantile Advertiser*, February 5, 1926.
39. *Singapore Free Press and Mercantile Advertiser*, October, 7, 1929.
40. Tarulevicz, "Hidden in Plain View," 134–153.
41. *Malayan Saturday Post*, November 12, 1932.
42. *Singapore Free Press and Mercantile Advertiser*, February 8, 1928.
43. *Singapore Free Press and Mercantile Advertiser*, September 19, 1930.
44. Drew and Joseph, *The Story of the Fly*.
45. *Singapore Free Press and Mercantile Advertiser*, February 20, 1929.
46. *Malayan Saturday Post*, June 2, 1932.
47. *Singapore Free Press and Mercantile Advertiser*, October 27, 1927.
48. Freidberg, *Fresh*, 45.

CULINARY INFRASTRUCTURE

49. Goh, *Serving Singapore.*
50. *Singapore Free Press and Mercantile Advertiser*, February 19, 1934.
51. Rioux and Myers, "Methylene Chloride Poisoning," 227–238.
52. Refrigeration Research Museum, accessed May 23, 2014, https://www.asme.org/about-asme/who-we-are/engineering-history/landmarks/207-refrigeration-research-museum.
53. *Straits Times*, June 11, 1934.
54. *Straits Times*, May 10, 1934.
55. *Straits Times*, June 9, 1936.
56. *Straits Times*, June 2, 1937.
57. *Straits Times*, February 12, 1937.
58. *Straits Times*, December 11, 1938.
59. *Straits Times*, June 1, 1934.
60. "Beer Adulteration Not Widespread," *Straits Times*, October 25, 1951.
61. "Steps Taken to Curb the Sale of 'Bad Beer,'" *Straits Times*, July 20, 1958.
62. Ibid.
63. Motorist, Letter to the editor, *Straits Times*, September 21, 1965.
64. K. Y. D. Gin, Acting Director of Public Works, Letter to the editor, *Straits Times*, March 13, 1965. Five footways are broad covered sidewalks in front of shophouses frequently used by merchants.
65. R. Wong, Letter to the editor, *Straits Times*, August 30, 1965.
66. M. Chong, Letter to the Editor, *Straits Times*, October 23, 1965.
67. V. M. S. Thevathasan, Senior Health Officer, Letter to the Editor, *Straits Times*, October 12, 1965.
68. See note 66 above.
69. "Fees Paid by 681 Hawkers," *Straits Times*, April 20, 1966.
70. "1,724 More Forms for Hawkers," *Straits Times*, March 3, 1966.
71. "Hawkers Code to Solve a Problem," *Straits Times*, March 12, 1966.
72. Kong, *Singapore Hawker Centres*, 19.
73. "A Shocking Record," *Straits Times*, September 19, 1913.
74. Edward Liu, "Warning to Shops, Hawkers: Profiteers May Lose Their Licences, Says Lim," *Straits Times*, February 18, 1974.
75. "A Litterbug's Mane of Shame," *Straits Times*, February 22, 1993.
76. Joseph Yeo, "Lee Calls For United Action By Consumers," *Straits Times*, February 17, 1974.
77. Madalene Hee, Letter to the Editor, *Straits Times*, November 5, 1977.
78. Fleeced, Letter to the Editor, *Straits Times*, November 10, 1978.
79. Lai Yew Kong, "Cleaning Spices; 'Onus on Factories,'" *Straits Times*, August 6, 1980.
80. Chew Tang Kiak, "Filth Mixed with Spices, says Case," *Straits Times*, August 5, 1980.
81. Loong Swee Ying, "Case to Ensure Food on Display Gives Value-For-Money," *Singapore Monitor*, May 17, 1984.
82. "Food Tests Planned to Help Set Minimum Standards," *Straits Times*, May 18, 1984.
83. "Making of a Good Consumer: Case to 'mould' Students with Quarterly Bulletin," *Straits Times*, August 28, 1983.
84. "Most Spices Sold Are Fit To Eat, Says Ministry," *Straits Times*, August 9, 1980.
85. Gopalan Nair, "Food Quality and Hygiene: Your Rights Under the Sale of Food Act," *Singapore Monitor*, October 30, 1983.
86. "Case Outlines 'Bill of Rights' for Consumers," *Straits Times*, September 18, 1989.

CULINARY INFRASTRUCTURE

87. "Here's How to Get the Most Out of Your Kitchen Aids," *Straits Times*, September, 18 1983.
88. "Men Who Visit Hawkers Six Times a Day," *Straits Times*, December 29, 1980.
89. "Here's How to Get the Most Out of Your Kitchen Aids," *Straits Times*, September, 18 1983.
90. Singapore Ministry of the Environment, *Food for Thought*.
91. Khng Eu Meng, "New Handbook on Food Hygiene for the Layman," *Straits Times*, December 12, 1989.
92. "Health Alert as Even More Eat Out," *Straits Times*, December 1, 2010.
93. Khng Eu Meng, "New Handbook on Food Hygiene for the Layman," *Straits Times*, December 12, 1989.
94. "Putting Right Food Forward," *Straits Times*, December 12, 1989.

Bibliography

Allen, Will. *The War on Bugs*. White River, VT: Chelsea Green, 2008.
Anderson, Benedict. *Imagined Communities: Reflections on the Origin and Spread of Nationalism*. Rev. ed. London: Verso, 1991.
Atlantic Constitution. 1941. "Flit Advertisement." July 27.
Bokhorst-Heng. Wendy. "Newspapers in Singapore: A Mass Ceremony in the Imagining of the Nation." *Media, Culture and Society* 24, no. 4 (2002): 563–564.
Chakrabarty, Dipesh. *Habitations of Modernity: Essays in the Wake of Subaltern Studies*. Chicago, IL: Chicago University Press, 2002.
Cheah, Boon Kheng. "Review of *Dateline Singapore: 150 Years of the Straits times*, by C.M. Turnbull." *Journal of the Malaysian Branch of the Royal Asiatic Society* 69, no. 2 (1996): 116–119.
Chua, Beng Huat. "Taking the Street out of Street Food." In *Food and Foodways and Foodscapes: Culture. Community and Consumption in Post-Colonial Singapore*, edited by Lily Kong and Vineeta Sinha, 23–40. Singapore: World Scientific, 2016.
Drew, Jason, and Justine Joseph. *The Story of the Fly: And How it Could Save the World*. Cape Town: Cheviot, 2012.
Duruz, Jean. "The Taste of Retro: Nostalgia, Sensory Landscapres and Cosmopolitianism in Singapore." In *Food and Foodways and Foodscapes: Culture. Community and Consumption in Post-Colonial Singapore*, edited by Lily Kong and Vineeta Sinha, 133–158. Singapore: World Scientific, 2016.
Duruz, Jean, and Gaik Cheng Khoo. *Eating Together: Food, Space, and Identity in Malaysia and Singapore*. Lanham, MD: Rowman and Littlefield, 2015.
Freidberg, Susanne. *Fresh: A Perishable History*. Cambridge, MA: Harvard University Press, 2009.
French, Michael, and Jim Philips. *Cheated Not Poisoned? Food Regulation in the United Kingdom, 1875–1938*. Manchester, NH: Manchester University Press, 2000.
Goh, Chor Boon. *Serving Singapore: A Hundred Years of Cold Storage, 1903–2003*. Singapore: Cold Storage, 2003.
Habermas, Jürgen. *The Structural Transformation of the Public Sphere*. Cambridge, MA: MIT Press, 1991.
Hoganson, Kristin L. *Consumers' Imperium: The Global Production of American Domesticity. 1865–1920*. Chapel Hill: University of North Carolina Press, 2007.
Jeffrey, Robin. "Testing Concepts about Print, Newspapers, and Politics: Kerala, India, 1800–2009." *The Journal of Asian Studies* 68, no. 2 (2009): 465–489.

Kenley, David. *New Culture in a New World: The May Fourth Movement and the Chinese Diaspora in Singapore, 1919–1932*. New York: Routledge, 2003.

Kong, Lily. *Singapore Hawker Centres: People, Places, Food*. Singapore: National Environment Agency, 2007.

Lai, Ah Eng. "The *Kopitiam* in Singapore: An Evolving Story about Cultural Diversity and Cultural Politics." In *Food and Foodways and Foodscapes: Culture. Community and Consumption in Post-Colonial Singapore*, edited by Lily Kong and Vineeta Sinha, 103–132. Singapore: World Scientific, 2016.

Laporte, Dominique. *A History of Shit*. Translated by Nadia Benabid and Rodolphe el-Khoury. Cambridge, MA: MIT Press, 2000.

Leong-Salobir, Cecilia. *Food Culture in Colonial Asia: A Taste of Empire*. New York: Routledge, 2011.

Malayan Saturday Post. 1932. "Flit Advertisements." June 2 and November 12.

McClintock, Anne. *Imperial Leather: Race, Gender and Sexuality in the Colonial Context*. New York: Routledge, 1995.

Neo, Harvey. "Placing Pig Farming in Post-Independence Singapore: Community, Development and Landscape Rurality." In *Food and Foodways and Foodscapes: Culture. Community and Consumption in Post-Colonial Singapore*, edited by Lily Kong and Vineeta Sinha, 83–102. Singapore: World Scientific, 2016.

Newell, Stephanie. "Articulating Empire: Newspaper Readerships in Colonial West Africa." *New Formations* 73 (2011): 26–42.

Petrick, Gabriella M. "'Purity as Life': H. J. Heinz, Religious Sentiment, and the Beginning of the Industrial Diet." *History and Technology* 27, no. 1 (2011): 37–64.

Pilcher, Jeffery M. "Culinary Infrastructure: How Facilities and Technologies Create Value and Meaning around Food." *Global Food History* 2, no. 2 (2016).

Rioux, John P., and Roy A. M. Myers. "Methylene Chloride Poisoning: A Paradigmatic Review." *The Journal of Emergency Medicine* 6, no. 3 (1988): 227–238.

Singapore Free Press and Mercantile Advertiser. 1926–1934. "Advertisements and Articles."

Singapore Ministry of the Environment. *Food for Thought: A Handbook on Food Safety and Hygiene*. Singapore: Ministry of the Environment, 1989.

Singapore Monitor. 1983–1985. "Advertisements and Articles."

Stallybrass, Peter, and Allon White. *The Politics and Poetics of Transgression*. Ithaca, NY: Cornell University Press, 1986.

Straits Times. 1934–1989.

Tarulevicz, Nicole. *Eating Her Curries and Kway: A Cultural History of Food in Singapore*. Champaign: University of Illinois Press, 2013.

Tarulevicz, Nicole. "Hidden in Plain View: Singapore's Race and Ethnicity Policies." In *The State, Development and Identity in Multi-Ethnic Societies*, edited by Nicholas Tarling and Terence Gomez, 134–153. New York: Routledge, 2008.

Tarulevicz, Nicole. "I Had No Time to Pick out the Worms: Food Adulteration in Singapore." *Journal of Colonialism and Colonial History* 16, no. 3 (2015): 1–24.

Times of India. 1926 [1966]. "Flit Advertisements." July 31 and July 15.

Tomes, Nancy. *The Gospel of Germs: Men, Women and the Microbe in American Life*. Cambridge, MA: Harvard University Press, 1999.

Turnbull, C. M. *Dateline Singapore: 150 Years of the Straits times*. Singapore: Singapore Press Holdings, 1995.

Turnbull, C. M. *A History of Modern Singapore: 1819–2005*. Singapore: National University of Singapore Press, 2009.

Waddington, Keir. "'We Don't Want Any German Sausages Here!' Food, Fear and the German Nation in Victorian and Edwardian Britain." *Journal of British History* 52, no. 4 (2013): 1017–1042.

Wong Hong Suen. *Wartime Kitchen: Food and Eating in Singapore 1942–1950*. Singapore: Editions Didier Millet, 2009.

A Museum's Culinary Life: Women's Committees and Food at the Art Gallery of Toronto

Irina D. Mihalache

ABSTRACT

This article explores the work of the Women's Committee and Junior Women's Committee at the Art Gallery of Toronto (AGT) in the 1960s to increase the visibility of the institution through the use of food. The committees organized numerous culinary events at the gallery, such as Men's Lunches, and off site, such as "The Art of Cooking" classes, in partnership with other important commercial actors in the city, primarily Consumers' Gas Company and Canada Packers. The communication tactics with AGT members, networks of relations with sponsors, and strategies for developing menus, creating recipes, and cooking the food established by the women's committees produced a culinary infrastructure inside the gallery and positioned the AGT as a significant cultural producer in Toronto. A focus on the museum's culinary infrastructure offers new knowledge about the work of museums which demonstrates their continuous concern for relevance and their centrality to larger social and cultural projects. Looking deeply and historically inside museums and engaging with its complex internal structure adds nuance accounts about museums which overlook the diversity of the institution's professional communities.

Introduction

The Art Gallery of Toronto's Women's Committee was founded in 1945 as "a subsidiary of the Men's Executive" with the aims to "keep the activities and opportunities offered by the Gallery before the public, and to increase the membership to the gallery."[1] Through the work of the Committee, the AGT, which was renamed the Art Gallery of Ontario (AGO) in 1966 and continues to be Toronto's main art institution, became the site of snack lunches, men's lunches, light suppers, afternoon teas, Sunday morning refreshments, cooking

CULINARY INFRASTRUCTURE

classes, costume balls with open bars and after hours parties which used food as a primary mode of engagement, entertainment, and moneymaking. This article explores the food work of the Women's Committee and the Junior Women's Committee (JWC)[2] at the AGT, focusing on the 1960s, which coincides with the two Committees' most active decade in terms of culinary programming, and observes how elements of culinary infrastructure – a kitchen, storage areas, a members' lounge/restaurant – supplemented the gallery's collecting, displaying, and public programming functions.

The gallery's culinary life is significant not only for its contributions to the AGT's growth – for example, money raised through culinary events were used to purchase some of the gallery's most famous acquisitions, including Henry Moore's "The Warrior" or Käthe Kollwitz's "Grief" – but also for positioning the gallery as a major cultural producer in the city. In this article, I define museums[3] as producers of cultures, with an active role in political, social, and cultural networks which inform their practices. To "matter," museum professionals are constantly searching for relevance in their curatorial, interpretive, educational, administrative, or commercial practice, which, ideally, connects with the contemporary visitor. The museum's relevance can go beyond that of collector, exhibitioner, and educator as the museum diversifies its repertoire of practices, taking on some unexpected tasks. Sarah Portnoy and Jeffrey M. Pilcher write that "the restaurant industry is also heavily influenced by an underlying infrastructure of media and food critics, culinary education and professional training, food distributors, transnational labor markets, and the local and national regulators that govern these diverse activities."[4] This infrastructure supporting the food cultures of cities is guided, in turn, by the work of cultural and political institutions, some of which are not directly connected to food, such as museums. The AGT became a significant participant to the culinary life of the city in the 1960s, at a time of intense modernization in Toronto,[5] through the work of the two women's committees, which integrated the museum to the city's culinary infrastructure and vice versa.

A focus on the museum's culinary infrastructure offers new knowledge about the work of museums and demonstrates their continuous concern for relevance and their centrality to larger social and cultural projects, much of which was the product of women's work in the 1950s and 1960s. Kendall Taylor writes about

> a second generation of women [who] entered the field between 1950s and 1970s… They tended to be generalists, rolling up their sleeves and performing the numerous activities that needed to be done in the expanding museum profession, such as organizing collections, renovating buildings, and developing public programs.[6]

Many of these women organized volunteer committees, transferring knowledge and skills acquired in the domestic sphere into the public space of the museum,[7] participating with agency to what Lori D. Ginzberg calls a "benevolent culture."[8] This article highlights the culinary work of the Women's Committee and its Junior counterpart who "ran" the gallery, as volunteers, alongside the male administrators, curators, and trustees. The committees' mandate to increase the AGT's visibility locally and to bring more members to the museum, sustained by constant efforts to engage audiences, is an opportunity to re-evaluate the relation between museums and their visitors, as it has been problematized in mainstream museum studies texts. The history of the women's committees at the AGT suggests another way to assess the complex work of museums to be relevant to their audiences and urban communities. A museum's own professional infrastructure is often invisible to its public just like the culinary history of the AGT remains relatively unknown, despite the fact that cooking and entertaining with food were central to the development of the institution.

This article is based on archival evidence[9] collected over the last two years in the Edward P. Taylor Library and Archives at the Art Gallery of Ontario and highlights two programs developed by the Women's Committee and JWC: The Men's Lunches,[10] monthly events planned and cooked by JWC members, served in the gallery and open only to men; and the Art of Cooking series, annual cooking demonstrations by renowned American and British chefs.[11] The Art of Cooking was a formative program for the AGT's positioning within the city's culinary culture, due to the collaborative character of such events, which engaged two unexpected commercial partners, Consumer's Gas Company and Canada Packers Limited, extending the museum's reach beyond its walls.[12] Culinary initiatives happen also inside the gallery and an in-depth look at the Men's Lunches reveals the gallery's culinary infrastructure, which is defined by the changing relations between *space* – kitchens, storage rooms and eating spaces; *material culture* – cooking utensils, serving tools, appliances, food, menus, cookbooks, and recipes; *culinary knowledge* – research methods, awareness of social and cultural trends, menu development; *tactics and strategies* – collaborations with non-museum institutions, communication and promotion of events, project management. I am particularly interested in how the relations with Toronto's major corporate players, which the women's committees developed in the 1960s through The Art of Cooking, generated new projects for the museum, such as a cookbook inspired by the Men's Lunches entitled *Can You Stand 25 for Dinner?* Such initiatives, produced in collaboration with key institutions in the city's culinary infrastructure, opened the AGT to a wider public while helping to shape Toronto's culinary culture.

The "Illusory Museum": Using Food and Women's History to Challenge Museum Studies Paradigms

The field of museum studies and the practice of museology have been dominated, at least in the past forty years, by a constant anxiety that museums are not doing enough to engage their audiences in a democratic and reflective fashion. James Cuno, president of the Getty Trust, writes, maybe a little too bluntly, that museums have also become the subject of considerable academic scrutiny and criticism. These critiques have rarely been subtle.... It is enough here to point out the directness of their claims that museums have the power and authority to control their visitors and that they do so in the service of the state and a Western-centric view of the world.[13]

Cuno's frustration with such criticism, which he calls a "fantasy,"[14] is tied to the paradigmatic modes of thinking about museums developed by some formative museum studies scholars. Such literature focuses on the museum's primary functions – to collect and display, leaving out of museum history less visible communities and practices, such as the women's work with education initiatives and with food. Likewise, spaces that are more marginal in the museum, such as the gift shop and the restaurant, are also left out from mainstream discussions in the field.

Tony Bennett positions the "birth of the museum" within the context of mechanisms developed by city officials in nineteenth-century Western Europe to control populations, especially the working classes.[15] In this perspective, the museum

> deploys its machinery of representation within an apparatus whose orientation is primarily governmental. As such, it is concerned not only to impress the visitor with a message of power but also to induct her or him into new forms of pro-gramming the self aimed at producing new types of conduct and self-shaping.[16]

Bennett points out very well one aspect of the museum's social and political function, which is to compliment the work of other cultural institutions, such as libraries, fairs, and colonial exhibitions, in shaping visitors by suggesting cer-tain ways of experiencing and looking at the world. In the nineteenth-century context discussed by Bennett, the dominant "practice of looking"[17] would have been informed by the colonial moment, which, as Timothy Mitchell argues, shows the "integral relationship between representation, as a modern tech-nique of meaning and order, and the construction of otherness."[18] It cannot be denied, despite Cuno's reluctance, that museums borrow discourses from the political culture that sustains them and contribute to systems of representa-tion, often tied to national interests. But that is only one side of the history of museums, what Henrietta Lidchi would call "the politics of exhibiting – the role of exhibitions/museums in the production of social knowledge."[19] Through practices of collecting and display, "the museum becomes an arbiter of meaning since its institutional position allows it to articulate and reinforce the scientific credibility of...discursive formations."[20] This speaks to the cultural relevance of museums, which allows them to have a voice in important social, cultural, and political matters. Historically, this voice has not always been inclusive or welcoming to cultural difference, as stated by Bennett and Mitchell, and has often been analyzed as authoritative rather than participatory.

A focus on "politics of exhibiting" based on commentaries on collecting and display limits the possibility of exploring museums in their fullness – for

CULINARY INFRASTRUCTURE

example, paying attention to other spaces in the museum, such as restaurants and gift shops, as significant in producing museum content – and shows a bias favoring theory over deep engagement with historical evidence, collected from the museums' archives. Josie Appleton writes that

> Foucauldian theories had an especially pernicious influence within the museum profession: the acts of collecting, categorizing and interpreting objects came to be seen not as the disinterested pursuit of knowledge, but as the striving for power on the part of Western culture.[21]

Cuno further elaborates that "while they might be witnesses to empire – not only in the year since their founding but, with their deep historical collections, ever since imperialism has existed in the world – they are not *instruments* of empire."[22] This theoretical slippage towards a criticism of "The Museum" rather than a meticulous interest in the history of museum practice in specific institutions is nicely summed up by Danielle Rice, who believes that

> the relationship between theory and practice is irrelevant to most theorists who see museums primarily as ideological symbols of the power relationships in today's culture…most museum practice continues to be deeply rooted in the politics of competing interests to respond to the structural issues discussed in theoretical literature.[23]

This disconnect between theory and practice produced, according to Rice, "an illusory museum."[24] A look at the culinary infrastructure of the AGT and its place in the broader conversations about cooking in Toronto, at a time when large national companies such as Consumer's Gas were intervening to the structure and consumer patterns of the city, troubles this "illusory museum," suggesting that a thorough reading of the museum's institutional memory reveals new and very important stories about the gallery.

Research which explores the gallery's culinary history problematizes another set of theoretical arguments critical of the museum's assumed authoritative tone and lack of engagement with its audiences. One main paradigm of the museum studies literature in the past forty years is the denouncing of "old museology" as being passive, undemocratic, and disengaged. Building on the work of Nick Merriman, Nicholas M. Pearson and Eilean Hooper-Greenhill,[25] Maxx Ross argues that after the 1970s, museums entered a climate of increasing reflexivity, labeled as "new museology," which he defines as "a transformation of museums from being exclusive and socially divisive institutions."[26] Peter Vergo warned in the very influential volume *New Museology* that "unless a radical re-examination of the role of museums in society…takes place, museums in this country, and possible elsewhere, may likewise find themselves dubbed 'living fossils'."[27] This concern can be tied back to Bennett's reading of museums as instruments of the state for civilizing citizens or with arguments that "the museum's primary function is ideologic."[28] Andrew McClellan offers a refreshing critique to these perspectives, arguing that "the monolithic museum posited by many critics, on both the left and the right, oversimplifies what museums do and overlooks their flexibility as institutions."[29] Danielle Rice advocates for a critical look at the museum history and practice informed by "the experiences of actual visitors and professionals" in order to challenge the "ossified and elitist institution posited by recent critical theory."[30] Thus, looking closely at the history of museums, including women's committees work with food, would allow scholars to observe the complexity of museological practice, the adaptability of the institutions and the continuity in discourse and practice rather than the (artificial) contrast to their "old" counterparts.

Using the museum's institutional memory collected and documented in its archives might just produce a more accurate and informed view of the museum's work, including areas of practice which are not typically associated with the scope of museums, such as food-related events. A close look at an institution's history also reveals the complexity of the museum's professional infrastructure, including the work of volunteer committees. In the AGT's history, the Women's Committee and the Junior Women's Committee were essential in building public visibility for the museum, creating a strong membership and building the collection. Much of their work was done by looking outside the museum, by establishing an Extensions Department, the first of its kind in North America, which would loan works of art and educational materials to organizations around Toronto and the Greater Toronto Area; by opening up the gallery for after hours parties, such as the Annual Ball;[31] or by partnering up with commercial companies and inviting famous chefs to cook gourmet recipes for Toronto audiences.

While the history of museums has been primarily documented in terms of their collections and their educational ethos, the story of museums can be told by focusing on practices such as culinary events. The AGT is a prime example of how food became central, in the 1960s, to the Women's Committees work to increase the visibility of the gallery. When the AGT invited visitors for culinary events in its galleries and planned cooking demonstrations off site, the institution captured the attention of those otherwise uninterested in art. For all the AGT visitors who left the museum with a copy of *Can you Stand 25 for Dinner?* – a cookbook published by the JWC in 1966, with support from the Consumer's Gas Company and Canada Packers Limited,[32] documenting menus and recipes cooked for the Men's Lunches, or who attended one of the seven very popular Art of Cooking classes, the lessons learned from their museum experience were in matters of marinating, roasting, and molding.

The AGT, its Publics, and Food Programming: "Toronto's Marvellous Art Awakening"[33]

On January 29, 1926, the citizens of Toronto were invited to enter the Sir Edmund Walker Memorial Court and adjoining galleries and see the Inaugural Exhibition celebrating the opening of the city's largest art museum. The plans for such an institution, which was thought of as "a force of inestimable value to the people of Toronto, if properly and adequately supported by its public-spirited citizens,"[34] go back to the early 1900s, when, soon after the gallery was incorporated by the City of Toronto, Professor and Mrs. Goldwin Smith expressed their desire to donate their home, the Grange, to the Museum.[35] Built around the nineteenth-century historic house, which is now the Member's Lounge of the AGO,[36] the museum grew significantly since the early twentieth century, going through multiple transformations, in terms of collections development, interpretive practice, architecture, and public programming. Food continues to be a very important component of the AGO experience: the museum has four eating spaces, numerous food-related events at FRANK, its main restaurant, thematic foods at the Night Market during First Thursdays after hours parties, and wine and dine opportunities during AGO Friday Nights, with tag line "art, dine, explore." Today, the AGO is one of Canada's largest and most active art galleries and a community hub, where visitors come to see art, listen to music, eat, drink, and learn.

From its first year of activity, the AGT showed awareness of its civic role in the city and of the imperative to think about its visitors, which is obvious from some "small" gestures, such as the inclusion of a section titled "The Gallery Visitors" in the first issue of the *AGT Bulletin* in 1926.[37] This section presents some preliminary thoughts on the museum's role in the city as "undoubtedly, Toronto contains no other meeting place of the nations quite like the Art Gallery, nor is the city's culture appraised by visitors by any more established barometer."[38] From the Education Department, readers learned that the museum was opened to different forms of entertainment, including music and even culinary events, as, during the Exhibition season, tea was served in the Grange House on Saturday afternoons for a charge of 25 cents. From the very beginning, the gallery developed a very strong education and public programming infrastructure, for both children and adults, to complement the exhibitions and permanent collection. In 1944, AGT President John M. Lyle spoke in his Report to the Annual Meeting about his vision for the gallery,

> I visualize our Gallery becoming a great one in a provincial and national sense, with a membership drawn from every walk of life and from the towns and cities of Ontario as well as the rural areas. In this way we would become a great 'people's Gallery.'[39]

The Women's Committee at the AGT was founded in 1945 "working to promote public interest in the Art Gallery of Ontario and to provide more services to the Gallery's public."[40] More specifically, some of the main activities of the committee are:

> To run and staff our two permanent projects, the Gallery Shop and the Art Rental Service; to raise money to provide works of art, equipment and special services for the Gallery; and to arrange events which would bring more people into the

CULINARY INFRASTRUCTURE

Gallery and into a consciousness of why our community and our province needs an expanding Art Gallery.[41]

The work of the Women's Committee was supported by that of the Junior Women's Committee, established in 1950, who also had

its own full regular programme: the annual costume ball; four lunches For Men Only; the sale of the cookbook *Can You Stand 25 for Dinner?*; a series of Saturday morning Gallery visits for children; and help at all the Gallery Wednesday Open Nights.[42]

Since 1945, among the regular and most popular events organized by the two committees were those that required the gallery's culinary infrastructure, usually hidden, to become visible. The 1960s were the most active years in the committees' culinary life, marked by the very successful "Art of Cooking"[43] series and Men's Lunches.[44] The Women's Committee was very active at the AGT until the early 1970s, when it was absorbed into the Volunteer Committee.

This social mission of the museum is further elaborated and refined, and also reflected in the exhibition and programming schedule of the museum to correspond with the expectations of "the individual citizen of Toronto... Everyone is welcome ... Our purpose is to bring out the true value of art in everyday living."[45] Making food a significant part of different museum experiences, primarily through the work of the two women's committees, was a strategy to create comfort and a sense of community. Little by little, cooking, shopping for food, communicating with food retailers, planning regular food events at the gallery, and collaborating with commercial companies became central to the AGT's efforts to increase its membership. Food came to structure many of the practices established by the committees, including the core organization of the Committee itself. In a letter inviting a new member to be part of the Committee and outlining the rules of membership, one "clause" states that "there is a Luncheon meeting on the fourth Monday or every month and the members are billed seventy-five cents for these lunches. It is expected that all members will attend these meetings."[46] Carmen Nielson Varty, and several other historians, would interpret such gestures as women making claims upon the public sphere, appropriating "certain accoutrements of publicness" through charity work, in a patriarchal context.[47]

The AGT's Women's Committees: Benevolence, Domesticity and Women in Museums

In a foundational text which reconsiders women's history in the nineteenth-century United States, Barbara L. Epstein writes that

middle-class women of this time constructed their own networks and a set of shared values...this culture was created rather than imposed upon women, though its limits were set by women's domesticity and dependence upon family relations and, more generally, by women's subordinate position within a male dominant society.[48]

Such networks of female agency are defined by Lori D. Ginzberg as "benevolent femininity," a "sisterhood which could undermine male dominance, in defining the middle class and in guarding property."[49] In the nineteenth century, the feminized work in religious organizations, charitable institutions, and temperance societies, was built on a set of values, which Barbara Welter groups under "the cult of the true womanhood," consisting of piety, purity, submissiveness, domesticity, which women assumingly acquired through socialization and exposure to Christian morality of Victorian times.[50] The domestic work of feeding families played an important role in enacting this notion of proper domesticity, and community cookbooks and meals were early means for raising funds for charitable works.[51] The AGT Women's Committees likewise used food work to move outside the domestic space and claim agency and power in the public venue of Toronto's leading art gallery.

Art galleries across North America functioned in the postwar years with the invisible work of volunteer committees, composed of women, typically white, middle and upper class with a good social standing.[52] Exploring the activities of the Woman's Board at the Art Institute of Chicago post-1950s, Gregory Nosan observes that "while creating fashionable public personae and benefiting from the wealth of the men who were their fathers, brothers, and husbands, these women also crafted their own brand of power and used it in individual and consistently creative ways."[53] Reflecting on the presence of women in museums at that time, Katherine Zankowicz explains that "historically white upper and middle class women were key players in founding education and docent departments because these were seen as 'appropriate' feminine duties within museums."[54] Work in museums, spaces with a very public character, could be seen as women's escape from the domestic spheres at a time when very few venues allowed such transgression. These transgressive moments, Zancowicz argues, were transformative for museums as "these women were necessarily the 'public' face of museums, providing a sphere of social and cultural influence that ended up transforming the very nature of who museums and galleries were for."[55] Despite the significant work women's committees did for museums in North America, the lack of professional credentials often positioned them as amateurs, "enthusiastic in their endeavours but not truly professional."[56] In fact, writes Zancowicz, women in museums were seen as ideal for such volunteer positions "because of perceived links to the feminine characteristics of motherhood"[57] rather than more professional skills, typically associated with male rationality.[58] The private/public divide, which underlines this separation of skills according to gender, has been both accepted and contested as appropriate for evaluating women's volunteer work.

In the introduction to *Gendered Domains*, Susan M. Reverby and Dorothy O. Helly question the "separate spheres" framework, which claims that "women's place everywhere was in part determined by the division of societies into public and private spheres."[59] Building on the work of Linda K. Kerber, who pointed out "that the language of separate spheres was vulnerable to sloppy use,"[60] the authors encouraged a reading of women's history which would account for the women's role in creating culture and negotiating the boundaries which they were expected to observe. In this context, the use of domestic skills, such as culinary knowledge and home management, can be observed as intentional and calculated strategies for gaining access to the male-dominated public domain. Therefore, by bringing the domestic into the public through the application of such skills, the two women's committees at the AGT exercised agency and creativity in shaping the culture of the art gallery, devising food-related programs to increase museum membership and diversify the audiences. Franca Iacovetta, Valerie J. Korinek, and Marlene Epp, in the preface to *Edible Histories, Cultural Politics*, state that "food, of course, is gendered in so many ways, and particularly in a feminine way, as grocery shopping, food preparation, and clean-up are all coded as women's responsibility."[61] By bringing food and its domestic connotations into the public space of the museum demonstrates the application of skills in areas of project management, communication, networking with important Toronto stakeholders, public relations and finances, with a constant re-evaluation of strategies and tactics for purposes of improvement. It is possible that this realization motivated Martin Baldwin[62] to state that "the pattern and general value of the Women's Committee has been a continued outspoken criticism of the gallery work, backed up by enthusiasm, support and initiative of the members of this committee."[63]

The Art of Cooking, 1961–1967: Creating Culinary Connections with Toronto

In the 1960s, the women's committees partnered with local businesses and guest celebrity chefs to develop The Art of Cooking, an annual series of cooking demonstrations, accompanied by a gourmet market and cookbooks with recipes from the events. Some leading chefs – James Beard, Dione Lucas, and Muriel Downes – visited Toronto at the invitation of the women's committees, and cooked for Toronto's citizens French-inspired gourmet dishes. *The Art of Cooking* recipe booklet, produced to document the 1964 event, featuring Muriel Downes,[64] thanked the main sponsors of the event, emphasizing that "the cooperation of these firms assists us in raising funds for our volunteer efforts in the Art Gallery. In thanking them we stress our gratitude and recognize our good fortune in their continued interest."[65] The history of these collaborations is very well documented in the Women's Committee archives through the rich and constant correspondence between members and Consumer's Gas and Canada Packers representatives. From 1961, when the first series of cooking demonstrations brought Dione Lucas to Toronto, the Women's Committee secured Canada

Packers Limited and the Consumer's Gas Company as the main sponsors for the events. In addition, the Committee also received donations from the T. Eaton Company's Hostess Shop which supplied "staple items and luxury goods used by Mrs. Dione Lucas in her series of demonstrations." [66]

In addition to the cooking demonstration, the Women's Committee organized the "Culinary Corner," a gourmet market opened only for the duration of the demonstrations, where "you will find many intriguing items which cannot be found in Toronto. This small exclusive selection of gourmet cooking utensils is available only in conjunction with these Demonstrations."[67] Among these items, participants could find larding needles, flan rings, molds for Lobster Washington, and truffle cutters.[68] Such networks of relations, which the women sustained through a sophisticated communication system, connected the museum with other organizations which were significant to the development of a consumer culture in Toronto in the 1950s and 1960s. A letter from July 20, 1954, written by Mrs. J. M. G Scott, the Chairman of the Junior Woman's Committee, addressed to Mr. R. C. Rice, Manager of the Schweppes Division of the Pepsi-Cola Company of Canada, invited him to consider sponsoring the Annual Ball, themed Le Bal Parisien. Scott wrote,

> The tremendous popularity of your products in Canada prompts us to suggest that you might be interested in sponsoring the Art Gallery Ball... The Robert Simpson Company, Limited, sponsored the Ball and in 1954 The T. Eaton Company, Limited, acted as sponsor. If you are agreeable to our suggestion... your products would be displayed at each of the four bars which are planned for the evening of the Ball.[69]

The cooking demonstrations and the Culinary Corner were held off site in the Blue Flame Room of the Consumer's Gas Company. The Blue Flame Room was an auditorium-type space which could be found in the 1960s at most of Consumer's Gas regional offices and was available to rent, for free, to community organizations. According to Jessie Lawrence, a home economist at the company in the 1970s, "It's our way of being of service in our community. The Room is booked by a lot of interesting people, and they stage some pretty interesting special events...book fairs, fashion shows, bridge parties."[70] The Blue Flame Room where the cooking demonstrations took place was located at 19 Toronto Street and was a very new addition to the city in 1960, built to replace a nineteenth-century office building located in the vicinity of the Consumers' Gas headquarters. The developing of the Blue Flame Room was closely tied to the clean-burning natural gas, which became available en masse in the 1960s, the decade which witnessed the construction pipelines across Canada.[71] The Room was one strategy for promoting new cooking technologies for domestic cooks and it "had a window display featuring mannequins wearing aprons and pearls standing over gas-ranges as if stirring a pot,"[72] thus connecting new technological developments with new cooking possibilities for the domestic "chef." By the 1960s, cooking with gas rapidly replaced stoves fueled with coal and

CULINARY INFRASTRUCTURE

wood[73] and competed with the electric stove alternative, allowing for cleaner and safer cooking environments. In fact, Consumer's Gas Company, which was essential in bringing natural gas to Toronto through the new networks of pipelines connecting Alberta to Ontario, redesigned its marketing strategies to promote natural gas as non-polluting, efficient and of high quality. Around this time, in the mid-1960s, the Women's Committee was partnering with the company to bring North American and British gourmet cooks to Toronto, linking the new development in cooking technology with the gourmet food trends at that time.[74] Building on the connections developed with major commercial players in the city, the women's committees brought the city's culinary culture into the galleries, organizing a very popular series of lunches, for men only.

Constructing a Culinary Infrastructure through Men's Lunches[75]

Staging culinary events in the AGT required equipment and serving utensils on site, threatening to disturb the normal setting of the gallery and raising concerns from the museum's administration, which was unwilling to invest in a kitchen for such events. Thus, the cooking for the many culinary events planned in the gallery was done by members of the committees in improvised spaces, as proper kitchen space was lacking. In addition, the ingredients for events such as Men's Lunches, which were purchased by the committees and stocked in the gallery, required storage space and records to keep track of what was consumed and what was needed.[76] The food served in the gallery for lunches and other smaller events was cooked by the committee members based on menus and recipes developed by them, drawing on culinary knowledge gained through domestic work. However, domestic knowledge was made public through a rigorous process of selecting recipes and ingredients which would appeal to the members they hoped to attract to the museum. The culinary infrastructure of the museum was sustained by continuous work to develop strong relations with external companies and business, including major retailers such as T. Eaton and food processing businesses such as Canada Packers. In addition, the communication networks extended to city organizations, such as the Liquor Control Board of Ontario or the Department of Buildings, and private businesses hired for gallery clean up, catering, and table and chair rentals for major events.

This culinary infrastructure, highly visible at times, needed to become invisible when not in use so that the food and the objects required for cooking and serving did not collide with art objects and the other museum happenings. The women's committee members were constantly developing strategies to maintain this culinary infrastructure with no financial support from the AGT's administration, which required constant search for new members. Successful events would create not only interest for the gallery but also repeating participants to these culinary initiatives, which would produce the revenue to sustain this infrastructure, especially the kitchen and the cooking supplies. Such challenges were often expressed by the members of the committees in their internal communication. For example,

> as our kitchen is small and we have no cafeteria the tables are put up in one of the offices for the day. Total money earned from the lunches is $4,038.40. This is spent on equipment for the lunches ($585.50), chairs and tables ($702.07) and last year the kitchen was modernized ($2404.12).[77]

An entire folder is full of research and financial plans for renovating the kitchen used by the two committees, located in the Grange.[78] The redesign of the kitchen was primarily motivated by the new needs required by the expanding of the culinary activities of the committees. For example, a close look at the plans for the new kitchen shows that the grouping of cooking and serving utensils, the relocation of the sinks, the purchase of a new stove, and reorganizing of kitchen cabinets was intended to accommodate the various lunch events planned at the museum.

Through the lunch events, several strategies were employed by the committee members to attract audiences which typically did not engage with AGT. One of these "difficult" audiences was composed of men, who could be invited into the AGT community as members but also as donors. With this in mind, in 1958, the two committees developed a series of food events targeting only men, Men's Lunches.[79] A close look at the Men's Lunches history demonstrates the employment of careful communication tactics with guests and their networks, the application of culinary knowledge in the selection of foods and drinks, and the use of the AGT's culinary infrastructure to create the ideal environment for men. An invitation sent out to husbands of the Women's Committee members in 1961 read

> On the first Friday of every month there is an informal men's luncheon in Grange House at the Art Gallery of Toronto. The bar opens at 12:15 and lunch will be served until 1:30 pm. The substantial luncheons are catered by the Gallery's Junior Women's Committee who, apart from serving the meal, remain unobtrusively behind the scene. After luncheon the current exhibition is toured.[80]

Communication with local media, such as *The Telegram, Globe and Mail, CKFH* revealed that "the purpose of these luncheons is primarily to attract more men to the Gallery and secondly to provide a new and unusual place for businessmen to lunch."[81] With these outcomes in mind, the Men's Lunches were organized to fully use the geography of the culinary spaces juxtaposed onto the museological space. The guests could start with a glass from the bar in the Grange, then they would be served a memorable lunch, cooked by the members of the JWC, some possibly their wives, thus bringing the domestic into the public, creating a sense of comfort and community, without the possibly intruding presence of women. The goal of such lunches was to create an attractive space for men at the AGT, reassuring them that an art gallery could be modified to suit their specific needs.

CULINARY INFRASTRUCTURE

The knowledge of food which would attract the interest of men was an important asset in securing regular attendance for such events. In a letter to Michael Hanlon, Entertainment Editor at *Globe and Mail* from September 17, 1964, Mrs. Gordon E. Cooper, Public Relations Chairman for the JWC, emphasized that "this luncheon will capture the atmosphere of Venice and the menu will consist of Venetian delicacies."[82] In another press release, JWC informed the guests that they would sample a French menu inspired by the visit of James Beard to Toronto, part of another event planned by the AGT later that month.[83] Several of these lunches were used to promote other events at the AGT, such as the 1967 Costume Ball, themed Silver Environment 2067 A.D. This Men's Lunch promised "home cooking with a gourmet touch ... accompanied by sparkling wine" with a menu featuring "chicken Italian style rice, Italian Garlic Bread, Green Salad, Fresh Fruit & Cheese Tray, Coffee, Wine."[84] The crafting of menus took on the tone of gourmet cooking, very popular in the 1960s, and visible in the structure of the menus, which includes dishes such as "tongue creole" or "pumpkin pie, whipped cream (homemade)" accompanied by "Spanish wine."[85] In all communication to guests and promotional materials, one very clear message was sent, that the gourmet meal, composed of a "hot buffet cooked and served by the Junior Women's Committee ... is designated to give busy men an opportunity to come to the gallery, sit amidst old master paintings, and enjoy a 'Men Only' lunch."[86]

The popularity and longevity of the Men's Lunches gave the JWC another idea: to write a community cookbook and sell it to secure funds for the Committee's other events. *Can you Stand 25 for Dinner?* further exemplifies the collaborative nature of the AGT's culinary events. The existing literature on community cookbooks agrees that community cookbooks represent relevant documents for community life and culinary culture through the work of women. Lynne Ireland, for example, believes that such cookbooks "make a statement about the food habits of the groups which produce them."[87] Anne Bower writes in *Recipes for Reading* that

> whether complicit with or pushing against the constraints and categories that bound them women acted to share the communities around them. Thus, what we might designate as fairly private activity or discourse (sewing, the writing of letters, contributing to a cookbook), may actually have been seen by women of the past as forms of public participation.[88]

Janet Theophano's discussion of "cookbook as communities," where cookbooks are "records of women's social interactions and exchanges,"[89] provides a good framework for understanding the significance of *Can you Stand 25 for Dinner?*

The story of the book is tied to the success of the Men's Lunches, inspiring the committee members to produce a book featuring ideas for eight menus, including recipes and grocery lists. In this book, the JWC "took a lighthearted simple approach. Each menu...includes a main course, one or two side dishes, a salad, bread, dessert, and a wine suggestion from an expert...Comments from well-known people, including Canadian artists, are quoted."[90] For example, the "Turkey Talk" menu, which features dishes such as "Sweet potato rum casserole" and "Canadian Pecan Pie" is accompanied by a quote from Canadian artist Dorothy Cameron, "an undressed turkey? How obscene!"[91] Just like *The Art of Cooking* recipe books, *Can you Stand 25 for Dinner?* was produced with the support of Canada Packers Limited, who provided the meat and dairy products used to test the recipes and Consumer's Gas Company, who allowed the cooks to use their kitchens. The book's back cover, playfully, sends thanks to the sponsors under the title "Thank you, Consumer's Gas, for your <u>gas</u>tronomical help"

> all recipes in this book were tested with fast, modern Natural Gas, thanks to the facilities provided by Consumer's Gas. We like the way it holds the exact temperature …responds instantly to temperature changes … controls heat without overcooking…broils smokelessly. In fact, we think it's a gas![92]

Cooking with natural gas, a relatively new practice in domestic kitchens in the 1960s, coincided with the excitement over cooking gourmet recipes at a time when chefs such as Dione Lucas, James Beard, and Julia Child were inviting North American audiences to cook fearlessly, even intimidating French dishes. In an interview with Canadian magazine *Maclean's* on March 23, 1963, James Beard spoke about "good food" which "is never more expensive than bad food dressed up. Good food can be achieved easily and quickly. Dozens of gourmet dishes can be made as quickly and even more cheaply than the inferior, prepackaged and jiffy –ready concoctions."[93] These words were collected during Beard's first major cooking demonstration held in Toronto, at the Consumers' Gas Company's Blue Flame Room, organized by the Women's Committee, only two years before this book was produced and sold to AGT visitors and Torontonians interested in gourmet cooking who were probably using natural gas stoves at that time.

Conclusions: Intersecting Infrastructures

From the mid-1940s until the 1970s, the members of the Women's Committee and the Junior Women's Committee modified the Art Gallery of Toronto to accommodate culinary spaces, adding a culinary infrastructure onto the other functions of the gallery, such as display and education. Outside the museum, the two committees developed a network of relations with institutions which were formative to the culinary infrastructure of the city, the Consumers' Gas Company and Canada Packers Limited. In collaboration with these companies, the two committees planned cooking demonstrations by some of the most famous chefs in the United States, such as James Beard and Dione Lucas, and invited new audiences in the gallery, to dine and hopefully to become members and donors. The work of these committees produced a new way of experiencing the museum, not as a site of "high" culture but as a space of entertainment, where paintings by Tintoretto and Monet would coexist with pop and hot dogs,

CULINARY INFRASTRUCTURE

which were served in the Sculpture Court during Christmas Parties, well into the 1970s.[94] Paying attention to the gallery's invisible culinary infrastructure, to collaborations between the AGT and the city, and to the resonance of events such as The Art of Cooking and the Men's Lunches inside and outside the museum opens up new avenues for thinking about museums, not as ideological tools but as complex, complicated, and connected institutions. Such culinary events offer an opportunity to further reflect on the public, yet voluntary, work of women in coopting male-dominated institutions, such as museums, where women used domestic skills and values to negotiate power and agency.

Acknowledgments

I gratefully acknowledge the support of Marilyn Nazar, Archivist at the Art Gallery of Ontario, for her guidance in my research; and Mary F. Williamson, for access to her collection of cookbooks. I am thankful to the article's reviewer for great feedback; to Donna Gabaccia, for reading recommendations; and to the Connaught Cross-Divisional/Cross-Cultural Seminar series (University of Toronto, 2016), for inviting me to present a working draft of the article.

Notes

1. Communication from Mrs. Graham Morrow, Corresponding Secretary to the Women's Committee, Box 1, Folder S4, Edward P. Taylor Library and Archives, Art Gallery of Ontario. All the archival documents consulted for this research are part of the Women's Committee and Junior Women's Committee Archives located in the AGO's Library and Archives.
2. The Junior Women's Committee was established in January 1950 to assist the Senior Committee with certain projects and to run its own initiatives, such as the Annual Balls and Men's Lunches. JWC was composed of younger women and had its own internal structure, based on that of its senior counterpart.
3. This article uses literature which theorizes large, well established museums with origins in the nineteenth century and focuses on the Art Gallery of Ontario as a case study representative of this literature.
4. Portnoy and Pilcher, "Roy Choi," 148.

5. For a detailed account of Toronto's urban and architectural modernization, see Armstrong, *Making Toronto Modern*.
6. Taylor, "Pioneering Efforts," 11.
7. Many scholars have problematized the private/public paradigm in the study of women's history arguing that "the language of separate spheres set up a binary framework that would need to be broken." See Helly and Reverby, *Gendered Domains*, 3. The "Introduction" to this volume offers a very comprehensive overview of the literature on this topic.
8. Ginzberg, *Women and the Work of Benevolence*, 2.
9. The Women's Committee and JWC activities (1945–1971) are documented in 41 boxes which include hundreds of folder with correspondence, meetings notes and minutes, reports of various sub-committees, memos, news releases, promotional materials for events, statements of revenue, miscellaneous materials relating to planning of events, and many others. My research focuses on Boxes 1–20, which cover the major culinary events organized by the committees. For this article, I consulted the folders which document the planning of Men's Lunches and The Art of Cooking events, as well as folders including minutes from the Volunteer Committees of Art Museums (VCAM) conference, where representatives of the two committees reported on their culinary activity. It is important to note that VCAM was launched in Toronto in 1952, with its first meeting held at the AGT and hosted by the Women's Committee.
10. Also referred to in some documents as "Men Only Lunches."
11. "The Art of Cooking" is an annual event initiated by the Women's Committee in 1961. Each event includes 7–8 cooking demonstrations over three days, conducted by very well-known chefs, some coming to Toronto for the first time. The event was canceled in 1967, after seven very successful years. Guest chefs: Dione Lucas (1961, 1962); James Beard (1963); Muriel Downes (1964); Alvin Kerr (1965); various Toronto chefs representing hotel restaurants (1966); and Michel Field (1967).
12. A close reading of the cooking demonstrations menus and recipes will be the subject of another study.
13. Cuno, *Museums Matter*, 3.
14. Ibid.
15. Bennett, *The Birth of the Museum*.
16. Ibid., 46.
17. Sturken and Cartwright, *Practice of Looking*, 9.
18. Mitchell, "Orientalism," 290.
19. Lidchi, "The Poetics and Politics," 184–5.
20. Ibid., 198.
21. Appleton, "Museums for 'The People'?" 116.
22. Cuno, *Museum Matter*, 89.
23. Rice, "Museums," 77.
24. Ibid.
25. Merriman, *Beyond the Glass Case*; Pearson, *The State and the Visual Arts*; Hooper-Greenhill, *Museums and the Shaping of Knowledge*.
26. Ross, "Interpreting the New Museology," 84.
27. Vergo, *New Museology*, 3, 4.
28. Duncan and Wallach, "The Universal Survey Museum," 448–69.
29. McClellan, *Art and Its Publics*, xviii.
30. Rice, "Museums," 79.

CULINARY INFRASTRUCTURE

31. The AGT was organizing after hours parties since the mid-1940s, showing continuity with contemporary after hours events, which are so popular in museums.
32. Canada Packers Limited is currently part of Maple Leaf Food, one of Canada's largest food processing companies.
33. "Inaugural Exhibition," 6.
34. "Notes from the Educational Committee," 14.
35. For more information on the history of the AGT, refer to: http://www.ago.net/fact-sheets.
36. For a brief history of the Grange, refer to: http://www.ago.net/grange.
37. In later issues of the *Bulletin*, information about visitors and members is integrated either in the "Report of the President" or reports from various departments and groups, such as the Educational Department, and later on, Extension Program and Circulating Exhibitions, and the Women's Committee.
38. "The Gallery Visitors," 14.
39. "Report of the President," *The Art Gallery of Toronto Annual Report for the Year 1944*. Reference Cabinet, AGO Library and Archive.
40. Stuart, "The Women's Committee, July 1st, 1967, to June 30th, 1968." *Art Gallery of Ontario Annual Report 1967–1968*, 21.
41. Ibid.
42. Ibid.
43. Attendance to the Art of Cooking demonstrations increased from 1033 tickets sold for the 1961 event (Dione Lucas) to 1709 in 1963 (James Beard). Numbers remained consistent until 1967, when the event was canceled.
44. In a letter dated January 18, 1972, J. R. Jennings, chairman of the JWC, wrote that in the 10 years since the Men's Lunches started, the event "accumulated a loyal group of men numbering approximatively 700 who fluctuate in attendance," Box 19, Folder S3C.
45. "The Art Gallery of Toronto," *Program*, 1947–1948. Reference Cabinet, AGO Library and Archive.
46. "Letter to Mrs. C. P. Fell to Mrs. Graham Morrow, Corresponding Secretary," June 2, 1948, Box 1, Folder S4.
47. Varty, "A Career in Christian Charity," 254.
48. Epstein, *The Politics of Domesticity*, 7.
49. Ginzberg, *Women and the Work of Benevolence*, 9.
50. Welter, "The Cult of True Womanhood."
51. Gabaccia and Aldrich, "Recipes in Context"; Bower, *Recipes for Reading*; Theophano, *Eat My Words*.
52. Most of the existing literature of women and museums focuses on the United States. I am using this literature to contextualize the work of women's committees at the AGO, which is a Canadian museum, due to the many similarities in institutional practices, development of women's committee and constituency.
53. Nosan, "Women in the Galleries," 50.
54. Zancowicz, "In Her Hands," 10. I am indebted to Zancowicz's work for many of the sources on women and museums and women history I use in this article.
55. Ibid., 12.
56. Taylor, "Pioneering Efforts of Early Museum Women," 12.
57. Zancowicz, "In Her Hands," 41.
58. Varty, "A Career in Christian Charity."
59. Reverby and Helly, "Introduction," 2.
60. Kerber, "Separate Spheres," 17.

CULINARY INFRASTRUCTURE

61. Iacovetta et al., "Introduction," 15.
62. Martin Baldwin was AGT director from 1948 to 1960.
63. "Report on the Conference of Women's Committees of America, held at the AGT in November 10th, 11th, 12th, 1952," Box 2, Folder S10B. It is common to find similar praise to the work of the committees from the AGT's leadership, primarily in the content of Annual Reports, called Bulletins at that time.
64. Muriel Downes was, at the time, the Co-Director of the Cordon Bleu School of Cookery, London, England.
65. Downes, "Acknowledgement." Private collection of Mary F. Williamson.
66. "Letter to Mr. Franck McEachren, Public Relations," Box 7, Folder S8.
67. "Culinary Corner" Promotional Brochure, Box 8, Folder S8.
68. Ibid.
69. Box 3, Folder S5.
70. "You Are Invited to Visit."
71. Bott, "Evolution of Canada's Oil"; see also Parr, "Shopping for a Good Stove."
72. Bell, "Belching Gas."
73. "The Consumers' Gas Company"; see also Bott, "Evolution."
74. For a discussion of the democratization of gourmet cooking in North America, see Johnston and Baumann, "Democracy versus Distinction"; Johnston and Baumann, *Foodies; Strauss, Setting the Table for Julia Child.*
75. In the 1960s, several men's clubs were operating in Toronto and it is very likely that husbands of many members of the women's committees were members of these exclusive clubs. The oldest such club in Toronto is the Toronto Club, which opened in 1837; others, such as the National Club and the Albany Club, date back to 1874 and 1882, respectively. Membership to these clubs was opened to women only in the early 1990s.
76. The W's C and JWC archives contain several inventories for the snack lunches, with very detailed recordings of types of ingredients, recipes, and prices.
77. "Thursday Morning Session," Box 3. Folder S10B.
78. Box 3, Folder S4B.
79. Men's Lunches are also referred as "men only" lunches in some of the archives.
80. "Invitation," Box 9, Folder S3C.; while there are no exact records of attendees to such events, it is fair to assume that the women used their personal networks to invite prominent Toronto men, some which were their husbands, brothers, and fathers.
81. Letter to Mr. Arthur Cole, City Editor, *The Telegram*, October 17, 1960, Box 9, Folder S3C.
82. Box 10, Folder S3C.
83. Letter to Ron Hewat, CKFH from Mrs. Mandel Sprachman, Publicity Chairman, January 18, 1963, Box 9, Folder S3C.
84. Promotional text for the event on Thursday, October 20, 1966 sent by Miss Janice M. Smiter, Public Relations & Information Officer for the JWC, Box 12, Folder S3C.
85. Promotional text for the Thursday, November 27, 1967 Men's Lunch, sent by Miss Janice M. Smiter, Public Relations & Information Officer for the JWC, Box 12, Folder S3C.
86. Letter to Mr. Scott Young, *Globe and Mail*, October 14, 1965, Box 10, Folder S3C.
87. Ireland, "The Compiled Cookbook," 108.
88. Bower, "Introduction," 6.
89. Theophano, *Eat My Words*, 13.
90. "For Immediate Release," December 10, 1966, Box 12, Folder S3C.

CULINARY INFRASTRUCTURE

91. Junior Women's Committee, *Can You Stand 25 for Dinner?*
92. Ibid.
93. "Jim Beard's $30 Cooking Course," 18.
94. Memo to Junior Women's Committee regarding Children's Christmas Party, Saturday, Dec. 9, 1972, Box 20, Folder S5.

Bibliography

Archival documents

Women's Committee and Junior Women's Committee Archives, Box 1-20, various folders, Edward P. Taylor Library and Archives, Art Gallery of Ontario.

Books and articles

Appleton, Josie. "Museums for 'the People'?" In *Museums and Their Communities*, edited by Sheila Watson, 114–126. London: Routledge, 2007.

Armstrong, Christopher. *Making Toronto Modern: Architecture and Design, 1895–1975*. Montreal: McGill-Queen's University Press, 2014.

Bell, Bruce. "Belching Gas Sustained a Glorious Architecture." *The Bulletin: Journal of Downtown Toronto*. http://thebulletin.ca/belching-gas-sustained-a-glorious-architecture/.

Bennett, Tony. *The Birth of the Museum: History, Theory, Politics*. London: Routledge, 1995.

Bott, Robert D. *Evolution of Canada's Oil and Gas Industry*. Calgary: The Canadian Center for Energy Information, 2004. http://www.energybc.ca/cache/oil/www.centreforenergy.com/shopping/uploads/122.pdf.

Bower, Anne L. "Introduction." In *Recipes for Reading: Community Cookbooks, Stories, Histories*, edited by Anne L. Bower, 1–14. Amherst: University of Massachusetts Press, 1997.

Collins, Kathleen. *Watching What We Eat: The Evolution of Television Cooking Shows*. New York: Continuum, 2009.

The Consumers' Gas Company Ltd. "History." In *International Directory of Company Histories*, edited by Thomas Derdak, vol. 6. Chicago, IL: St. James Press, 1992. http://www.fundinguniverse.com/company-histories/the-consumers-gas-company-ltd-history/.

Cook, Nathalie, ed. *What's to Eat: Entrees in Canadian Food History*. Montreal: McGill-Queen's University Press, 2009.

Cuno, James. *Museums Matter: In Praise of the Encyclopedic Museum*. Chicago, IL: University of Chicago Press, 2011.

Downes, Muriel. "Acknowledgement." *The Art of Cooking: Muriel Downes*. Toronto: Consumer's Gas Company, 1964.

Duncan, Carol, and Alan Wallach. "The Universal Survey Museum." *Art History* 3, no. 4 (1980): 448–469.

Duncan, Dorothy. *Canadians at Table: A Culinary History of Canada*. Toronto: Dundurn Press, 2006.

Epstein, Barbara L. *The Politics of Domesticity: Women, Evangelism and Temperance in Nineteenth Century America*. Middletown, CT: Wesleyan University Press, 1986.

Gabaccia, Donna, and Jane Aldrich. "Recipes in Context: Solving a Small Mystery in Charleston's Culinary History." *Food, Culture and Society* 15, no. 2 (2012): 197–221.

The Gallery Visitors. *The Art Gallery of Toronto Bulletin* 1, no. 1 (1926): 14.

Ginzberg, L. D. *Women and the Work of Benevolence: Morality, Politics and Class in the Nineteenth Century United States*. New Haven, CT: Yale University Press, 1990.

Helly, Dorothy O., and Susan M. Reverby. "Introduction." In *Gendered Domains: Re-thinking Public and Private in Women's History*, edited by Dorothy O. Helly and Susan M. Reverby, 1–24. Cornell University Press, 1992. Ithaca: Cornell University Press.

Hooper-Greenhill, Eilean. *Museums and the Shaping of Knowledge*. London: Routledge, 1992.

Hooper-Greenhill, Eilean. "Education, Communication, Interpretation: Towards a Critical Pedagogy in Museums." In *The Educational Role of the Museum*, edited by Eileen Hooper Greenhill, 3–27. London: Routledge, 2003.

Iacovetta, Franca, Valerie J. Korinek, and Marlene Epp, eds. *Edible Histories, Cultural Politics: Towards a Canadian Food History*. Toronto: University of Toronto Press, 2012.

Inaugural Exhibition. *The Art Gallery of Toronto Bulletin*, 1, no. 1 (1926): 6.

Ireland, Lynne. "The Compiled Cookbook as Foodways Autobiography." *Western Folklore* 40, no. 1 (1981): 107–114.

Jim Beard's $30 Cooking Course. *Maclean's*, March 23, 1963, 18.

Johnston, Josée, and Shyon Baumann. "Democracy versus Distinction: Omnivorousness in Gourmet Food Writing." *American Journal of Sociology* 113, no. 1 (2007): 165–204.

Johnston, Josée, and Shyon Baumann. *Foodies: Democracy and Distinction in the Gourmet Foodscape*. New York: Routledge, 2015.

Junior Women's Committee. *Can You Stand 25 for Dinner?* Toronto, 1966.

Taylor, Kendall. "Pioneering Efforts of Early Museum Women." In *Gender Perspectives: Essays on Women in Museums*, edited by Jane Glaser and Artemis Zenetou, 11–27. Washington, DC: Smithsonian Institution Press, 1994.

Lidchi, Henrietta. "The Poetics and Politics of Exhibiting Other Cultures." In *Representation: Cultural Representations and Signifying Practices*, edited by Stuart Hall, 151–208. London: Sage, 2010.

Kerber, Linda K. "Separate Spheres, Female Worlds, Woman's Place: The Rhetoric of Women's History." *Journal of American History* 75, no. 1 (1988): 9–39.

McClellan, Andrew. "Introduction." In *Art and Its Publics: Museum Studies at the Millennium*, edited by Andrew McClelland, xiii–xviii. Malden: Blackwell, 2003.

Merriman, Nick. *Beyond the Glass Case*. Leicester: Leicester University Press, 1991.

Mitchell, Timothy. "Orientalism and the Exhibitionary Order." In *Colonialism and Culture*, edited by Nicholas B. Dirks, 289–318. Ann Arbor: The University of Michigan Press, 1992.

Nosan, Gregory. "Women in the Galleries: Prestige, Education and Volunteerism at Mid-Century." *Art Institute of Chicago Museum Studies* 29, no. 1 (2003): 46–71, 92–95.

Notes from the Educational Committee. *The Art Gallery of Toronto Bulletin* 1, no. 1, (1926): 14.

Parr, Joy. "Shopping for a Good Stove: A Parable about Gender, Design, and the Market." In *A Diversity of Women: Ontario, 1945–1980*, edited by Joy Parr, 75–97. Toronto: University of Toronto Press, 1995.

Pearson, Nicholas M. *The State and the Visual Arts: A Discussion of the State Intervention in the Visual Arts in Britain 1760–1981*. Milton Keynes: Open University Press, 1982.

Portnoy, Sarah, and Jeffrey M. Pilcher. "Roy Choi, Ricardo Zárate, and Pacific Fusion Cuisine in Los Angeles." In *Global Latin America*, edited by Matthew Gutmann and Jeffrey Lesser, 146–62. Berkeley: University of California Press, 2016.

Rice, Danielle. "Museums: Theory, Practice, Illusion." In *Art and Its Publics: Museum Studies at the Millennium*, edited by Andrew McClelland, 77–95. Malden, MA: Blackwell, 2003.

Ross, Max. "Interpreting the New Museology." *Museum & Society* 2, no. 2 (2004): 84–103.

CULINARY INFRASTRUCTURE

Strauss, David. *Setting the Table for Julia Child: Gourmet Dining in America, 1934–1961*. Baltimore, MD: The Johns Hopkins University Press, 2011.

Stuart, Mary Alice. *"The Women's Committee, July 1st, to June 30th, 1968"*. Art Gallery of Ontario Annual Report. Toronto: Art Gallery of Toronto, 1967.

Sturken, Marita, and Lisa Cartwright. *Practice of Looking: An Introduction to Visual Culture*. Oxford: Oxford University Press, 2009.

Taylor, Kendall. "Pioneering Efforts of Early Museum Women." In *Gender Perspectives: Essays on Women in Museum*, edited by Jane R. Glaser and Artemis A. Zenetou, 11–27. Washington, DC: Smithsonian Institution Press, 1994.

Theophano, Janet. *Eat My Words: Reading Women's Lives through the Cookbooks They Wrote*. New York: Macmillan, 2003.

Varty, Carmen N. "'A Career in Christian Charity': Women's Benevolence and the Public Sphere in a Mid-nineteenth-century Canadian City." *Women's History Review* 14, no. 2 (2005): 243–264.

Vergo, Peter, ed. *New Museology*. New York: Reaktion Books, 1989.

Wasson, Haidee. "Every Home an Art Museum: Mediating and Merchandizing the Metropolitan." In *Residual Media*, edited by Charles Acland, 159–184. Minneapolis: University of Minnesota Press, 2007.

Welter, Barbara. "The Cult of True Womanhood." *American Quarterly* 18, no. 2 (1966): 151–174.

You Are Invited to Visit Consumer's Gas. 1976. *Pickering Bay's News*, Pickering, August 25, 1976. http://www.pada.ca/books/page/?id=674&view=text&page=3.

Zancowicz, Katherine. "In Her Hands: Women's Educational Work at the Royal Ontario Museum, the Canadian National Exhibition, and the Art Gallery of Toronto, 1900s–1950s." PhD diss., University of Toronto, 2014.

Developing Constipation: Dietary Fiber, Western Disease, and Industrial Carbohydrates

Sebastián Gil-Riaño and Sarah E. Tracy

ABSTRACT

This paper focuses on the rise of what we call the *dietary fiber paradigm,* as championed by British medical researcher Denis Burkitt, a.k.a. "Dr Fiber," and his collaborators working in Uganda and South Africa. We situate this attention to fiber intake in nutritional advice within a longer history of white Euro-American anxieties about the corrosive physiological effects of modernization. We examine how former colonial medical experts transformed dietary fiber from an object of negligible nutritional value – mere "roughage" – to one whose presence could mean the difference between health and disease. In the 1960–70s, Burkitt and his collaborators developed the concept of Western "diseases" to describe a series of chronic bodily ailments they linked to modern culinary infrastructure, or the consumption of what they called "refined carbohydrates" – particularly, commercially produced white bread. Chief among these were afflictions of the intestinal tract: diverticulosis coli, colon and bowel cancer, ulcerative colitis, and appendicitis. Startled by the observation that colonic disorders were practically absent in the "Third World" yet ubiquitous in modern affluent societies, these researchers hypothesized that the transit-time in which food was consumed, digested, and evacuated could be used to track these disparities. Is digestive dysfunction a necessary by-product of industrialized food systems, they asked? Is constipation an unavoidable feature of modernity? Through hospital questionnaires and observational prison studies, Burkitt and others surveyed the bowel movements, stool size, and diets of a variety of racial groups in several African countries and in Britain, and identified dietary fiber as a prophylactic for the hazards of modern eating. Burkitt's influential studies, we suggest, tell a resonant story of culinary modernization gone wrong – of a corrosive disconnect between the architecture of the human gastrointestinal tract and that of the quickly absorbed carbohydrates refined for purity and for whiteness.

CULINARY INFRASTRUCTURE

diet and disturbance and derangement of function – obstructions, debility and irritations, are among the most important elements of those diseases. William Sylvester Graham, 1837[1]

The whiter your bread, the sooner you're dead. Sir William Arbuthnot Lane, 1924[2]

The hon. member says that we made fine promises to the people in connection with white bread etc. We promised them a white civilisation [and] I just want to say to the hon. member that he can expect a completely white policy from this side. Minister of Agriculture and Forestry, South Africa, 1951[3]

Introduction

In his reflections on half a century's work on nutritional disorders in Africa, the white South African biochemist Alexander P. Walker relayed one of his most remarkable memories. During fieldwork in South Africa in the 1950s, he discovered that a huge majority of "rural African schoolchildren" were able to "pass a stool on request!"[4] This unexpected finding led Walker to wonder whether the children of "Western" ancestors were also able to defecate with such aplomb. Though separated by hundreds of years of history, Walker speculated that children in the pre-modern "West" and rural African children were similarly "accustomed to a high fiber, low fat diet" – a diet he believed was now tragically lost to the modern, industrialized West.

In the late 1960s, Walker's insights on the relationship between low-fiber diets and what came to be known as "Western diseases" were tested and popularized by Denis K. Burkitt (1911–93), a world-renowned cancer epidemiologist. Burkitt's scientific trajectory is well known among cancer researchers, as is his influence on the development of medical research in Uganda.[5] In this paper, however, we examine how the expansive and comparative outlook Burkitt developed through his medical service in the British colonial system across Africa was later mobilized to critique the culinary infrastructures of what he called the West. Picking up on the hypothesis of Walker and other colonial physicians about the impact of dietary fiber on health, Burkitt utilized his vast network of colonial contacts in Africa and other parts of the southern hemisphere to map global distributions of colonic disorder and their relationship to the consumption of dietary fiber. The "Western diseases" under scrutiny were primarily afflictions of the intestinal tract like diverticulosis coli, bowel and colon cancer, ulcerative colitis, appendicitis, and – leading them all – constipation, which Burkitt proclaimed "the commonest western disease."[6] As Burkitt and others accumulated comparative data, they became increasingly startled by the observation that the colonic disorders of the modern and affluent West were practically absent in the impoverished "Third World."[7] To explain this disparity, Burkitt and Walker began to investigate the hypothesis that the transit-time in which food was consumed, digested, and evacuated was a key variable accounting for the presence of colonic disease. In seeking to make sense of the damaged colons of Western populations, these scientists sought to understand the causal relationship between diet, economic development, and bowel movements. Are diseased gastrointestinal (GI) tracts a necessary by-product of industrialized food systems, they asked? Is constipation an unavoidable feature of modernity?[8]

This paper situates the rise of what we call the *dietary fiber paradigm,* as championed by Burkitt, a.k.a. "Dr Fiber," and his collaborators in Uganda and South Africa, within a longer history of white Euro-American anxieties about the potentially corrosive physiological effects of modernization. We examine how former colonial medical experts transformed dietary fiber from an object of negligible nutritional value – mere "roughage" – to one whose presence in human diets could mean the difference between health and disease. The physiological virtues of dietary fiber became visible to these experts as they began to track the embodied differences between human populations living in differing conditions of economic and technological scarcity and affluence. As they excavated these professed environmental features of diet and defecation, they linked the widespread manufacture and consumption of what they called "refined carbohydrates" in industrial societies to persistent disruptions of the human digestive infrastructure.

Since the 1970s, "Dr Fiber's" research has been credited with "chang[ing] the breakfast tables of the western world."[9] His work, we suggest, also tells a resonant story of culinary modernization gone wrong, and one that demonstrates how the concept of culinary infrastructure can enrich our histories of contemporary global foodways. The relevance of Burkitt's work to wider discussions of culinary infrastructure is that he *ontologized* dietary fiber as a marker of what we the authors see as infrastructural *failure.*[10] By comparing the diets, defecation patterns, and diseases of populations differentiated by wealth and privilege, Burkitt established a quantitative relationship between the proportion of dietary fiber and the prevalence of specific internal diseases. Burkitt's work thus posited an ontology of health regulated by the circulation of fiber in both bodies and economies.

Curiously, this framework was one that sought to understand the epidemiological import of "race" as a social category and in so doing revealed unexpected correlations between racial categories and intestinal well-being. It did so by tracking disparities in fiber consumption and defecation as a feature of environment and lifestyle rather than as the outcome of race-specific physiologies, as medical experts might have done in the colonial era. In so doing, fiber researchers echoed the ways that human biologists and social scientists after the Second World War refashioned "race" and rendered it a social rather than biological object.[11] However, although their work was consistent with postwar critiques of biological determinism, fiber researchers conceptualized their populations of study as either "primitive" or "modern" and thus retained

CULINARY INFRASTRUCTURE

categories that, during the colonial era, marked relative degrees of societal development (described then as "race" progress). This postwar framing of nutritional science revealed unexpected findings. Instead of a racial hierarchy privileging white modernity, Burkitt's study of fiber and defecation revealed that greater economic progress – irrespective of racial phenotype – entailed greater digestive fallout.[12] Through careful analysis of differing transit-times, Burkitt and his collaborators thus demonstrated empirically that modernization, in this dimension of human digestion and elimination, was going wrong. Chronic ill health became directly associated with the refined-grain dietary staples iconic of modernization, while intestinal well-being was linked with the unrefined grains of traditional agrarian populations. In other words, though they scrupulously treated race as a an innocuous social category, their work was nevertheless invested in meticulous comparisons of intestinal physiologies collected, labeled, and analyzed in terms of race. Drawing on epidemiological contrasts between racially-specific populations in the UK, the US, Uganda, and South Africa, the fiber paradigm hypothesized a corrosive disconnect between the ecological infrastructure of the human GI tract and the culinary infrastructures that produced one of the dietary pillars of modern, affluent societies: soft, uniform, shelf-stable white bread.

Building a Farinaceous World: On Culinary Infrastructure

The word *infrastructure* comes to us from the French, its usage originating in railroad engineering in the late-nineteenth century and spreading to many different domains before its adoption in other languages after 1950.[13] In his intellectual history of infrastructure, historian of science Bill Rankin considers the term as specific to postwar intellectual debates around economic development, and now best understood as an intrinsically international – or, rather, post-national – category that signals "the increasing misalignment between bounded geographical units, cultural groups and economic markets."[14] Invoking a framework that similarly looks beyond the nation-state, some scholars of food have recently described infrastructures as those often-imperceptible configurations that "create conditions for economic activity, produce collective security, and introduce reliability and predictability into the world."[15] We likewise understand infrastructure to exceed the realms of consumer choice and national and corporate interests, and simultaneously attend to the ideas and material forces within which historical actors have operated. Infrastructure conceived in this way bleeds into concepts of hegemony, embodying, to use the incisive words of the editors of a recent *Limn* issue on Food Infrastructures, the "tacit conventions of need and entitlement" that, in a self-fulfilling way, "inscrib[e] a certain end-user or consumer." For example, the consumer desirous of edible artifacts of affluence – refined, packaged, and necessary luxuries, for example white bread or polished white rice – was accompanied by the material infrastructure of industrial wheat agriculture, milling, and baking.[16] And, crucially, neither was eroded by the widespread medical acceptance of wartime research demonstrating the nutritional deficiencies of refined grains. [17] Burkitt's refined carbohydrates were not desirable so much because they were healthy; they were desirable because, historically, they had been scarce – which is to say that only the elite few could access them.

We understand culinary infrastructures as dynamic, "vital systems" that are "vulnerable and in need of protection." Infrastructures become most visible to most of us who live within them when the arrangement's organization is *changed, goes out of order, or fails* – because such infrastructures are "essential to the smooth operation of society."[18] The physiology of the human gut – itself a built environment cum infrastructure necessary to human living processes – became newly legible to scientists and then to the lay public only with the accretion of statistical data linking a paucity of dietary fiber to digestion gone wrong. Like other scholarship reflecting on the stakes of contemporary food infrastructures, we maintain that questions of ethics and politics are key to a historical study of global culinary infrastructures. In other words, focusing on infrastructure gives us traction for our critical reflections on the lived stakes (e.g. constipation) of "Big Food" – that "simultaneously varied and monolithic, indispensable and frightening" arrangement of scaling up food production and distribution with the end of "managing risk, avoiding disruption, nourishing families, and transmitting pleasure."[19]

Finally, in engaging the idea of failure within a networked space or infrastructure, this paper builds on the established concepts of food systems and actor-network-theory by focusing on an object that is of both alimentary and medical significance: for example, white bread. Science and technology studies scholars have demonstrated how medical facts are contingent upon medical networks that bring a variety of actors both human and non-human into relation. For instance, in their discussion of the role of medical networks in producing facts about the incidence of anemia (iron deficiency) in the Netherlands and in African countries such as Zimbabwe and Mozambique, Annemarie Mol and John Law demonstrate how knowledge of anemia relies on a hemoglobin measuring network comprised of measuring devices, skilled technicians to operate them, physicians, and ailing patients.[20] In this paper, we examine how nutritional research linking food production and intestinal failure was made possible through epidemiological networks forged during the last gasps of British colonial rule in Africa. However, rather than theorizing the workings of those medical networks themselves, we focus on how such networks were instrumental to the efforts of medical experts to accumulate evidence of the geographic distribution of a macro (modern production) and micro (digestive) infrastructural incompatibility. Through their epidemiological research on fiber and feces, Walker and Burkitt established a comparative network of intestinal variation that asked: Is chronic constipation and the erosion of human digestion a universal feature of modernization?

CULINARY INFRASTRUCTURE

There are, of course, historical precedents to the emergence of dietary fiber as a nutritional prescriptive in the 1960–70s. We cannot do justice to them in this brief account, but will instead provide some highlights from Anglo-American nutritional discourse that illustrate the effects of the industrialization of bread production on the philosophical and dietetic traditions Burkitt and Walker would have been versed in. Generally speaking, prior to the 1870s, wheat grains were ground by millstones powered by water or wind – if not in handmills.[21] Grain was produced and consumed locally, because the coarser, whole-grain flour (containing germ, bran, and endosperm) that stone mills produced contained oils (in the germ) that made it liable to spoilage. This flour's relatively short shelf-life was incompatible with what has been normalized today: national and international food commodity markets. To illustrate, the flour trade in England in the mid-to-late-nineteenth century is estimated to have operated within a radius of thirty miles from the local mill – and this only in the case of the largest mills.[22] The "roller-mill revolution" came to the US by way of the milling community of Minneapolis, through a case of industrial espionage in which American millers poached technology then being pioneered in Hungary.[23] A firm called Washburn Crosby and Company were the first to popularize this new sifting, grinding, and purifying process intended to optimize flour's baking qualities, aesthetic appearance (whiter, cleaner-looking), and production output. Theirs was the first advertised "patent" flour (signifying it was the result of a patented technical process), setting a new consumer standard of white, industrially milled flour.[24] The influx of hard spring wheat from the prairies provided incentive for leading mills throughout the United States to likewise adopt roller mill systems.[25] From the 1830–70s, the unprecedented, state-sponsored settlement of not only the North American plains, but also those of Argentina and Australia,[26] prompted a massive increase in the cultivation of hard spring wheat varieties, which were well suited to the new roller milling techniques. The Minneapolis region, poised between new railroad networks and the water-power of the Mississippi River (at the St. Anthony waterfalls, previously used by the logging industry, and the emerging urban markets of the eastern US), birthed a model for an export-based, modern milling industry in the 1870–80s.[27]

In 1890, an estimated 80 percent of all bread consumed in the US was baked at home (typically by women). However, between 1850 and 1900, the number of commercial bakeries grew by 700 percent and became predominantly male; by 1900 the largest could turn out 15,000 loaves/day – a figure dwarfed by that of 1920, by which point the largest bakeries were producing 100,000 loaves/day.[28] Formal academies of baking proliferated following the founding of the first in 1780s France by Antoine August Parmentier, an army apothecary, who set out to train those "to whom the health of the nation is entrusted."[29] The National Association of Master Bakers (UK, since 2013 the Craft Bakers Association), founded in the 1880s, convened member meetings on the latest scientific thinking in wheat chemistry, rational cost accounting, the effect of salt on fermentation, accurate weighting and measuring, efficient movement, the physiology of taste, bacteriology, etc. Rationalization entailed new controls over weights, measurements, and quality of ingredients, and electricity meant unprecedented control of temperature. Enter production-line baking: dough mixed in refrigerated conditions to prevent overheating, transferred to temperature-controlled proofing and fermentation chambers, and then baked in some of the most accurate ovens in human history.[30] A final key technological innovation was millers' development of the Alsop Process of chemical bleaching in 1904, which greatly accelerated the natural process – always fraught with the risk of spoilage – of flour whitening as it aged.[31] The result was that by the mid-twentieth century in the UK, the US, and South Africa, at least, a lot more wheaten bread flour was traveling farther and sitting longer before being turned (however laboriously) into fecal matter.[32]

This is all to say that modern culinary infrastructures encompassing the imperial seizure of land, the rationalization of a science of baking, and the scaling up of wheat milling and industrial bakeries was connected to the knowledge infrastructure that assembled around dietary fiber in the postwar period. One material and the other discursive, they are both (post)colonial formations – made possible by the violent acquisition of vast resources worldwide through European settler colonialism. In the 1920–30s, the newly cohered discipline of nutrition science enjoyed some of its most significant discoveries: for example, the isolation and identification of what we now call vitamins, or what physiologists and chemists had chased for years under the name of "accessory factors." Many of these were driven by the evidence of sickness in the wake of heavy dependence on industrially produced foods – particularly among the urban working classes: polished white rice, condensed and pasteurized milk, even white bread.[33] In a sense, the modernization of eating in the early twentieth century provided a giant Petri dish that made possible the success (i.e. international recognition, government and private research funding, institutional homes, formal publications and programs of education, translation into public health campaigns, etc.) of the science of nutrition, with its elucidation of the chemical constituents of foods and their effects on health. In particular, colonial networks and sites of governance were enabling of these insights – with their shared imperative of managing far-flung outposts, institutions (corporate housing, schools, prisons), and seemingly clearly-delineated populations under supervision: natives, settlers, soldiers, prisoners.

Overlaying this history were *civilizationist* discourses centered on diet, at their height in the mid-to-late-nineteenth century but continuing on through the close of Second World War. From dietetic (prescriptive eating for health) and moralist crusaders like William Sylvester Graham (1795–1851) and John Harvey Kellogg (1852–1943), to culinary and home economics writers like Sarah Josepha Buell Hale (1788–1879), bread was considered vital to the

CULINARY INFRASTRUCTURE

integrity of the Anglo-American body politic. Nineteenth-century commentators frequently referred to this in the all-encompassing shorthand of "the bread question" – in which bread referred to the baked loaf and to sustenance in general. Would there be enough? What did it cost? And was it good enough?[34] For Graham, bread "signified domestic order, civic health, and moral well-being."[35] Wheaten bread was perceived as a healthy staple that did not overtax digestion or aggravate the nerves. Frequently cited examples of this popular wisdom in the US are Eliza Leslie's (1787–1858) 1840 *Directions for Cookery* and Catharine Beecher's (1800–1878) *Treatise on Domestic Economy*, which in 1841 actually elaborated a food category called "farinaceous substances," wheat being the most nutritive, safe, and acceptable for "all classes and in all circumstances" – this to be eaten in the form of bread, every day, through the entire life cycle.[36]

The most iconic *refined carbohydrate*, as Burkitt and others would term the enemy of healthy digestion, then, was white wheaten bread. White bread embodied an ambivalence about modernization: coveted as a delicious luxury made so affordable by industrial, scientific baking that it appeared on even the humblest table by the 1930s, and also reviled as an artifact of modern degeneration. In his recent history of white bread in the United States, Aaron Bobrow-Strain writes that through the Progressive Era (roughly 1880–1920) and into the interwar period, nutrition experts, health columnists, and social reformers variably took up the refining of wheat flour as source of danger to American society. These included potential contagion (fear about yeasty fermentation in an era of intense hygiene campaigns to prevent communicable disease); commercial adulteration (by greedy industrialists in the early days of food regulation); and chemical exposure (by unknown industrial processing techniques).[37]

By the early twentieth century, white flour was both miracle and abomination, purity and poison, paradoxically depriving its eater of both nourishment and contagion. Anti-white bread campaigners, whose efforts Bobrow-Strain claims peaked around 1920 in the United States, often framed their position in anti-modern terms, romanticizing the dark bread of "savage" Others while assuming white bread as an icon of progress.[38] In a telling insight, Bobrow-Strain notes that, since the Middle Ages, whiteness has had a "Janus-faced social and religious symbolism in the west," standing for both life or death, purity or pallor. However, by the 1930s, industrially produced white bread had emerged victorious, which historians attribute to the moral and aesthetic valorization of whiteness as sign of cleanliness, purity, and progress – at a time of great threatened racial intermixture and Darwinian fears of the demise of the white race.[39] Some early twentieth century social commentators extended this racism to claim that eating white bread might not only "Americanize" undesirable immigrants, it could literally lighten their complexions.[40] Whiteness was good and attractive; darkness was suspect and undesirable.

CULINARY INFRASTRUCTURE

However, despite modernist enthusiasm for patent flour white bread and white skin, there remained doubters. Experts in the US like Henry Clapp Sherman (1875–1955) attacked "America's rage for whiteness," reminding his readers of the threat of white bread acidosis, a disease of nutritional deficiency caused by eating too much white bread in isolation. But even brown (i.e. whole grain) bread champion and author of a "sensible self-defense manual for consumers swimming in a sea of food-industry deceit,"[41] Alfred McCann deplored the practice whereby bread adulterers would exploit the "dusky color" of their loaves to conceal impurities. This practice fueled the ability of the white bread manufacturer to "point to his immaculate loaf, free from the faintest tint of color," or to "contrast the 'chastity' of that white loaf with the 'defilement' of the dark one."[42] Thus, a generation before "Dr Fiber" conducted his seminal research on dietary fiber and digestive health, even the stoutest critics of the white loaf could not overcome the lurking threat of darkness and the lure of the taste of white affluence.

The Dietary Fiber Paradigm

According to historian of medicine James Whorton, the idea of disease as the result of digestion gone wrong has lived in the medical imagination since Pharaonic Egypt. However, the preoccupation reached fever pitch after the acceptance of germ theory by the late-nineteenth century, which provided a new vocabulary and set of experimental methodologies for investigating the effects of what *The People's Medical Lighthouse* in 1856 called, "the disease of civilization." That is, constipation.[43] If germs had been demonstrated to cause putrefaction of organic tissue outside of the body, what could they be doing on the *inside*, exposed to that teeming cesspool that was the gut? When it was learned in the 1880s that gut microbes broke down proteins into compounds that proved toxic when injected into lab animals, vague concern flowered into a full-blown theory of "autointoxication," or self-poisoning by way of undigested matter in the intestines. From roughly 1900–20 (after which point studies discredited the theory that bowel toxins could leak into the circulatory system), autointoxication became a leading catchall for many chronic complaints unexplainable by other means (for instance, headache, indigestion, impotence, nervousness, insomnia) and as an explanation for an overall loss of quality of life and longevity.[44] The general physician's recommendation to eat more fresh fruits and vegetables and whole grains, to exercise regularly, and to evacuate the bowels promptly competed with more convenient commercial offerings in the popular constipation arsenal. These ranged from All Bran cereal, introduced in the early 1900s for specifically this purpose, yeast, yoghurt, a host of laxative products (phenolphthalein was introduced for use as a cathartic in 1900, and the 1920–30s was reportedly a "golden age of purgation"), colonic irrigation tools, electrical stimulators, rectal dilators, abdominal support belts,

110

abdominal massage machines – and even a surgical procedure called colectomy, popularized by the celebrated surgeon of London's Guy's Hospital, Sir William Arbuthnot Lane. Its purpose was to "streamline" the human "drainage scheme."[45] Lane was convinced that constipation was a disease specific to urban, industrial civilization – in which living habits "distorted the colon's anatomy in a way not suffered by 'savage races.'"[46]

After the Second World War, these longstanding concerns about the corrosive physiological effects of constipation were reactivated in the comparative observations of colonial medical officers like Denis Parsons Burkitt. Prompted by wartime policies that re-introduced "brown bread" into the diets of Britain and its former colonies, medical researchers posted in the southern hemisphere started questioning the supposed advantages of industrially produced staples like white bread and examining the physiological consequences of dietary fiber intake. However, whereas previous theories were based on anecdotal observations, Burkitt and his collaborators accumulated epidemiological data on the differences in stool size and bowel transit-time between urban populations in industrialized societies and rural populations in the southern hemisphere. By rigorously and methodically tracking patterns of defecation, they crafted a medical geography that problematized the inherent benefits of economic development and industrialization – a process they often referred to as westernization. Through observations of the connections between culinary infrastructures and intestinal health, this research repositioned the digestive systems of Western populations as pathological and the bowels of decolonizing populations as high-functioning exemplars of culinary and digestive harmony. As they pursued the hypothesis that an overabundance of refined carbohydrates was the cause of "Western diseases," Burkitt and others romanticized the unrefined diets of so-called primitives as a model of natural harmony between macro and micro infrastructures.

In the 1970s and 1980s, after compiling extensive evidence on the dietary determinants of "Western disease" Burkitt articulated an ambitious policy agenda that called for refocusing Western medicine on disease prevention. In an oft-cited analogy from his lectures and publications, Burkitt compared the prevalence of disease in what he called the Western world to an overflowing sink (Figure 1). Rather than "turning off the tap" – and thus addressing the issue at its source – Western medicine was instead focused, ineffectively, on mopping up the floor.[47] Given that the majority of diseases Burkitt and his colleagues identified as prevalent in the West were non-infective and considered reflective of lifestyle choices, the emphasis on prevention and reform of eating habits often meant realigning modern diets with those imagined proper to a pre-industrial past.

The guiding principles of the dietary fiber hypothesis and its relation to Western disease were first articulated by the British biochemist Alexander R. P. Walker, who developed an obsession with nutrition and human fecal variation

Mopping up the floor rather than turning off the tap.

Figure 1. Burkitt's visual depiction of Western medicine's misplaced emphasis on symptom treatment as opposed to prevention. Burkitt, "Economic Development," 12.

while working as a government scientist in South Africa during Second World War. In 1938 Walker and his wife left an economically depressed England and immigrated to Johannesburg where Walker found work in the laboratories of the Municipal Department of Health and later at the South African Institute for Medical Research. During the war years, Walker's observations and studies led him to develop a keen interest in the differences in health between black and white populations and the degree to which they could be accounted for by nutritional and especially intestinal differences. In a retrospective of his life's work, Walker reminisced that it was amidst the human waste he encountered on a daily basis in the municipal laboratories that he became gripped with a passion for understanding the significance of fecal variation. Recalling his duties at the laboratories, he explained that he was tasked with analyzing the "various effluents and sludges from sewage, the end product of human metabolism." As he observed this constant flow of waste he detected feces "of various sizes and consistencies" and began to wonder whether "such variability [had] any significance to health?" In the half century of research he then pursued at the South African Institute for Medical Research, he was driven by a desire to understand what happens "in between" – from the "amount and nature of food eaten, the purpose it serves, to the ultimate passing of excreta."[48]

Walker's first foray into this research program came in 1943 when the South African Government introduced a wartime measure that made a brown loaf of bread of "90% extraction rate" the only bread available for consumption to the public.[49] In an attempt to anticipate the potential consequences of this

CULINARY INFRASTRUCTURE

policy the government asked Walker to conduct nutritional studies on whether brown bread would be harmful to the calcium and iron balance of black South Africans whom he classified as "Africans" in contrast to "whites." Existing research demonstrated that the intakes of mineral salts among Africans were already low. The South African government's request stemmed from a recent experiment performed by Robert McCance and Elsie Widdowson, nutritional scientists in Cambridge, who showed that test subjects on a diet of breads with a high extraction rate (92 percent) absorbed less minerals (such as calcium, magnesium, and potassium) than those on a diet of bread with low extraction rate (59 percent).[50] This research worried South African officials, and Walker was tasked with determining whether the newly introduced brown-loaf policy would further diminish the mineral intake of what they termed the country's African population.

To address the government's anxieties about this potential nutritional deficiency, Walker set out to replicate McCance and Widdowson's experiment on black and white prison inmates. Much to the relief of South African officials, Walker's studies showed that although brown bread initially appeared to cause negative calcium and iron balances in both white and black subjects, this effect was temporary and after a few weeks both groups tended to adapt and show positive mineral balances. However, the study also yielded some unexpected results about the different excretory patterns of white and African prisoners. Whereas the young "African prisoners" in the study typically voided 200–400 g of wet feces, two to three times daily, their young "white" counterparts voided 100 g of feces, usually once daily.[51] Even more surprising, these differences in bowel behavior seemed to correspond with other differences in health. For instance, the study found that whereas white prisoners often requested laxatives for constipation, the African prisoners never made such a request. In fact, the so-called African prisoners seemed to enjoy better overall health. In the ten years previous to the study, only one case of appendicitis had been reported among thousands of African prisoners, whereas six cases had been reported in the previous three years among white prisoners. Similarly, no elderly African prisoner had ever developed colon cancer nor had a heart attack, whereas both of these afflictions were common among elderly white prisoners. As Walker explained in his reminiscences, such contrasting phenomena greatly stimulated South African scientists' interest in "the patterns of bowel physiology and pathology associated with dietary and other differences in our interethnic populations."[52]

The impact of gross disparities in treatment – and medical perceptions – of black vs. white prisoners in apartheid South Africa (1948–94) on the data Walker accumulated in these studies is difficult to assess. We should understand from prison writing under apartheid that the conditions of black inmates in this period were markedly more wretched than those of whites.[53] How to reconcile this with the recorded lower incidence of health outcomes like heart attack

113

and colon cancer among black inmates is a puzzle that our medical archives do not make clear. The relationship of race to, for example, the life expectancy of prisoners, and on access to and collection methods of (stool) samples are important questions we wish to reflect upon in greater depth in future iterations of this project. For it was the apparently stark contrast between the excretory and disease patterns of black vs. white populations that sparked the interest of researchers in the 1970s to extrapolate these findings onto a global scale. How transferrable were such results? The difficulty of categorizing citizens within the apartheid government's hierarchical four-race legal typology (European, Asiatic, colored or mixed race, and local/Bantu) must have been reflected in the racial designations of medical research subjects. From Burkitt and Walker's published papers we see little to nothing of how black inmates were distinguished – by subjective visual assessment? through documented lineages in passbooks? – from white, and white from Indian or Asiatic, and colored from white.[54] As we discuss further later on, the simultaneous power and ambiguity of such racial categories coexisted with Walker and Burkitt's preferred emphasis on lifestyle and environment (rather than race as a causative variable for disease in itself). The result is a loose racial topology of digestion, elimination, and disease – but one that claims race to not be a determining factor at all.

In the decades after his studies on the effects of brown bread, Walker continued to wonder about the different disease patterns among the "Whites, Blacks, Coloreds, and Indians living in South Africa." He found that appendicitis was thirty times more common among "Whites than Blacks" and that a similar pattern held true for diabetes, gallstone, and obesity.[55] Though his work relied heavily on comparisons between South Africa's racial populations, Walker also began to compile evidence that these differences had little to do with biological differences between these populations but rather with the lifestyle choices and environmental exposures associated with differing levels of economic affluence. By the early 1960s, Walker had begun identifying specific socioeconomic mechanisms that could account for these differences in population health. For instance, in a 1962 editorial piece Walker provided an alarming inventory of "health hazards" associated with the "urbanization of the African." Among the "indigenous inhabitants" of Africa, Walker explained, "changes are taking place at varying speed – from primitiveness to sophistication, and from savagery to commerce."[56] Such changes were particularly marked in South Africa, where he observed rural Bantu groups migrating to cities such as Johannesburg at unprecedented rates. Though he conceded that there were certainly benefits – such as increased access to health, education, food, and employment – Walker argued that "many results of the urbanization of the African are disquieting to say the least."[57] In the city, most Bantu abandoned their traditional social institutions, Walker suggested, and were subsequently plagued by problems of crime, delinquency, family instability, and sexually transmitted disease. Walker's chief concern, however, were the problems that arose as a result of changes in

CULINARY INFRASTRUCTURE

nutrition. In the city, Bantu mothers buckled under the pressure of advertising and tended to give up breastfeeding in favor of "processed foods." However, these foods were "almost invariably" prepared in too dilute a manner, thus predisposing – "if not causing" – *kwashiorkor* among Bantu children.[58] Other diseases that Walker identified as on the rise among urban Bantu were rickets, which he linked to insufficient vitamin D caused by "overclothing of babies" and alcoholic pellagra and beriberi, which he associated with greater consumption of illegal alcoholic beverages coupled with reduced levels of B complex vitamins due to a replacement of the traditional diet of lightly milled and fermented maize porridge called *mielie* with industrially produced white bread. According to the Wheat Industry Control Board (formed in 1935) of South Africa, white bread consumption doubled between the 1940s and 1970s in great part due to a government subsidy that enabled poor South Africans to enjoy "the cheapest bread in the world."[59] The general opinion in South Africa at the time was that the wheat-to-bread chain needed to be "rationalized" because of the inefficient and wasteful effects of poor coordination, harmful competition, and resulting volatile prices from traders speculating in an uncontrolled market.[60]

For Walker, what was most alarming about the rise of white bread and the trend toward urbanization was the rise in "diseases of civilization" such as dental caries, diabetes, coronary heart disease, and lung cancer among urbanized Bantus. He found the increased incidence of these kinds of diseases particularly galling because they seemed related to lifestyle choices and thus entirely avoidable. Instead of using their increased wealth on better housing and more nourishing food, Walker observed that urbanized Bantu were spending their incomes on seemingly frivolous items such as expensive clothing, cigarettes, gramophone records, and transistor radios – social markers of affluence. Worse still, he noted, urbanized Bantu seemed to rely on nutritionally deficient food such as "white bread, sugar, soft drinks, and European liquor."[61] As he looked to the future and pondered what could be done about this lamentable situation, Walker did not attend to the regulatory changes in food production or to the psychic effects of (de-) colonization that made such historically elite (and European) products so enticing, but rather to the Bantu consumers who seemed so enthralled by them. "The crucial difficulty lies in endeavouring to inculcate into these people," Walker explained, "the capacity to choose more wisely in their pattern of living, and to be governed less by snobbish thinking, by the acquisition of status symbols, and by personal pleasure." Though these motives certainly influenced the lives of "civilized" people, Walker conceded, they were more dominant in "backward populations" in the process of "becoming westernized."[62]

By 1969, when the Irish surgeon Denis Burkitt came to visit Walker in South Africa, Walker had already accumulated much in the way of anecdotal and statistical evidence to support his contention that in sub-Saharan Africa the migration of rural populations to cities and subsequent adoption of Western diets introduced a new set of diseases to these populations. However, it was the epidemiological networks and contacts that Burkitt had built up through his prior research that catapulted these ideas to a global scale and eventually transformed them into a field of medical research recognized as "Western Diseases."[63] When Burkitt visited Walker in South Africa for the first time, he was beginning the transition from nearly two decades of research in Uganda on a rare form of cancer to his own experimental and statistical forays into the field of comparative nutrition. A devout evangelical Christian who came from a family with a strong tradition of service in the British empire, Burkitt served as a surgeon with Britain's Royal Army Medical Corps in East Africa during Second World War. At the end of the war, Burkitt joined the Colonial Medical Service in Uganda where he conducted research and taught for the next two decades. Though he professed himself a "simple bush-surgeon," he eventually gained international prestige and recognition for his epidemiological research on the geographic distribution and treatment of a rare lymphoma that affected many Ugandan children. This condition came to be known as Burkitt's Lymphoma. By the late 1960s, when he took up a research position in the Department of Morbid Anatomy at St. Thomas Hospital in London, Burkitt had transformed from a little-known "bush surgeon" to a prestigious epidemiologist who attracted the attention of leading cancer researchers throughout the world.[64]

Burkitt's interest in comparative epidemiology and the role played by diet in the causation of disease was sparked after returning to London and being struck by how different the pattern of illness was in the city's St. Thomas Hospital compared to what he had encountered at the Mulago Hospital in Kampala. His interest in the different patterns of disease between Africa and Britain was further stimulated by an encounter with a little known figure in the medical establishment – a retired surgeon and former naval captain named Thomas L. Cleave. Burkitt met Cleave at St. Thomas Hospital in 1967 and became intrigued by his hypothesis that an overconsumption of refined sugars was the cause of several diseases that were prominent in economically developed countries yet absent in the developing world. Cleave also had some suspicions about the importance of dietary fiber and allegedly garnered the nickname "Bran Man" during the Second World War after bringing sacks of bran onboard to cure the constipated soldiers on his battleship.[65] When he met Burkitt, Cleave had recently published a co-authored book titled *Diabetes, Coronary Thrombosis, and the Saccharine Disease* (1966) with a South African diabetes specialist named G. D. Campbell. Cleave and Campbell's book argued that many diseases found in the affluent Western countries were rare or non-existent in rural areas of the so-called Third World and that these diseases were caused by an overconsumption of refined carbohydrates, with sugar being the worst culprit.[66] Burkitt's encounter with Cleave proved transformative. Recalling his own experience in East Africa and Uganda, he became convinced that the "diseases of civilization" that Cleave claimed to exist only in the modern affluent West – namely coronary heart

CULINARY INFRASTRUCTURE

disease, gallstones, appendicitis, diverticular disease of the colon, diabetes, varicose veins, hemorrhoids, and ulcers – were indeed practically non-existent in sub-Saharan Africa and other parts of the southern hemisphere. He was also convinced by Cleave's observation that because these non-infective diseases had similar geographic and socioeconomic distributions and often afflicted the same patients, they must share a common cause. However, whereas Cleave believed these diseases were being caused by an overconsumption of sugars and other refined carbohydrates to which the human body was not evolutionarily adapted, Burkitt suspected that it was not so much overconsumption of refined sugars but rather the under-consumption of fiber that accounted for the prevalence of diseases of the bowel.

In the years that followed his encounter with Cleave, Burkitt set about compiling statistical evidence substantiating Cleave's insights about the geographic distribution of non-infective diseases. He also began conducting historical research on the history of fiber and constipation. Through his previous epidemiological work on the global distribution of cancer, Burkitt had established connections with more than 150 hospitals in Africa, South East Asia, and Latin America that sent him monthly figures on the incidence of cancer among their patients.[67] Now interested in the geographic distribution of the diseases that Cleave hypothesized as specific to economically developed nations, Burkitt developed a new questionnaire asking the hospitals to track the occurrence in their patients of the family of diseases hypothesized to be endemic to the affluent West.[68] He sweetened this request with "generous gifts of drugs and equipment."[69] Around this time, Burkitt also travelled to Chicago to meet with Raymond Knighton, the founder and president of the Medical Assistance Program (MAP), a non-profit Christian organization that collected unused stocks of medicine and medical equipment and sent them to more than one thousand mission hospitals throughout the southern hemisphere for free. Taking advantage of these shipment routes already in place, Burkitt arranged to have MAP enclose one of his questionnaires with each shipment.

With these epidemiological networks in place, Burkitt also began looking into the history of dietary fiber, or "roughage" as it was most commonly referred to then. Prior to the 1970s, fiber was a substance that most nutritional scientists had paid little attention to and believed to be of little nutritional value. However, by delving into the economic history of bread consumption and milling practices and correlating it with disease patterns, Burkitt began to craft a narrative that elevated dietary fiber into a crucial and necessary element of nutrition. Through this epidemiological and historical research Burkitt pieced together a story about how the industrial removal of dietary fiber was causing constipation among populations in the Western world and thus the various diseases of the bowel that Cleave had linked to overconsumption of refined carbohydrates in affluent societies. He was keen to decipher the precise physiological effects that distinguished low from high fiber diets, and so he developed a method that involved measuring the time it took for food to pass through the alimentary tract. When Burkitt visited Walker in South Africa in 1969, Walker was quick to share the methodology he had developed during his brown bread studies on prisoners. In order to test whether there was a difference in transit-time between the white volunteers and the black prisoners who were recruited for the study, Walker asked the participants in both groups to ingest capsules with food coloring and recorded the time it took for the dye to appear in the stools. As he suspected, the "bowel transit-time" was much quicker in the "Africans on their unrefined diet." During this meeting Walker also outlined a potential explanation of the mechanism by which fiber-depleted diets cause so-called diseases of civilization. Echoing the theories of Lane and Kellogg, Walker postulated that "the increased length of time that food remains in the bowel in a fiber-deficient, constipated person, allows more opportunity for ingested carcinogens to act on the lining cells of the bowel."[70]

Walker and Burkitt's mutual interest in the temporality of the digestive tract led to a co-authored paper, along with surgeon Neil S. Painter, that appeared in *The Lancet* and has since been celebrated as a "citation classic" in nutritional science.[71] It was also a foundational piece in what came to be known as the dietary fiber paradigm.[72] Matter-of-factly titled, "The effect of dietary fibre on stools and transit-times, and its role in the causation of disease," the 1972 article succinctly laid out the evidence that Burkitt had been accumulating about the geographic and socioeconomic specificity of diseases of the bowel and advanced the argument that the removal of dietary fiber from foods in the Western diet was to blame.[73] Based on an analysis of "over a 1000 transit times of various ethnic groups at home and abroad, together with the weight of the stool passed daily" the *Lancet* article posited that in countries "little affected by industrialisation," diets containing the "natural amount of fibre are eaten and result in large, soft stools that traverse the intestine rapidly." In contrast to the natural and untarnished diets of populations in the non-industrialized world, the authors postulated that the "refined low-fibre foods of the economically developed countries" produce an unnatural and undesired effect: "small firm stools which pass through the gut slowly." Though they had previously experimented with different methods for measuring transit-times, in this paper Walker, Burkitt, and Painter were keen to demonstrate their use of a new and cutting-edge method – Hinton's method – that produced rapid and reproducible results. Instead of relying on millet seeds, carmine, or barium salts to measure transit-time, Hinton's method used "radio-opaque plastic pellets" the size of rice grains. Participants in the study swallowed twenty-five of these pellets after a meal and then voided their next five or six stools into "numbered plastic bags" and recorded the time at which the stool was passed. The researchers then weighed and x-rayed each stool and eventually calculated a transit-time based on the time elapsed between when the subject swallowed and passed twenty of the pellets.

CULINARY INFRASTRUCTURE

Using this method, the authors calculated the transit-times for over a thousand test subjects. Though they sought to dispel the notion that race played any part in the differing transit-times and stool size, their collected data nevertheless relied upon familiar racial categories. The data on the transit-times and stool weight was presented in a statistical table that classified all of the groups tested by race (either White, Indian, or African) and type of diet (either "refined," "mixed," or "unrefined") and sorted them in a hierarchy according to the weight of the stools passed per day. With the lowest mean stool size, the test subjects on a "refined" diet (all identified as "white") occupied the top tier of their table. This upper echelon consisted of British naval ratings and their wives, British teenage boarding school pupils, and white South African students. The middle tier of the table was comprised by a combination of Indian, African, and White test subjects from Uganda and South Africa who typically ate a "mixed" diet. This group included South Indian nurses working in South Africa who consumed a "less refined diet than that of the Western world," black urban school-children in South Africa who ate a "partly Europeanized diet," black boarding school pupils from Uganda who ate a "traditional Ugandan diet plus refined sugar, white bread, jam, butter," and white vegetarians from the UK whose transit-time and stool size were deemed noteworthy for their similarity to those of rural Africans. Occupying the bottom tier of this apparent excretory hierarchy were black school children and villagers from rural South Africa and Uganda who consumed unrefined diets and were not yet "supplementing their diet with processed foods of Western type." In this way, Burkitt, Walker and Painter's staging of modernization (specifically in eating and defecating habits) reflected colonial legacies in which social privilege, affluence, and power were inversely related to the darkness of one's skin (Figure 2).

However, the authors concluded that this graph demonstrated an inverse relationship between daily stool weights and transit-times. "The bulky stool containing more fiber weighs more and is propelled through the bowel faster," they explained – an inverse relationship that held true, they insisted, "regardless of race."[74] The example of white British vegetarians whose stool weights and bowel behavior were "essentially similar to those of Ugandan boarding-school pupils" served as the most striking example of how this presumed physiological relation between stool weight and transit-time was indifferent to skin color. Instead of hereditary racial makeup as a determinant, Burkitt and Walker argued that differences in this physiological function were shaped by specific historical and socioeconomic factors that informed the diets of different populations. The article also suggested that these differences in stool weight and transit-time correlated with specific disease patterns and with the degree to which a population had adopted a Western diet. For instance, Burkitt, Walker, and Painter suggested that in Britain coronary-artery disease, diverticulosis coli, appendicitis, and gallbladder disorders arose only after 1870 following the

CULINARY INFRASTRUCTURE

TABLE II—TRANSIT-TIMES AS SHOWN BY HINTON'S METHOD

Subjects	Country	Race	Type of diet	No. of subjects	Time of appearance of first pellets (hr.)		Transit-time (hr.)		Weight of stools passed per day (g.)		Comments
					Range	Mean	Range	Mean	Range	Mean	
Naval ratings and wives	U.K.	White	Refined	15	22–110	45·7	44–144	83·4	39–223	104	Shore-based personnel (compare Steigman [1])
Teenage boarding-school pupils	U.K.	White	Refined	9	18–103	57·4	35–120	76·1	71–142	110	Institutional diet together with cakes, sweets, and so on from school shop
Students	South Africa	White	Refined	100	13–54	30·5	28–60	48·0	120–195	173	These ate more fruit than is usual in the U.K.
Nurses	South Indian	Indian	Mixed	13	9–34	27·6	23–64	44·0	..	155	Less refined diet than that of Western world
Urban school-children	South Africa	African	Mixed	500	9–40	28·5	24–59	45·2	120–260	165	Partly Europeanised diet
Manor House Hospital patients	U.K.	White	Mixed	6	15–24	22	27–48	41·0	128–248	175	U.K. diet plus wholemeal bread and added bran
Senior boarding-school pupils	Uganda	African	Mixed	27	4–54	27·6	22–118	47·0	48–348	185	Traditional Ugandan diet plus refined sugar, white bread, jam, butter
Vegetarians	U.K.	White	Mixed	24	8–49	22·0	18–97	42·4	71–488	225	Note similarity of values to those of African groups
Rural school-children	South Africa	African	Unrefined	500	5–28	12·8	20–48	33·5	150–350	275	
Rural villagers	Uganda	African	Unrefined	15	4–32	19·8	19–68	35·7	178–980	470	Villagers not yet supplementing their diet with processed foods of Western type

Figure 2. Transit-time table from the *Lancet* article of 1972. Burkitt, Walker, and Painter, "Effect of Dietary Fibre," 1408.

"introduction of improved milling techniques, lower consumption of bread, and increased use of sugar."[75]

Burkitt, Walker, and Painter claimed that information obtained from "more than two hundred hospitals in over twenty countries" confirmed that: "appendicitis, diverticular disease of the colon, and both benign and malignant tumors of the colon and rectum, which are common in the Western nations, are rare in the developing countries."[76] They observed that in developed countries these diseases afflicted people of all racial backgrounds. In the US, for example, such diseases afflicted "both white and coloured Americans, although the American Negro was less prone to them only a generation ago." In rural Japan, "where eating habits have changed but little" these diseases of the bowel were very rare but were increasing among "Japanese who live in Hawaii and California" and among those in Japan "who have changed to a Western diet." Through their epidemiological and physiological evidence, Burkitt and Walker thus posited that the shift to low-fiber diets associated with economic development was a potent catalyst of intestinal disease, regardless of racial identity (Figure 3).

So, despite efforts to disavow a link between race and diseases of the bowel, Burkitt, Walker, and Painter's analysis betrayed a romantic colonial nostalgia. In their canonical *Lancet* piece they depict rural populations in the developing world as anachronistic societies living in harmony with nature and threatened by the imminent encroachment of Western civilization and its technological excesses. "We conclude," Burkitt, Walker, and Painter wrote,

> that the transit-times and stool weights of the villager in the developing countries, who still eats his traditional unrefined carbohydrates, are normal and that the small stiff stools and prolonged transit-times of the citizens of the Western world are abnormal.[77]

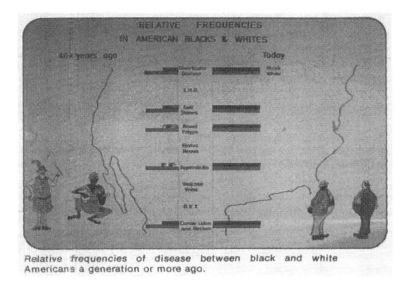

Relative frequencies of disease between black and white Americans a generation or more ago.

Figure 3. Visual representation of Western disease patterns in the US from a 1976 article. Burkitt, "Economic Development – Not all Bonus," 8.

Through this formative article of the dietary fiber paradigm, the bowels of the Western world were thus rendered abnormal – an about-face from colonial medicine that had typically cast colonized bodies as ill-suited to and resistant to progress by virtue of their racialized (and it was understood, inferior) physiology.[78] Walker, Burkitt, and Painter retained the colonial binary of primitive and civilized, but valorized the freely defecating rural villagers and their presumed harmony with nature. The authors figured traditional villagers as exemplars of intestinal normality and as an instructive contrast to the constipated moderns made dysfunctional by economic progress. Burkitt and Walker thus mapped a history of progressive loss of bowel efficiency – a retrogression in dietary health that cast doubt on the promised benefits of economic development. By measuring the averaged transit-time of glow-in-the-dark pellets through the internal infrastructure of the raced human gut, Burkitt, Walker, and Painter assembled a temporal disconnect between our industrial and physiological infrastructures.

Through its excavations into the physiology of defecation, the dietary fiber paradigm thus unwittingly disrupted a body of medical work on imperial hygiene, in which defecation had been construed a symbol of corporeal distinction between colonizer and colonized, and thus an important element of colonial rule and its resistance. For instance, in the context of the US conquest of the Philippines, Warwick Anderson has shown how US health officers relied on a "poetics of defecation" to distinguish the pure, retentive, hygienic (and somehow, paradoxically, also virile) body of the colonizer, who wiped, flushed, and sanitized, from the polluting, open, and grotesque body of the colonized, who were imagined as "promiscuous defecators."[79] In the Philippines, medical control of defecation and the production of clean bodies became an important element of US imperial rule. However, as Achille Mbembe has argued, in African nations emerging from colonial rule, defecation has also been mobilized in the service of a politics of the grotesque – that is, the embrace of wasteful excess, hedonistic display, and unapologetic vulgarity as a means of affirming or subverting masculinist state power.[80] The excremental and its "aesthetics of vulgarity" is also, according to Joshua Esty, a common trope in postcolonial literature from sub-Saharan Africa to a degree that the anus often serves as synecdoche (a part standing for the whole) for the native, while the brain symbolizes the ordering presence of the white male.[81]

When situated within such changing politics of defecation in postcolonial societies, the dietary fiber paradigm can be interpreted as an attempt to sanitize the vulgar and revalorize the dietary and hygienic practices of subalterns still imagined as part of – rather than above – the natural world. By extolling the virtues of dietary fiber, white male medical experts like Burkitt and Walker revalorized primitive eating and defecating practices and abstracted them into a global theory of digestive health and preventive medicine. In so doing, they inverted the value of "shit," which according to Esty has served a "as a material sign of underdevelopment; as a symbol of excessive consumption; as an image of wasted political energies" in the postcolony or, as Anderson notes, as a sign of "failed development."[82] By redeeming and revaluing promiscuous defecation, the dietary fiber paradigm challenged facile notions of progressive modernization, with its inexorable, universally desirable reward of more wealth, more health, and less visible shit – not to mention a more deliciously varied selection of processed foods. The dietary fiber paradigm, as exemplified by the work of Denis Burkitt, was thus reflective of the epidemiological documentation of the ease of digestive movement in African postcolonies. It de-pathologized the open, defecating body beyond the margins of modernization, and instead pathologized the retentive body of the modern citizen, holding fast to the white loaves of progress.

Conclusion

In our studies of food, we have become accustomed to the about-faces of alternative food trends since the 1960s. Slow foods, organic foods, and whole foods, to name a few, all privilege an imagined and pristine prior to the industrial food systems that govern our lives. These trends reflect, in part, a wish to "get back" somehow to somewhere or something we moved away from.[83] What we get less frequently are critical historical accounts of the science in dialog with these trends in food culture. In this paper, we have sketched how dietary fiber was assembled into a direct, causal relationship with a host of conditions for

CULINARY INFRASTRUCTURE

which there was previously no clear, scientific rationale or preventative measure. The accretion of epidemiological evidence and medical consensus in the 1970s around dietary fiber as a preventative for bowel disease casts into relief similar preoccupations in our present. Namely, contemporary framings of metabolic disorder (e.g. overweight, diabetes, irritable bowel syndrome (IBS)) as a syndrome of effects linked to the impoverishment of our microbiota and the erosion of our shared biotic infrastructure: the gut.[84] The premise in Burkitt's day – and now today in the twenty-first century – is that processed foods low in dietary (or, as it is frequently termed today, insoluble) fiber make us unhealthy. Burkitt and his contemporaries implicitly conceptualized the effect of these eating habits as a failure in transit, a defective internal infrastructure whose pathologies correlated with the strength of the culinary infrastructures specific to modern society.

Even after the mainstream uptake of Burkitt's work and the wide availability of vitamin-enriched white bread and mass-produced whole wheat bread, research continues on the incompatibility of our digestive system – now linked more closely to arenas like cognition, mood, immunity, and longevity – with a highly processed, industrially-produced diet. This processed diet is generally characterized as containing relatively high refined-sugar, fat, and refined-grain content, not to mention preservatives, texturizers, flavor and color additives, etc. Today, we understand a new host of endemic pathologies as the result of a simplification of the diversity of our colonies of gut microbes, brought about in part by consuming large quantities of refined grains and simplified sugars. This fiber-poor diet, when combined with a chronic lack of physical activity, is now believed to result in decreased activity of the gut and inadequate (and inadequately-diversified) food for gut microbes, which instead eat away at the mucosal lining of the gut, causing inflammation. In other words, now we conceptualize our internal infrastructure a bit differently; there are more actors lining its sidewalks. Digestive stasis and stagnation does not wreak internal degradation on its own – now microbial actors bring about chemical and physiologic transformation that manifests in us as chronic disease. However, we have retained Burkitt's imagining of the gut as a transit system whose structural form – and integrity – we partially determine through our dietary behavior. Our gastrointestinal tracts became, in the era of Burkitt's work, a built space. And they remain thus.

The work of Burkitt and his collaborators offered new valuation of the bowels (and stool) of those allegedly outside such a definition of modernity. To play with the title of Warwick Anderson's recent paper on postcolonial excrementalism,[85] Burkitt's fiber studies put crap *back on the map* – as an object of scientific and medical importance. Defecating was no longer just a vulgar and distasteful process that exposed populations to disease and contagion: something to be cleaned up, hidden away, and made rational. Its production – rather than its inhibition – became a valuable metric of a population's health and wellness. The redemptive quality of Burkitt's studies for the culinary traditions and toilet habits of non-modern populations continues into our present and is reincarnated in comparative studies of the human microbiome of "isolated populations," believed to hold the secret to restoring the modern world's lost microbiotic diversity, and thus health.[86] In tracking one particular permutation of racial categories in medical science – black pooping, brown pooping, and white – we have aimed to contribute to a critical project shared across food and science studies: to undo biological essentialisms, including – to borrow the words of literary critic Kyla Wazana Tompkins – an "epidermal ontology of race,"[87] as well as other racial essentialisms anchored beneath the skin, into bone structure, immunity, moral character, genetics – or, in this case, digestion. In this piece, we have hoped to illuminate how, at a historical moment in which race had been debunked as having no basis in biology, in the calculus of trend-setting nutritional research, even pooping was raced.

Acknowledgments

The authors would like to express their gratitude to participants of the Culinaria group's Connaught Seminar workshop on Culinary Infrastructures; to two anonymous reviewers; to Chin Jou, Warwick Anderson, and the incomparable Michelle Murphy, for their insightful feedback on improving this paper.

Funding

This work was supported by the Australia Research Council [grant number FL110100243]; Sarah Tracy's research was sponsored by an Ontario Graduate Scholarship.

Notes

1. Graham, *Treatise on Bread and Bread-Making*, 52.
2. Lane, "Against White Bread," 1179.

CULINARY INFRASTRUCTURE

3. Stanwix, "Wheat, Bread, and the Role of the State," 16.
4. Walker, "Nutrionally Related Disorders/Diseases in Africans."
5. See for instance: Varmus, "Medical Research Centers," 2014.
6. Burkitt and Trowell, *Western Diseases*, 427.
7. Hereafter we try to avoid the tiresome use of scare quotes around a range of terms used historically to distinguish between the spaces and inhabitants of formerly colonized regions of the world broadly identified today as the Global South, and those identified as the Global North (referring most frequently to the affluent countries of Western Europe and the United States); however, we flag the periodicity of each of these usages throughout the paper, and in every instance employ the terms in their constructed sense (rather than in a self-evident or factual sense).
8. The idea of a connection between constipation and civilization has been ably explored by historian of medicine Whorton, *Inner Hygiene*. See also his article, "Civilization and the Colon," 424–427.
9. This accolade is quoted in Whorton, "Civilization and the Colon," 2000, 427; Ferguson "D. P. Burkitt [obituary]," 996.
10. We use ontology to refer to a specific bringing-into-being or declaration of the nature of a thing. This usage understands that ontologies are multiple. For example, Burkitt's research *ontologizes* colon disease as an effect of gastrointestinal irritation (due to stool stasis) associated with deficient dietary intake. This is in contrast to colon disease being ontologized as an auto-immune disease, or as a genetic disease, or as a symptom of impoverished gut microbiota. Annemarie Mol, for one, has explained the importance of attending to not only the *methods* of the sciences, but also the *objects* those methods produce – i.e. the different things that different scientific methods make thinkable, doable, possible. For example, the microscope (method) made germ theory (ontology) and surgical sterilization and food pasteurization (practices) thinkable. See Mol, *The Body Multiple*, or her brief discussion, "A Reader's Guide to the 'Ontological Turn.'"
11. For historical accounts of the ways that racial conceptions were refashioned after the Second World War through scientific agencies like UNESCO see Gil-Riaño, "Historicizing Anti-Racism"; Yudell, *Race Unmasked*; Brattain, "Race, Racism, and Antiracism," 1386–413; Selcer, "Beyond the Cephalic Index," S173–84.
12. For larger discussions of the persistence and stakes of racial categories in late-twentieth century biomedical research, see the work of TallBear, *Native American DNA*; Pollock, *Medicating Race*; Duster, "Buried Alive," 258–277; Reardon, *Race to the Finish*; Nelson, *Reckoning*.
13. Laak 1999: 61, cited in Rankin, "Infrastructure."
14. Rankin, "Infrastructure," 63.
15. The quoted passages in this section are attributed to Frohlich et al., "Preface: Food Infrastructures."
16. For more on rice and modern culture, identity, and nutrition science in Asia, see Ohnuki-Tierney, *Rice as Self*; Bay, "Beriberi, Military Medicine," 107–152.
17. See, for example, Carpenter, "A Short History of Nutritional Science, Part 3," 3023–32; Carpenter, "A Short History of Nutritional Science: Part 4," 3331–42.
18. These phrasings are once again borrowed from Frohlich et al., "Preface: Food Infrastructures." For another example of how infrastructures become visible through failure and excrement see Benson, "Generating Infrastructural Invisibility," 103–30.
19. Benson, "Generating Infrastructural Invisibility."
20. See "Regions, Networks and Fluids," 641–71.

CULINARY INFRASTRUCTURE

21. This method predominated in Britain and the US; however, the hard wheat varieties that fared better in parts of Eastern Europe prompted Hungarian inventers to investigate a milling technology to produce a more desirable flour from hard wheats.
22. Winson, *The Industrial Diet*, 98.
23. In the late 1870s, Washburn sent an engineer named William de la Barre to Hungary, where he posed as a worker and sketched the new roller-milling machinery at work there. These drawings he brought back to the United States, where they were reproduced through the 1880–90s with considerable resultant savings in production costs, particularly labor.
24. Winson, *Industrial Diet*, 2013. See also Bobrow-Strain, "Kills a Body Twelve Ways," 46.
25. Hard, spring wheat processed well in roller mills, in contrast to stone milling, which tended to pulverize part of the hard, friable husk of the grain, producing a darker and lower-priced flour than that of soft wheats.
26. The Canadian Government sponsored a settlement program for the territories west of Lake Superior in an effort to check the spread of its acquisitive southern neighbor with its mandate of "manifest destiny." Such incentives as 160-acre land grants on the prairies prompted settlers from eastern Canada, the US, the British isles, and from the European continent to try their hand – many for the first time – at wheat farming. These years of western migration turned the Canadian prairies into one of the largest wheat-growing regions of the world. Winson, *Industrial Diet*, 98.
27. The development of this new milling technology drove the creation of large milling trusts with the buying power to negotiate preferential transportation rates from railroad companies and large flour contracts with overseas buyers. The roller milling technology gradually reduced and separated the different parts of the wheat – first splitting open the husk, then separating the floury "middlings" from the bran. Further sifting removed any coarse material, and all while expending far less power than a stone mill and producing a much larger proportion of fine white "patent" flour. An interesting insight on historical commercial bread practice is that a strong flour yields greater gluten, and thus greater expansion, and a lighter bread, which absorbs more water and thus weighs more – equating to more income for baker, who traditionally sold bread by weight. Winson, *Industrial Diet*, 99, 230, quoting Kuhlmann, *The Development of the Flour-Milling Industry*, 113, 423–4, 428; Wazana Tompkins, *Racial Indigestion*, 63, citing Knopf, *Changes in Wheat Production*, 49.
28. This statistic is provided by self-styed "historian of white bread," Bobrow-Strain, "White Bread Bio-politics," 29, and elaborated in his book, *White Bread*.
29. For example, the Wahl-Henius Institute of Fermentology, the Wahl Efficiency Institute, the Chidlow Institute, the Siebel Institute of Technology (scientific study of bread chemistry, biology, and technology) had been founded. Bobrow-Strain, "White Bread Bio-politics," 29.
30. According to Bobrow-Strain, by 1930, only fermentation still defied control, the living nature of the yeast set limits on the quantity of dough that could rise at one time so industry researched chemical dough conditioners and other processes that would "break through the yeast ceiling." Bobrow-Strain, "White Bread Bio-politics," 29–30.
31. A 1930 issue of *Scientific American* reported that a patent whitening agent ("Do-White"), chlorine gas, nitrogen trichloride, and nitrogen peroxide were

CULINARY INFRASTRUCTURE

all in widespread use as flour bleaching agents. Bobrow-Strain, "White Bread Bio-politics," 31–32.

32. As would later be acknowledged, the health implications of this paradigmatic shift (the widespread removal of wheat germ and bran in the refining processes) was the simultaneous loss of many essential nutrients, such as the B vitamins, calcium, iron, phosphorous, and magnesium – not to mention, as Burkitt would come to impress upon the nutritional community, fiber. Winson, *Industrial Diet*, 100–101.

33. See, for example, Carpenter, "Short History of Nutrition"; Bay, "Beriberi."

34. Bobrow-Strain elaborates this subject in the introduction of his book, *White Bread*, 3.

35. Graham was trained as an evangelical minister, a staple of the northeastern lecture circuit by 1840 (wrote 8 books in 1830s): he was an advocate of sobriety, Sunday school, and stopping the spread of cholera. He linked vice directly to diet, and articulated a "Grahamite" dietetic program, the foundation of which was the "brown or dyspepsia bread" that in 1839 Sarah Hale described as best known as "Graham bread," because the minister had had been "unwearied successful in recommending it to the public." Wazana Tompkins, *Racial Indigestion*, 64–5; quoting Hale, *Good Housekeeper*, 17.

36. Wazana Tompkins, *Racial Indigestion*, 62.

37. For example, Christian and Christian, *Uncooked Foods*, described bread rising when "infected with the yeast germ because millions of these little worms have been born and have died, and from their dead and decaying bodies there rises a gas just as it does form the dead body of a hog." Schlink's widely read *Eat, Drink, and Be Wary* (1935) described industrial bread as "chemical fluff" and advocated making your own or buying Shredded Wheat, Grape Nuts, or other 'healthy' wheat products. Bobrow-Strain, "Kills a Body," 44, 51.

38. Bobrow-Strain, "White Bread Bio-politics," 31; Bobrow-Strain, "Kills a Body," 46.

39. Whiteness was coveted, represented in modern appliances (kitchens, water closets), schools, hospitals, clothing, women's magazines, advertisers, home economists' supplications to housewives to relentlessly bleach their laundry aprons, and towels. White wash and white paint were frequently discussed with respect to their merit for revealing surface dirt or garbage – boasting even the capacity for shaming "the Polacks and Hungarians in the district to get rid of [their refuse] in some way" (Woods Hutchinson, ironic *American Magazine article*). Bobrow-Strain, "White Bread Bio-politics," 33–34.

40. Bobrow-Strain, *White Bread*, e.g. 7.

41. Bobrow-Strain, "Kills a Body," 51.

42. The debate about refined wheat flour even reached the US Supreme Court, with critics and supports both framing debate in terms of national health. McCann himself brought suits against bread manufacturers, working with New York City and state officials to seize loads of "unsound" flour. Bobrow-Strain, "White Bread Bio-politics," 34.

43. Whorton, "Civilization and the Colon," 424, citing H. Root.

44. This is elaborated in Whorton, "Civilization and the Colon," 425.

45. Whorton, "Civilization and the Colon," 426; Lane, "An Address on Chronic Intestinal Stasis," 1126.

46. Whorton, "Civilization and the Colon," 426; Lane, *The Operative Treatment of Chronic Constipation*, 36–37.

47. Burkitt. "Economic Development," 12.

48. Walker. "Nutritionally Related Disorders/Diseases in Africans," 1.

CULINARY INFRASTRUCTURE

49. An "extraction rate" is a measure of how much of a total wheat berry a flour contains. For example, a whole wheat flour is considered to be of 100 percent extraction.

50. McCance and Widdowson performed their experiment on group of four men and four women deemed to be "healthy adults." Their test subjects were predominantly Cambridge scientists. See McCance and Widdowson, "Mineral metabolism of healthy adults," 44–85.

51. Walker, "Nutritionally Related Disorders/Diseases in Africans," 4.

52. Ibid.

53. For example, Makhoere, *No Child's Play*.

54. For more on racial classification under apartheid (and, in particular, the banal violence of the necessity of non-white South Africans to always carry a passbook – a tome containing one's medical, employment, legal, and housing documentation), see Bowker and Star, "The Case of Race Classification."

55. Nelson, *Burkitt: Cancer, Fiber*, 165.

56. Walker, "Health Hazards," 551.

57. Ibid.

58. *Kwashiorkor* is a state of severe malnutrition resulting from a deficiency of protein. Ibid, 552.

59. In the 1930s, galvanized by the Depression and droughts throughout the US, Africa, and Australia, the UK, Holland, and South Africa all legislated national regulatory frameworks to centralize wheat purchase from farmers (1937 Marketing Act in South Africa), set nationwide bread prices, and protect domestic farmers against fluctuating price of imported grain. The Union of South Africa was under British Colonial Rule official in 1910. The late-twentieth century discovery of diamonds and gold in South Africa spurred exploration and settlement and economic growth and speculation– also drove demand for bread, and thus wheat. In late-nineteenth century SA was importing more than it produced, so domestic production beyond Western Cape (traditional area of wheat cultivation, formed a wheat farming cooperative called *Wesgraan* in 1912) was encouraged by the colonial government. Stanwix, "Wheat, Bread, and the Role of the State."

60. De Swardt, 1962, De Swardt, 1983: 17; quoted in Stanwix, "Wheat, Bread, and the Role of the State," 9.

61. Walker, "Health Hazards," 552.

62. Ibid.

63. Up until the 1970s the kinds of diseases researched by Burkitt and Walker were referred to as "diseases of civilization." The term "Western Diseases" was introduced by Hugh Trowell in 1951, one of Burkitt's collaborators who had also worked as a physician in Uganda and found it "obnoxious to teach African and Asian medical students that their communities had a low incidence of these diseases because they were uncivilised." See Temple and Burkitt, *Western Diseases*.

64. Biographical information on Burkitt is drawn from Epstein and Eastwood, "Denis Parsons Burkitt"; Smith, "Denis Parsons Burkitt"; Nelson and Temple, "Tribute to Denis Burkitt"; Nelson, *Burkitt: Cancer, Fiber*. The finding aid to the Denis Burkitt collection at the Wellcome Library also has a good biography. http://archives.wellcomelibrary.org/DServe/dserve.exe?dsqIni=Dserve.ini&dsqApp=Archive&dsqCmd=Show.tcl&dsqDb=Catalog&dsqSearch=(Sources_guides_used=%27Far%20East%27)&dsqPos=189

65. Wellcome Library biography.
66. Nelson, *Burkittt: Cancer, Fiber*, 154.
67. Ibid., 159.
68. Ibid.
69. Burkitt, "The Emergence of a Concept," 8.
70. Nelson, *Burkitt: Cancer, Fiber*, 165.
71. Neil S. Painter was a surgeon who specialized in the study of pressure in the colon of patients with diverticular disease. He published a book titled *Diverticular disease of the colon: a deficiency disease of Western civilization* in 1975 that revolutionized treatment of this disease according to his biography for the Royal College of Surgeons of England. http://livesonline.rcseng.ac.uk/biogs/E007560b.htm.
72. Trowell, Burkitt, and Heaton, *Dietary fibre*. For contemporary journalistic coverage of the emergence of the dietary fiber paradigm, see Galton, *The Truth About Fiber*.
73. Burkitt, Walker, and Painter, "Effect of Dietary Fibre."
74. Ibid., 1409.
75. Ibid., 1410.
76. Ibid., 1409.
77. Burkitt, Walker, and Painter, "Effect of Dietary Fibre," 1410.
78. See, for example, Fanon, *A Dying Colonialism*; Adas, "Contested Hegemony"; and Vaughn, *Curing Their Ills*.
79. Anderson, "Crap on the Map"; and, previously, Anderson, "Excremental Colonialism."
80. Mbembe, "The Banality of Power."
81. Esty, "Excremental Postcolonialism."
82. According to Anderson, still other postcolonial critics problematize wealth and development by describing money as mere "polished waste" – excessive debris that carries only a superficial veneer of value. Anderson, "Crap on the Map," 173.
83. See, for example, Carruth's discussion of what she terms the "post-industrial pastoral" in *Global Appetites*.
84. O'Keefe et al., "Fat, fibre and cancer risk"; Sonnenburg and Sonnenburg, *The Good Gut*; John Swansburg, "Cute Family"; Velasquez-Manoff, "How the Western Diet has Derailed"; Pollan, "Some of my Best Friends are Germs."
85. Anderson, "Crap on the Map."
86. Velasquez-Manoff, "How the Western Diet has Derailed."
87. Wazana Tompkins, Racial Indigestion, 3.

Bibliography

Adas, Michael. "Contested Hegemony: The Great War and the Afro-Asian Assault on the Civilizing Mission Ideology." In *Decolonization: Perspectives from Now and Then*, edited by Prasenjit Duara, 78–100. London: Routledge, 2004.

Anderson, Warwick. "Crap on the Map, or Postcolonial Waste." *Postcolonial Studies* 13, no. 2 (2010): 169–178.

Anderson, Warwick. "Excremental Colonialism: Public Health and the Poetics of Pollution." *Critical Inquiry* 21 (1995): 640–669.

Bay, Alexander. "Beriberi, Military Medicine, and Medical Authority in Prewar Japan." *Japan Review* 20 (2008): 107–152.

CULINARY INFRASTRUCTURE

Bobrow-Strain, Aaron. "Kills a Body Twelve Ways: Bread Fear and the Politics of What to Eat?" *Gastronomica* 7, no. 3 (2007): 44–52.

Bobrow-Strain, Aaron. "White Bread Bio-politics: Purity, Health, and the Triumph of Industrial Baking." *Cultural Geographies* 15 (2008): 19–40.

Bobrow-Strain, Aaron. *White Bread: A Social History of the Store-bought Loaf.* New York: Penguin Random House, 2013.

Bowker, Geoffrey C., and Susan Leigh Star. "The Case of Race Classification and Reclassification under Apartheid." In *Sorting Things out: Classification and Its Consequences*, 195–225. Cambridge: MIT Press, 1999.

Brattain, Michelle. "Race, Racism, and Antiracism: UNESCO and the Politics of Presenting Science to the Postwar Public." *American Historical Review* 112, no. 5 (2007): 1386–1413.

Burkitt, Denis, and H. Trowell (eds.). *Western Diseases: Their Emergence and Prevention.* London: Arnold, 1960.

Burkitt, Denis P. "Economic Development-not All Bonus." *Nutrition Today* 11 (1976): 6–13.

Burkitt, Denis P. "The Emergence of a Concept." In *Western Diseases: Their Dietary Prevention and Reversibility*, edited by Norman J. Temple, 1–13. Totowa, NJ: Humana Press, 1994.

Burkitt, Denis P., A. R. P. Walker, and N. S. Painter. "Effect of Dietary Fibre on Stools and Transit-times, and its Role in the Causation of Disease." *The Lancet* 300, no. 7792 (1972): 1408–1411.

Carpenter, Kenneth J. "A Short History of Nutritional Science: Part 3 (1912–1944)." *Journal of Nutrition* 133, no. 10 (2003): 3023–3032.

Carpenter, Kenneth J. "A Short History of Nutritional Science: Part 4 (1945–1985)." *Journal of Nutrition* 133, no. 11 (2003): 3331–3342.

Carruth, Allison. *Global Appetites: American Power and the Literatures of Food.* Cambridge: Cambridge University Press, 2013.

Duster, Troy. "Buried Alive: The Concept of Race in Science." In *Genetic Nature/ Cuture: Anthropology and Science beyond the Two-culture Divide*, edited by Alan H. Goodman, Deborah Heath and M. Susan Lindee, 258–277. Berkeley: University of California Press, 2003.

Epstein, Anthony, and M. A. Eastwood. "Denis Parsons Burkitt. 28 February 1911–23 March 1993." *Biographical Memoirs of Fellows of the Royal Society* 41 (1995): 88–102.

Esty, Joshua D. "Excremental Postcolonialism." *Comparative Literature* 40 (1999): 22–59.

Fanon, Frantz. *A Dying Colonialism.* Translated by Haadon Chevalier. New York: Grove Press, [1959] 1965.

Ferguson, A. "D. P. Burkitt [Obituary]." *British Medical Journal* 396 (1993): 996.

Frohlich, Xaq, Mikko Jauho, Bart Penders, and David Schleifer. 2014. "Preface: Food Infrastructures." *Limn* January 4. Accessed May 10, 2015. http://limn.it/preface-food-infrastructures/

Galton, Lawrence. *The Truth about Fiber in Your Diet.* New York: Crown, 1976.

Gil-Riaño, Sebastián. "Historicizing Anti-racism: UNESCO's Campaigns against Race Prejudice in the 1950s." PhD diss., University of Toronto, 2014.

Graham, William Sylvester. *Treatise on Bread and Bread-making.* Boston, MA: Light & Stearns, 1837.

Lane, William A. "Against White Bread." *Journal of the American Medical Association* 83 (1924): 1179.

Lane, William A. "An Address on Chronic Intestinal Stasis." *British Medical Journal* 2 (1913): 1126.

CULINARY INFRASTRUCTURE

Lane, William A. *The Operative Treatment of Chronic Constipation*. London: Nisbet, 1909

Lock, Margaret, and Patricia Kaufert. "Menopause, Local Biologies, and Cultures of Aging." *American Journal of Human Biology* 13, no. 4 (2001): 494–504.

Makhoere, Caesarina Kona. *No Child's Play: In Prison under Apartheid*. London: Women's Press, 1988.

Mbembe, Achille. "The Banality of Power and the Aesthetics of Vulgarity in the Postcolony." Translated by Janet Roitman *Public Culture* 4 (1992): 1–30. Revised as chapter 3 in Achille Membe. *In the Post-colony*. Berkley: University of California Press, 2001.

McCance, R. A., and Elsie M. Widdowson. "Mineral Metabolism of Healthy Adults on White and Brown Bread Dietaries." *Journal of Physiology* 101 (1942): 44–85.

Mol, Annemarie. *The Body Multiple*. Durham, NC: Duke University Press, 2003.

Mol, Annemarie. 2014. "A Reader's Guide to the 'Ontological Turn'-Part 4." *Somatosphere*, March 19. Accessed May 10, 2015. http://somatosphere.net/2014/03/a-readers-guide-to-the-ontological-turn-part-4.html

Mol, Annemarie, and John Law. "Regions, Networks and Fluids: Anaemia and Social Topology." *Social Studies of Science* 24 (1994): 641–671.

Nelson, Diane. *Reckoning: The Ends of War in Guatemala*. Durham, NC: Duke University Press, 2009.

Nelson, Cliff L., and Norman J. Temple. "Tribute to Denis Burkitt." *Journal of Medical Biography* 2 (1994): 180–183.

Nelson, Ethel R. *Burkitt: Cancer, Fiber*. Brushton, NY: Teach Services, 1998.

Ohnuki-Tierney, Emiko. *Rice as Self*. Princeton, NJ: Princeton University Press, 1993.

O'Keefe, Stephen J. D., Jia V. Li, Leo Lahti, Junhai Ou, Franck Carbonero, Khaled Mohammed, Joram M. Posma, James Kinross, Elaine Wahl, Elizabeth Ruder, et al. "Fat, Fibre and Cancer Risk in African Americans and Rural Africans." *Nature Communications* 6 (2015): 6342. doi:10.1038/ncomms7342.

Pollan, Michael. 2013. "Some of My Best Friends Are Germs." *New York times*, May 15.

Pollock, Anne. *Medicating Race: Heart Disease and Durable Preoccupations with Difference*. Durham, NC: Duke University Press, 2012.

Rankin, William. "Infrastructure and the International Governance of Economic Development, 1950–1965." In *Internationalization of Infrastructures*, edited by Jean-François Auger, Jan Jaap Bouma and Rolf Künneke, 61–75. Delft: Delft University of Technology, 2009.

Reardon, Jenny. *Race to the Finish: Identity and Governance in an Age of Genomics*. Princeton, NJ: Princeton University Press, 2005.

Selcer, Perrin. "Beyond the Cephalic Index: Negotiating Politics to Produce UNESCO's Scientific Statements on Race." *Current Anthropology* 53, no. S5 (2012): S173–S184.

Smith, Owen. "Denis Parsons Burkitt CMG, MD, DSc, FRS, FRCS, FTCD (1911–93) Irish by Birth, Trinity by the Grace of God." *British Journal of Haematology* 156 (2012): 770–776.

Sonnenburg, John, and Erica Sonnenburg. *The Good Gut: Taking Control of Your Weight, Your Mood, and Your Long Term Health*. New York: Penguin, 2015.

Swansburg, John. 2015. "Cute Family. And You Should See Their Bacteria." *New York Magazine*, April 23. Accessed May 10, 2015. http://nymag.com/scienceofus/2015/04/sonnenburg-family-stomach-bacteria.html

Stanwix, Benjamin. "Wheat, Bread, and the Role of the State in Twentieth Century South Africa." MA thesis, Harvard University, 2012.

TallBear, Kim. *Native American DNA: Tribal Belonging and the False Promise of Genetic Science*. Minneapolis: University of Minnesota Press, 2013.

CULINARY INFRASTRUCTURE

Temple, Norman J., and Denis P. Burkitt (eds.). *Western Diseases: Their Dietary Prevention and Reversibility*. Totowa, NJ: Humana, 1994.

Tompkins, Kyla Wazana. *Racial Indigestion: Eating Bodies in the 19th Century*. New York: New York University Press, 2012.

Trowell, H. C., D. P. Burkitt, and K. W. Heaton. *Dietary Fibre, Fibre-depleted Foods and Disease*. London: Academic Press, 1985.

Vaughn, Megan. *Curing Their Ills: Colonial Power and African Illness*. Stanford, CA: University of Stanford Press, 1991.

Velasquez-Manoff, Moises. 2015. "How the Western Diet Has Derailed Our Evolution." *Nautilus*, November 12.

Walker, Alexander R. P. "Nutritionally Related Disorders/Diseases in Africans: Highlights of Half a Century of Research with Special Reference to Unexpected Phenomena." In *Dietary Fiber in Health and Disease*, edited by David Kritchevsky and Charles Bonfield, 1–14. New York: Plenum Press, 1997.

Walker, Alexander P. "Health Hazards in the Urbanization of the African." *The American Journal of Clinical Nutrition* 11 (1962): 551–553.

Whorton, James C. *Inner Hygiene: Constipation and the Pursuit of Health in Modern Society*. New York: Oxford University Press, 2000.

Whorton, James C. "Civilization and the Colon: Constipation as 'the Disease of Diseases.'" *Western Journal of Medicine* 173 (2000): 424–427.

Winson, Anthony. *The Industrial Diet: The Degradation of Food and the Struggle for Healthy Eating*. Vancouver: University of British Columbia Press, 2013.

Yudell, Michael. *Race Unmasked: Biology and Race in the Twentieth Century*. New York: Columbia University Press, 2014.

Index

Note: Page numbers in *italics* refer to figures

abdominal support belts 110
actor-network-theory 106
Adri, Ferran 19
adulteration: beer 65–6; food 58; milk 66;
 spice 70–1
African slaves 9
Africans: urbanization of 114; Bantu
 groups 114–15
aging meats 12
agroecological knowledge 4
All Bran cereal 110
Alsop Process of chemical bleaching 108
American refrigeration industry 37
Anderson, Warwick 121, 123
anti-Communist propaganda 14
Appadurai, Arjun 7
appendicitis 3, 103, 119, 120
Appleton, Josie 84
Armour & Company 43
Art Gallery of Ontario (AGO) 80, 82
Art Gallery of Toronto (AGT) Women's
 Committee: Art of Cooking series 82,
 89–91; food programming by 85–7;
 introduction to 80–2; Men's Lunches
 91–4; paradigm challenges through
 82–5; summary of 94–5; women's history
 and 87–9
artistic independence of chefs 15
Art of Cooking, The recipe booklet 89
Art of Cooking series 82, 89–91
autointoxication 110

bacterial contamination of meat 13
Baldwin, Martin 89
Bantu groups, in Africa 114–15
B complex vitamins 115
Beecher, Catharine 109
beer adulteration 65–6

benevolent femininity 88
Bennett, Tony 83
Berlin Low Temperature Syndicate 43
Big Food 106
Birdseye, Charles 2, 32
Bobrow-Strain, Aaron 109
bowel cancer 103
bowel transit-time 118–21, *120*
Bower, Anne 93
Brandt, Karl 40–1
bran, in diet 116
bread: brown 109–10, 112–14; importance
 108–9; white *vs.* dark 109–10, 112–14
breastfeeding 115
brigade de cuisine 17
British East India Company 56
British Empire Marketing Board 14
brown bread 109–10, 112–14
bureaucracy of food inspectors 67–8
Burkitt, Denis Parsons 103–5, 111, *112*,
 115–25
Burkitt's Lymphoma 116

Cameron, Dorothy 94
Campbell, G.D. 116
cancer 3, 103, 117, 120; bowel 103, colon 3,
 103, 113, 120
carbohydrates, refined 3, 104, 109
Carême, Antonin 15
Carrene, refrigerant 63
cellophane-packed frozen food 39
Charabarty, Dipesh 59
chefs, artistic independence of 15
Chicago Board of Trade 8, 11
Chinese vegetables 14
Choi, Roy 20
cholera 67
Christian morality of Victorian times 88

INDEX

civilizationist discourses on diet 108
Claflin, Kyri 13, 34
Cleave, Thomas L. 116–18
cold chain 11–12, 21
Cold Storage Company 62–3
Collingham, Lizzie 34
colon cancer 3, 103, 113, 120
colonialism 108
colonic irrigation tools 110
commercialization of authenticity 18
Common Market 12
constipation 3
consumer advocacy *vs.* responsibility 70–3
Consumers Association of Singapore 71–2
contamination of food 58, 59
Continental European economy 41
cookbook culture 16
coronary-artery disease 119
corporate supermarket chains 14
corporate technology and food safety 62–5
corruption of food 58
Cronon, William 6
culinary cultures 15
culinary infrastructure: fast freezing
    32–48; introduction to 1–4; knowledge
    infrastructure 14–20; museum in 3;
    overview 5–9; physical infrastructure
    9–14; summary of 20–2
culinary labor 16
culinary professionalism 16–17
culinary tourism 21
cultural hierarchies 19
Cuno, James 82–3

Dart, Joseph 6
defecation, and fiber 104–5
dehydration 34
*Diabetes, Coronary Thrombosis, and the
    Saccharine Disease* (Cleave, Campbell)
    116
digestion: electrical stimulators for 110;
    microbial actors in 109, 123
dietary fiber paradigm: defecation and
    fiber 104–5; edible artifacts of affluence
    105–10; introduction to 3, 102–5;
    overview of 110–22, *112, 120, 121*;
    summary of 122–4
dietary health: bran in diet 116; brown
    bread 109–10, 112–14; dietary fiber 117–
    18; gut microbes 110, 123; introduction
    to 3; nutrition science 34
Directions for Cookery (Leslie) 109
diseases: appendicitis 3, 103, 119, 120;
    cancer 3, 103, 117, 120; chronic disease
    3; of civilization 116–18, 121, *121*;

diverticulitis 3, 103, 119, 120; dysentery
    67; enteric fever 67; gallbladder
    disorders 119; gastroenteritis 67; heart
    attack 113; sexually transmitted disease
    114; ulcerative colitis 103
diverticulitis 3, 103, 119, 120
Dojima rice exchange 11
Donofrio, Greg 13
Dr. Seuss *see* Geisel, Theodore
Dupont Corporation 13
Duruz, Jean 59
Dutch spice traders 9
dysentery 67

earthenware amphora 10
edible artifacts of affluence 105–10
Edible Histories, Cultural Politics (Iacovetta,
    Korinek, Epp) 89
Edward, Paul 14–15
Edward P. Taylor Library and Archives 82
electrical stimulators for digestion 110
Emblik, Eduard 39–40
endemic pathologies 123
Enlightenment philosophes 16
enteric fever (typhoid) 67
entrepreneurial women 18
Epp, Marlene 89
Epstein, Barbara L. 87–8
Escoffier, Auguste 17–19
Esty, Joshua 122
European agricultural land 33
European food economy 48
European Grossraumwirtschaft 38

fair trade label 19
fast freezing 32–48
fecal waste studies 111–12
femininity, benevolent 88
Ferguson, Priscilla 17
fiber, and defecation 104–5
fiber-poor diet 123
Field Cookbook (Feldkochbuch) 38
Field Kitchen Recipes 39
Finstad, Terje 33
flies, and food safety 60–2, 67
Flit insecticides 56, 60–1
food adulteration 58
food, contamination of 58, 59
food deserts 14
Food for Thought handbook 72–3
food inspectors, bureaucracy of 67–8
food markets, regional 11
food regulation 57–60
Food Research Institute at Stanford
    University 40

INDEX

food safety, and flies 60–2, 67
food safety in Singapore: adulteration of beer 65–6; aid by corporate technology 62–5, bugs and vermin 60–2; consumer advocacy *vs.* responsibility 70–3; for developing economies 68–70; introduction to 2, 55–6; newspaper sources 57; scholarly sources 57–60; state regulation of food safety 67–8; summary of 73–4
Franco–Prussian War 6
French, Michael 57–60
French agriculture 2, 41
French culinary hegemony 19
French fishing industry 41
French gastronomical meal 19
fresh label 19
Friedberg, Susanne 62
Friedman, Harriet 7
frozen fish acceptance 34; Norwegian 34
frozen food: cellophane-packed 39; processing plants 2; vitamin-rich foods 39; *see also* fast freezing

gallbladder disorders 119
Gandulfo, Doña Petrona de 18
gastrodiplomacy 19–20
gastroenteritis 67
gastrointestinal (GI) tracts 104
Gault Henri 19
Geise, Theodore 60–1
Gendered Domains (Reverby, Helly) 88–9
German Refrigeration Association 42
German Syndicate of Freezing Companies for France 43
germ theory 61
Gil-Riaño, Sebastián 102
Ginzberg, Lori D. 81, 88
globalized food systems 2, 9, 56
global linkages of supply 6
Global North/South 19
Goody, Jack 15
grading standards, uniform 8
Graham, William Sylvester 108
grain elevator 5–6, 8
grain processing of wheat 107
Grunow Refrigerators 63
Guthman, Julie 19
gut infrastructure, human 106
gut microbes 110, 123

Hale, Sarah Josepha Buell 108
handmills 107
Harlon, Michael 93
Harvey House 18

Hawker Code 68
heart attack 113
Heinz Company 58
Helly, Dorothy O. 88–9
Hinton's method 118
Hitler, Adolf 37–8
Hoganson, Kristin L. 59
hookworm 67
Hovemann, Charles 42
Howard Johnson's 18
Hughes, Thomas P. 8
human gut infrastructure 106
hunger, during World War I 36

Iacovetta, Franca 89
imperial bureaucracies 10
Imperial China 10
India 61
industrial infrastructure 18
industrialization: dietary fiber paradigm 111; European economy 40; food processing 5; food production 3; professionalization of culinary labor 16; regional food markets 11; rise of 58
inflammation 123
insecticides, Flit 56, 60–1
intellectual property 14
international grain trade 3
international political economy 7
International Refrigeration Institute 42, 43
Ireland, Lynne 93
irritable bowel syndrome (IBS) 123
Italian olive oil 14

Japanese occupation in World War II 63
Junior Women's Committee (JWC) 81, 82, 85, 87, 93, 94

Kellogg, John Harvey 108
Kerber, Linda K. 89
knowledge infrastructure 14–20
Korinek, Valerie J. 89

labels 19
Lancet journal 118, 120
Lane, William Arbuthnot 111
Lebon, André 46
Lee, Heather 17
Leong-Salobir, Cecilia 59
Les Eleveurs Vendéens 45–6
Leslie, Eliza 109
Lewis, Max 66
Lidchi, Henrietta 83
Limn magazine 7
long-distance supply chains 48

INDEX

Lucas, Dione 89–90
Lyle, John M. 86

marginalized populations 19
Maya chocolate pots 10
Mbembe, Achille 122
McCance, Robert 113
McCann, Alfred 110
McClellan, Andrew 84
McClintock, Anne 59
McMichael, Philip 7
meat processing: aging meats 12; bacterial
    contamination concerns 13; fast-frozen
    "bricks" of meat 39; monopolistic tactics
    in 12; thawing instructions 38–9
meat trades, in Paris 13
Medical Assistance Program (MAP) 117
Men's Lunches 91–4
mercantilist empires 9
Mexican peasant cooking 19
Michelin guide 18, 20
microbial actors in digestion 109, 123
migrant networks for food 14
Mihalache, Irina D. 80
military *Field Cookbook (Feldkochbuch)* 38
military provisioning 35, 37
milk adulteration 66
Millau, Christian 19
millstones 107
Milward, Alan 40
Mintz, Sidney 7
monopolistic tactics in meat packaging 12
Monthulet, Henri 45
Moore, Henry 81
Mosolff, Hans 37
Murton, James 14
museum in culinary infrastructure 3

National Association of Master Bakers 107
nationalism 57
National Socialists expansionism 32–48
Nazi-occupied France 2
neo-colonialism 12
neoliberalism 21
Newfoundland cod fisheries 9
New Museology (Vergo) 84
non-governmental organizations 70
Norwegian frozen fish acceptance 34
Nosan, Gregory 88
nouvelle cuisine 19
nutrition science 34

olive oil, Italian 14
organic label 19
Organisational Committee for
    Refrigeration Enterprises 46

Orientalist fashions 59
Orvell, Miles 58
Otter, Chris 37

Painter, Neil S. 118–22
parasitic infections 67
Paris meat trades 13
Parmentier, Antoine August 107
pasteurization 13
People's Refrigerator (Volkskühlschrank)
    37
Pétain, Maréchal Philippe 33–4, 41
Petrick, Gabriella M. 58
Phillips 57–60
physical infrastructure 9–14
Piettre, Maurice 42–6
pig farming 59
Pilcher, Jeffrey M. 1, 5, 81
Plank, Rudolf 36
poison gases 36
politics of exhibiting 83–4
politics of food distribution 9
populist movements 11
Portnoy, Sarah 81
Portuguese spice traders 9
practice of looking 83
privatization of supply chains 13, 14
professionalization of culinary labor 16
Progressive Era 109
protein gap 34
protein-rich food 12

Qing dynasty 17

Rankin, Bill 105
Recipes for Reading (Bower) 93
rectal dilators 110
refined carbohydrates 3, 104, 109
refrigeration industry: American 37; food
    safety and 62–3; during World War I and
    37–8; *see also individual companies and
    institutions*
Refrigeration Research Museum 63
regional food markets 11
regionalism 57
Reich Institute for Food Conservation
    36–7
restaurant professionality 16–17
Reverby, Susan M. 88–9
Rice, Danielle 84, 85
Ritz, Cesar 18
roundworm 67

Scholliers, Peter 17
Scientific Research Center (Centre de la
    Recherche Scientifique) 44

136

INDEX

Scott, J. M. G., Mrs. 90
Seabridge, George 57
self-poisoning 110
self-service shopping 13
sewage systems 9
sexually transmitted disease (STD) 114
Sherman, Henry Clapp 110
shop keeper responsibility 70
Singapore *see* food safety in Singapore
Singapore Monitor newspaper 71, 72
Singapore Tourist Promotion Board 70
slaves, African 9
social inequalities 18
Song dynasty 17
soybean cultivation 34
Spang, Rebecca 16
specialty food items 14
spice adulteration 70–1
Spices of the Orient 70
spice traders 9
Spiekermann, Uwe 35
state regulation of food safety 67–8
Stockholm School of Economics 13
Straits Times newspaper 57, 58, 65, 71, 73
street hawking prohibitions 68
suburbanization 18
supermarket chains, corporate 14
supermarket supply chains 9
supply chains 6, 9, 13, 14, 48; privatization of 13, 14

Tarulevicz, Nicole 55
Taylor, Kendall 81
techno-scientific solutions 36
Tetra Pak 13
Theophano, Janet 93
Thoms, Ulrike 34, 35
Tomes, Nancy 61
Tompkins, Kyla Wazana 125
Torrie, Julia S. 32
tourism, culinary 21
Tracy, Sarah E. 102
transnational labor markets 81

Treatise on Domestic Economy (Beecher) 109
Tudor, Frederick 12
Turnbull, C. M. 57

ulcerative colitis 103
UNESCO 19, 20
uniform grading standards 8
urbanization of Africans 114

value chains 8
Varty, Carmen Nielson 87
vegetables, Chinese 14
Vergo, Peter 84
Verlot, Jean Bernard 46–7
Victorian times, Christian morality of 88
vitamin-rich foods: freezing of 39

Waddington, Keir 58
Walker, Alexander 103, 111–21
Wallerstein, Immanuel 6
wartime food patterns 34
Westinghouse refrigerator 63–5
wheat grain processing 107
Wheat Industry Control Board 115
white bread acidosis 110
white *vs.* dark bread 109–10, 112–14
Whorton, James 110
Widdowson, Elsie 113
Wilk, Richard 10
winemakers 18–19
Woman's Board at the Art Institute of Chicago 88
women, entrepreneurial 18
Wong Hong Suen 59–60
world systems theory 6
World War I 33, 41, 46; hunger during 36
World War II 2, 9, 104, 111; Japanese occupation in 63; wartime food patterns 34

Zankowicz, Katherine 88
Ziegelmayer, Wilhelm 35
Zukin, Sharon 18